Medical Office Billing

A Self-Study Training Manual

Sarah J. Holt, PhD, FACMPE

Medical Group Management Association
104 Inverness Terrace East
Englewood, CO 80112-5306
877.275.6462
mgma.com

MGMA®
Defining Your Profession™

Production Credits
Senior Content Manager: Susan Sarapata, MA
Editorial and Production Manager: Anne Serrano, MA
Compositor: Virginia Howe
Proofreader: Joyce Dunne
Cover Design: Ian Serff, Serff Creative Group, Inc.

Library of Congress Cataloging-in-Publication Data

Holt, Sarah J.
Medical office billing : a self-study training manual / Sarah J. Holt.
p. ; cm.
Summary: "This workbook explains the fundamentals of how to work effectively as a medical office insurance staff member. It introduces individuals to the various steps of filing a claim and the role that insurance staff members play in claims processing and thus in the organization's financial health"--Provided by publisher.
ISBN 978-1-56829-388-2
1. Medical fees. 2. Health insurance claims. 3. Medicine--Practice--Finance. 4. Medicine--Practice--Accounting. I. Medical Group Management Association. II. Title.
[DNLM: 1. Reimbursement Mechanisms--United States. 2. Insurance Claim Reporting--United States. 3. Patient Credit and Collection--methods--United States. 4. Practice Management--economics--United States. W 80]
R728.5.H665 2012
610.68'1--dc23

2011024693

Item 8421
ISBN: 978-1-56829-388-2

Material in several chapters has been reprinted/adapted from: Holt, Sarah J. 2010. *Get the Money in the Door: Physician Billing Basics*. Englewood, Colo.: Medical Group Management Association. © 2010 Medical Group Management Association. Reprinted/adapted with permission.

Printed in the United States of America
10 9 8 7 6 5 4 3 2 1

Contents

List of Exhibits

Introduction

Competent staff trained to handle physician billing is necessary to ensure that physicians receive financial remuneration for the services they provide. At the same time the need for competent staff is increasing, the role of insurance staff members has been enlarged and the demands on these individuals intensified.

The days of filing an insurance claim with the reasonable expectation that the claim will be paid are gone. The American Medical Association has publicized that one in five insurance claims is paid incorrectly.[1] This astounding fact will not surprise those who understand the healthcare insurance processes. Billing for physician services is a highly complex, yet ambiguous, activity.

The 21st-century environment of rising cost and decreased payments in healthcare is a reality. Physicians in strong medical groups face the dilemma of practice costs rising each year and the uncertainty of decreased payment. Independent physician groups depend on competent insurance staff to bring in the revenue for the services the physicians provide. Without the efforts of an expert insurance staff, physicians may face financial jeopardy. In addition, healthcare reform has encouraged integrated delivery systems as a desirable model for care delivery. Many physicians, even those in strong groups, feel threatened, and those in less stable groups are likely to seek employment with hospital systems.

Historically, members of the medical office insurance staff have been trained on the job. This training can be excellent; however, the quality of learning is dependent on the trainer. Occasionally, a knowledge gap exists between what a medical office insurance staff person thinks he or she "knows" to be correct and what is correct. In addition, there is often a broad disparity between the knowledge base of staff members in a single insurance department. Sometimes terms may be defined incorrectly, or terms within a single insurance department are coined and used as if they are industry-wide terms. Those situations are very uncomfortable for even an experienced person as a new employee in an insurance department. The training course in this book ensures that *every* insurance department member has consistent and accurate training in healthcare insurance basics and a working vocabulary of industry terms.

Managers of medical office insurance departments have placed and will continue to place great emphasis on experience. Equal training provides a starting point of fairness and equal opportunity for success.

---

1. Dolan, Pamela Lewis. 2010. "AMA Meeting: Health plans process 1 in 5 claims incorrectly," *American Medical News,* June 28. www.amednew.com. (Accessed 8/2/11.)

This workbook explains the fundamentals of how to work effectively as a medical office insurance staff member. It introduces individuals to the various steps of filing a claim and the role that insurance staff members play in claims processing and thus in the organization's financial health. Most people are surprised and shocked when they learn that many health insurance claims are not paid correctly and, of the large number of claims that are initially denied, many are not followed up on and re-filed.

Reading and working through this book, you will understand why an insurance claim is filed, gain a framework for thinking about the major types of health insurance, and learn about the various elements of health insurance. You will also learn about what constitutes fraud and abuse and how to avoid each. In addition you will come to understand the elements of coding and how to read an Explanation of Benefits. You will learn how to deal effectively with account follow-up, known as working insurance, and why it is a critical component of your success as a member of the medical office insurance staff.

WHY TRAINING?

Hiring a new employee is a huge investment, so medical practices should want to invest in well-trained staff. Knowledgeable staff members have the best opportunity to be successful in their position and give the organization the best chance of a positive return on its investment.

When organizations advertise for and hire staff, they may not have sufficient assurance that the person they select has good knowledge and experience, even when the insurance person says he or she has 20 years of experience. How successful was the individual in bringing in revenue to the organizations for which he or she worked?

TRAINING IS FOR MORE THAN JUST NEW EMPLOYEES

Certainly, new employees must be trained, but it is important to remember that training should not just be focused on new employees. Once a new employee has been trained and integrated into the organization, an opportunity exists to expand training for employees across the organization to ensure that all staff members share the same chance to acquire knowledge.

Cross-training provides a good occasion for expanding knowledge and for making staff more inclined to work as a team. For example, I heard an insurance staff member who had been covering at the front desk express in response to a complaint from another insurance staff person, *"If she had any idea what the people at the front desk do, she wouldn't be so critical. I have covered up there when I thought I was just going to cry."*

Cross-training benefits both the organization and the employee, allowing employees to learn new tasks and better understand how all the jobs in the practice fit together. Cross-training also gives managers more flexibility in moving employees around to get the work done. For insurance staff in particular, cross-training gives complete knowledge of the interlocking roles in the medical practice that affect their work.

THE ROLE OF THIS TRAINING MANUAL

This book provides a comprehensive introduction to the role of medical office billing staff. It presents a basis for understanding the fundamentals of the insurance claim process (Lesson 1), the different types of commercial and government insurance (Lessons 2–5), the revenue cycle (Lessons 6–9), how to read an Explanation of Benefits (Lesson 10), coding (Lessons 11–12), and insurance regulations (Lesson 13). Exercises and scenarios are presented at the end of each lesson, so that readers can test their knowledge and solidify their understanding. It is hoped that this manual will both provide an introduction to new medical office insurance staff and serve as a reference for existing insurance staff members and practice managers.

HOW TO USE THE CD

As an extra bonus, a CD comes with this book. It contains pre-tests and post-tests for training purposes.

The pre-tests are on the CD only and should be used by the billing staff employee and/or his or her manager to test knowledge about medical office billing before working through each lesson. Once the individual has completed the lesson, he or she should take the post-tests to gauge billing knowledge acquired. The post-tests on the CD are the same as those that follow each lesson.

In addition, the CD contains a master list of "Key Terms and Definitions," which combines into one list the glossaries that appear at the end of each lesson.

The tests and reference material on the CD are extremely useful tools for managers — not only to help the billing staff member train himself or herself about the intricacies of medical office billing, but to strengthen their own knowledge of this complicated skill set.

Overview of Medical Office Insurance Staff Work

OBJECTIVES

- Describe what constitutes an encounter.
- Summarize the steps through which claims are filed and processed.
- Identify factors that may affect the processing of a claim.
- Define the three major types of insurance in the United States.

WHAT IS AN ENCOUNTER?

When a patient seeks medical care from a healthcare provider, commonly in a face-to-face visit, this is an encounter. The provider may be a physician or a midlevel provider providing services on behalf of the physician. The midlevel provider may be a nurse practitioner or a physician assistant; regardless, the provider must be licensed in the state where service is provided.

WHAT ARE THE STEPS OF FILING AND PROCESSING A CLAIM?

Primarily physicians get paid for the services they provided to patients from insurance carriers. Filing the insurance claim is an essential step in resolving payment. This training manual starts with the claim, the fundamental work of insurance staff. An insurance claim is filed to get payment for services because services were provided, usually through an encounter.

After service is provided, the process of documentation and coding must be completed. The provider must document in detail the services that were provided. This documentation gets translated into a code called a *Current Procedural Terminology (CPT®*)* code, which clearly describes the service that was provided. In addition to the CPT code, a corresponding diagnosis code(s), called an *International Classification of Diseases (ICD-9-CM)* code, that describes the medical condition(s) and why the patient sought treatment are attached. After that information is recorded in the practice management (PM) system the claim is ready to be filed, or in other words, sent to the insurance carrier for payment. The claim may be sent either electronically or on paper. But before the claim can be filed, work has already occurred behind the scenes. The PM system must be set up in the proper format with the correct information about the provider, the patient, and the insurance carrier to ensure that the claim gets to the carrier for payment consideration.

The claim will be sent to the insurance carrier or to its agent, such as a third-party administrator (TPA), for adjudication. *Adjudication* is the process of determining if the claim will be paid. When the claim arrives, the decision is made whether the claim is able to be processed. A claim that can be processed or is *processable* is called a *clean claim*. A claim that is not able to be processed is *unprocessable*. If the claim can be processed, it will be put through several edits to see how much will be paid. For example, the edits will determine if the provider is a *participating provider* and take *assignment*, meaning that the payment amount is predictable for the carrier, and the money will be sent directly to the provider. If the provider is *non-participating*, the claim is non-assigned — the provider has not made an agreement with the insurance carrier for payment — and the check for payment is sent to the insured instead of the provider.

IMPACTS ON PAYMENTS

Payment of a claim may be affected for many reasons. Those include:

- If the patient was not *eligible* for coverage on the date of service,
- If the insured patient had other coverage that could be a source of payment — the determination must be made if the carrier pays as the *primary payer* or the *secondary payer*,
- If the service provided is a *covered service* or an *excluded service* — the carrier will not pay for services that are excluded from coverage,
- If the claim is for treatment of a *pre-existing* condition,
- If the provider was in-network or out-of-network,
- If the service met precertification requirements,
- If the patient has met deductible requirements as outlined in the benefits package, or
- If the patient has met the out-of-pocket maximum.

Other payment considerations relating to the CPT and diagnosis code billed are based on modifiers and place of service. The considerations outlined above are not an exhaustive list but provide information about the complexity of the insurance filing and payment process.

After the insurance carrier has applied all edits, a payment determination is made and a check is sent out. Let's assume that the check has been received in the physician's office. The check will be accompanied by an Explanation of Benefits (EOB) that explains the payment amount. Then it is up to the medical office insurance staff members to decide if they agree with the payment determination. If payment has been denied or if staff members do not agree with the amount, the payment determination must be appealed. If the payment amount is correct, then an adjustment must be made to reconcile the difference between the amount charged and the amount paid. The practice management system may be set to automatically take the adjustment between the charged amount and the contracted amount. If not, medical office insurance staff must manually make the adjustment between the charge and the payment. Any remaining balance on the account is probably the coinsurance that is the patient's responsibility to pay. A statement is sent to the patient for the coinsurance, if it has not already been collected. It is the medical practice's responsibility to follow up on the balance until it is resolved.

Complexity is a reality relating to healthcare insurance, and the body of knowledge is so large that no one individual can master it totally. "But gaining a working knowledge and building on that through experience is the best way to become proficient. The difficulty in learning how to work in a medical office insurance department reminds me of the saying, *"How do you eat an elephant? One bite at a time."* We can apply that philosophy to the study of healthcare insurance by creating a framework to use in thinking about the fundamentals of healthcare insurance and then learning how to find the resources to use when questions arise.

WHAT TYPES OF INSURANCE ARE USED IN THE UNITED STATES?

A good rule of thumb when thinking about healthcare insurance is to break it down into major types. The three major types for consideration here are government insurance, commercial for-profit insurance, and non-governmental not-for-profit insurance. Use Exhibit 1.1 on the next page to help sort out the major types of insurance and their elements.

This training manual deals specifically with government insurance and commercial insurance. A good understanding of these two types of insurance allows individuals working in a medical office insurance department to have a broad base of knowledge from which they can draw in dealing with the situations that they will face during the course of their work.

KEY TERMS AND DEFINITIONS

Adjudication — The process of determining whether a claim will be paid.

Adjustment — The amount of a charge that is written off based on the difference between the fee-for-service charge amount and the contracted amount.

Appeal — A written request asking the insurance carrier to review or critically examine the initial determination of payment for services provided. Claims that were paid incorrectly are appealed by the medical practice to ask the payer for reconsideration on payment. Every claim that pays incorrectly should be appealed.

Assignment — An agreement to accept as payment in full the allowed amount established by Medicare for services provided. Assignment also refers to the situation when a patient agrees to have payment sent directly to the provider for services provided.

Benefits Package — The collection of services an insurance carrier has agreed to pay for under the insurance contract.

Clean Claim — A claim containing all relevant and correct information needed for processing.

Coding — Transforms a verbal description of treatment by assigning alpha or numeric identifiers from a recognized classification system to diagnostic and procedural clinical documentation.

EXHIBIT 1.1 ■ Major Types of Insurance and Their Elements

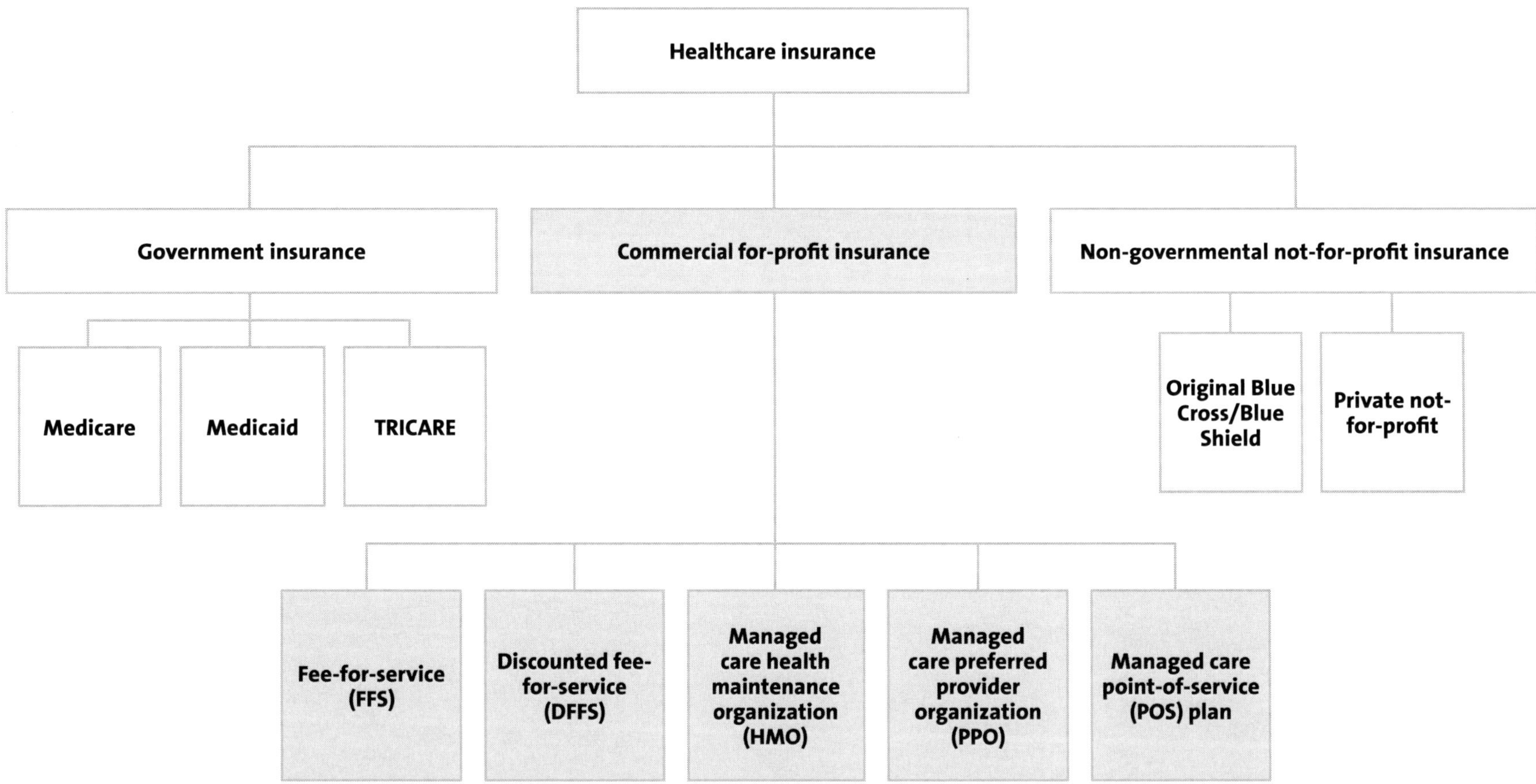

Covered Service — An approved medical service that will be paid by insurance.

Current Procedural Terminology (CPT) Codes — The official standard system of codes maintained annually by the American Medical Association of the medical industry. Descriptive terms are coupled with numeric codes and paired with diagnosis codes to bill for services provided.

Date of Service — The date a healthcare service was provided.

Deductible — The amount an insured individual must pay before insurance begins to pay for covered services. Deductibles are met at the beginning of each plan year and are defined by the insurance contract.

Documentation — The record of medical services provided to satisfy documentation guidelines as defined by either the 1995 or 1997 Medicare Documentation Guidelines for Evaluation and Management Services.

Eligible — A person who has met all the criteria to receive healthcare coverage for services.

Encounter — A face-to-face contact between a patient and a provider during which medical services are provided and the provider documents those services.

Excluded Service — Services not covered by insurance.

Explanation of Benefits (EOB) — A written description of payment made by a health plan that is sent to both provider and patient.

In-Network — A provider among a group of providers that have contracted with a health plan so that its insured can access healthcare services at discounted rates.

International Classification of Diseases, Ninth Revision (ICD-9) Codes — An international coding system for diagnosis codes used for billing and tracking purposes. They are paired with CPT codes and used to bill for services provided.

Midlevel provider — A nonphysician medical provider licensed to treat and diagnose patients under the supervision of a licensed physician.

Modifiers — Numeric codes that increase or decrease the relative value unit (RVU) of a Current Procedural Terminology (CPT) code. A complete list of modifiers with definitions is found in the CPT codebook.

Non-participating Provider — A provider who has not agreed to accept assignment on all Medicare claims.

Nurse Practitioner (NP) — A registered nurse who has completed additional educational training and is licensed to work as a midlevel provider under the supervision of a licensed physician.

Out-of-Network — A provider who has not contracted with an insurance company at a negotiated rate for reimbursement on services provided.

Out-of-Pocket Maximum — The maximum amount the insured will have to pay personally. The out-of-pocket amount is dictated by the health plan's benefits package. Once healthcare services expenses have reached this amount, insurance pays 100 percent of future expenses during the current healthcare contract.

Participating Provider — A medical services provider who has voluntarily agreed to accept assignment on all claims benefits considered a covered service for Medicare beneficiaries.

Payment Determination — The decision of how much will be paid on a claim based on criteria to fulfill the responsibility of the insurance carrier in accordance with the benefits package of the insured.

Physician Assistant (PA) — A person prepared in an accredited academic and clinical program and certified to practice medicine under the supervision of a licensed physician.

Place-of-Service Codes — Codes used on providers' claims to identify where a service to the patient was provided.

Pre-existing Condition — A medical condition acquired before the individual was enrolled in a health plan to receive insurance benefits.

Primary Payer — A carrier whose benefit plan pays first on medical care for an insured individual.

Processable — A claim that is considered a clean claim and can be processed for payment.

Secondary Payer — The carrier that will pay after the primary insurance on a claim for services when a beneficiary has two or more payers.

Third-Party Administrator (TPA) — An entity contracted to make payment or perform claims administration for a plan or an entity.

Unprocessable — A claim that contains incomplete or invalid information.

REVIEW OF OBJECTIVES

- **Describe what constitutes an encounter.**
  - A patient receives services, usually face-to-face, from a physician or midlevel provider.
- **Summarize the steps through which claims are filed and processed.**
  - An encounter occurs with supporting documentation and coding.
  - Charges for the encounter are entered then batched for filing.
  - After edits, claims are filed and sent to a clearinghouse, which sends the claim on to the carrier.
  - Once received by the carrier, payment determination is made.
  - The claim is paid, accompanied by an EOB provided to both provider and patient.
  - Then the major work of the insurance department starts. Payment is posted, and the insurance department assesses the appropriateness of payment. It may be necessary to move the charges to the patient's account or appeal the claim. In any case, follow-up is required.
- **Identify factors that may affect the processing of a claim.**
  - Benefit conditions such as eligibility, covered services, deductibles met, in-network or out-of-network provision of services.
  - Factors affecting payment such as documentation, coding requirements, modifiers, place of service.
- **Define the three major types of insurance in the United States.**
  - Government
  - Commercial (for-profit)
  - Not-for-profit commercial

REVIEW EXERCISES: LESSON 1

MULTIPLE CHOICE

Please circle the best answer.

1. A face-to-face contact between a provider and a patient is:

- **a.** An encounter
- **b.** A covered service
- **c.** An eligible service

2. A record of services provided is:

- **a.** Adjudication
- **b.** Assignment
- **c.** Documentation

3. The identification of a patient's medical condition or disease is:

- **a.** Pre-existing condition
- **b.** Diagnosis
- **c.** CPT code

4. The process of determining whether a claim will be paid is:

- **a.** Adjustment
- **b.** Adjudication
- **c.** Clean claim

5. A claim that is processable and can be paid is:

- **a.** A clean claim
- **b.** A medically necessary claim
- **c.** An edited claim

6. A written description of payment made by a health plan that is sent to both provider and patient is:

- **a.** A payment
- **b.** An EOB
- **c.** A record

7. A provider who has not agreed to accept assignment on all Medicare claims is:

- **a.** Non-participating
- **b.** An ordering physician
- **c.** A midlevel provider

8. **A written request asking the insurance carrier to review or critically examine the initial determination of payment for services provided is an:**
   a. Edit
   b. Adjudication
   c. Appeal

9. **Codes used on providers' claims to identify where a service to the patient was provided are:**
   a. ICD-9
   b. Modifiers
   c. Place of service

10. **Payment of a claim may be impacted for many reasons. Those include:**
    a. Place of birth
    b. Deductible requirement
    c. Medical liability insurance

11. **Which of the following is not a major type of insurance?**
    a. Government
    b. Commercial
    c. Protected health

12. **A claim is filed to:**
    a. Record the service
    b. Seek payment for services provided
    c. Create a health record

13. **An approved medical service that will be paid by insurance is:**
    a. An unbundled service
    b. An excluded service
    c. A covered service

14. **The collection of services an insurance carrier has agreed to pay for under the insurance contract is:**
    a. A benefits package
    b. Bundling services
    c. Subscribed services

15. **A registered nurse who has completed additional educational training and is licensed to work as a midlevel provider under the supervision of a licensed physician is a:**
    a. Physician assistant
    b. Nurse assistant
    c. Nurse practitioner

(Answers on page 15)

CASE STUDIES

Case study 1: All the physicians of XYZ Medical Group are participating providers with Very Best Benefits insurance carrier. Mrs. Smith has called Jane in the insurance department of the medical practice saying that she has received a check from Very Best Benefits for services provided to her by Dr. Phillips, one of the physicians of the medical practice, and she is asking if the money is hers. What should Jane tell Mrs. Smith?

a. The money is hers, and she can cash the check.

b. The insurance carrier mistakenly sent the payment to her rather than the medical practice. Mrs. Smith can sign the check over to the medical practice, and Jane can call the carrier about the situation.

c. Jane should tell the carrier that it has to send the physician a check for the same amount; now the service that Mrs. Smith received has cost it double.

Case study 2: Jane is posting payment from Very Best Benefits insurance carrier. It has made a zero dollar payment for the services XYZ Medical Group provided to patient Paul Barnes because the cost of services was applied to the deductible. What action should Jane take on the account?

a. Set aside the lack of payment for review at a later time.

b. Call the insurance carrier and ask it why it didn't pay.

c. Move the responsibility on the charges to the patient.

Case study 3: An insurance claim has been filed for payment of services. The carrier has not yet paid. Jane realizes that the claim was filed with the wrong date of birth recorded for the patient. What action should Jane take?

a. Correct and re-file the claim.

b. Call the patient to tell her that she will receive payment because the wrong date of birth was filed.

c. Call the carrier and tell it to correct the date of birth for the patient.

(Answers on page 15)

COMPLETION QUESTIONS

Please fill in the blank.

1. What is a face-to-face visit called?

____

2. What does *adjudication* mean?

____

3. Which set of documentation guidelines must a physician satisfy when documenting face-to-face services provided to a patient?

____

____

4. Define *midlevel provider.*

____

____

5. What is meant by a *processable* claim?

____

____

6. What does it mean to be a participating provider with Medicare?

____

____

____

7. Physicians who participate with Medicare have agreed to accept assignment. What does that mean?

____

____

____

8. What does assignment mean for patients other than Medicare patients?

____

____

____

9. What does the term *date of service* mean?

____

____

10. What does the term *covered service* mean?

____

____

11. Define *deductible.*

____

____

12. Modifiers serve a purpose when attached to a CPT code. What is that purpose?

____

____

13. List at least 10 benefit situations that may affect the payment of claims.

____

____

14. What is an *appeal*?

____

____

15. What is an *adjustment*?

____

____

(Answers on page 15)

MATCHING

Please match the letter of the definition to the term.
Write the letter of the definition next to the term.

CPT codes_____	**a.** A face-to-face contact between a patient and a provider during which medical services are provided and the provider documents those services.
Encounter_____	**b.** A nonphysician medical provider licensed to treat and diagnose patients under the supervision of a licensed physician.
Coding_____	**c.** A registered nurse who has completed additional educational training and is licensed to work as a midlevel provider under the supervision of a licensed physician.
Midlevel provider_____	**d.** A person prepared in an accredited academic and clinical program and certified to practice medicine under the supervision of a licensed physician.
Pre-existing condition_____	**e.** The record of medical services provided to satisfy documentation guidelines as defined by either the 1995 or 1997 Medicare Documentation Guidelines for Evaluation and Management Services.
ICD-9 codes_____	**f.** Transforms a verbal description of treatment by assigning alpha or numeric identifiers from a recognized classification system to diagnostic and procedural clinical documentation.
In-network_____	**g.** The official standard system of codes maintained annually by the American Medical Association of the medical industry. Descriptive terms are coupled with numeric codes and paired with diagnosis codes to bill for services provided.
Nurse practitioner (NP)_____	**h.** An international coding system for diagnosis codes used for billing and tracking purposes. They are paired with CPT codes and used to bill for services provided.
Out-of-network_____	**i.** An entity contracted to make payment or perform claims administration for a plan or an entity.
Benefits package_____	**j.** The process of determining whether a claim will be paid.
Out-of-pocket maximum_____	**k.** A claim that is considered a clean claim and can be processed for payment.

Physician assistant (PA)_____	**l.** A claim containing all relevant and correct information needed for processing.
Deductible_____	**m.** A claim that contains incomplete or invalid information.
Documentation_____	**n.** A medical services provider who has voluntarily agreed to accept assignment on all claims benefits considered a covered service for Medicare beneficiaries.
Adjudication_____	**o.** An agreement to accept as payment in full the allowed amount established by Medicare for services provided. Assignment also refers to the situation when a patient agrees to have payment sent directly to the provider for services provided.
Non-participating provider_____	**p.** A provider who has not agreed to accept assignment on all Medicare claims.
Excluded service_____	**q.** A person who has met all the criteria to receive healthcare coverage for services.
Unprocessable_____	**r.** The date a healthcare service was provided.
Secondary payer_____	**s.** A carrier whose benefit plan pays first on medical care for an insured individual.
Eligible_____	**t.** The carrier that will pay after the primary insurance on a claim for services when a beneficiary has two or more payers.
Modifiers_____	**u.** An approved medical service that will be paid by insurance.
Processable_____	**v.** Services not covered by insurance.
Place-of-service codes_____	**w.** A medical condition acquired before the individual was enrolled in a health plan to receive insurance benefits.
Date of service_____	**x.** A provider among a group of providers that have contracted with a health plan so that its insured can access healthcare services at discounted rates.
Payment determination_____	**y.** A provider who has not contracted with an insurance company at a negotiated rate for reimbursement on services provided.
Participating provider_____	**z.** The amount an insured individual must pay before insurance begins to pay for covered services. Met at the beginning of each plan year and are defined by the insurance contract.
Explanation of Benefits (EOB)_____	**Aa.** The collection of services an insurance carrier has agreed to pay for under the insurance contract.

Appeal_____	**Ab.** Numeric codes that increase or decrease the relative value unit (RVU) of a Current Procedural Terminology (CPT) code.
Primary payer_____	**Ac.** Codes used on providers' claims to identify where a service to the patient was provided.
Clean claim_____	**Ad.** The decision of how much will be paid on a claim based on criteria to fulfill the responsibility of the insurance carrier in accordance with the benefits package of the insured.
Adjustment_____	**Ae.** A written description of payment made by a health plan that is sent to both provider and patient.
Assignment_____	**Af.** A written request asking the insurance carrier to review or critically examine the initial determination of payment for services provided. Claims that were paid incorrectly are appealed by the medical practice to ask the payer for reconsideration on payment. Every claim that pays incorrectly should be appealed.
Third-party administrator (TPA)_____	**Ag.** The amount of a charge that is written off based on the difference between the fee-for-service charge amount and the contracted amount.
Covered service_____	**Ah.** The maximum amount the insured will have to pay personally. The out-of-pocket amount is dictated by the health plan's benefits package. Once healthcare services expenses have reached this amount, insurance pays 100 percent of future expenses during the current healthcare contract.

(Answers on page 16)

ANSWERS: LESSON 1

MULTIPLE CHOICE

1-a; 2-c; 3-b; 4-b; 5-a; 6-b; 7-a; 8-c; 9-c; 10-b; 11-c; 12-b; 13-c; 14-a; 15-c

CASE STUDIES

Case study 1-b; Case study 2-c; Case study 3-a

COMPLETION QUESTIONS

1. An encounter
2. It is the process of determining if a claim will be paid.
3. Physicians may use either the Medicare Documentation Guidelines for Evaluation and Management Services of 1995 or 1997.
4. A nonphysician medical provider licensed to treat and diagnose patients under the supervision of a licensed physician
5. A processable claim is a clean claim that can be processed for payment.
6. A participating provider is one who has voluntarily agreed to accept assignment on all claims benefits that are covered services.
7. It means that physicians have signed an agreement to accept as payment in full the allowed amount established by Medicare for services provided.
8. Assignment refers to the situation when a patient agrees to have payment sent directly to the provider for services provided rather than have the money sent to the patient and then the patient must pay the provider.
9. The date a healthcare service was provided
10. A covered service is one that is an approved medical service and will be paid by the insurance carrier.
11. The deductible is the amount an insured individual must pay before insurance begins to pay for covered services.
12. The use of modifiers signals that payment for the CPT code will be increased or decreased.
13. The following may affect payment of claims: eligibility; primary or secondary insurance; covered or excluded services; pre-existing condition; in-network or out-of-network; pre-certification requirements; deductible requirements; and/or out-of-pocket maximum. *(Any from the list)*
14. An appeal is a written request asking the insurance carrier to review or critically examine the initial determination of payment for services provided.
15. An adjustment is the amount of a charge that is written off based on the difference between the fee-for-service charge amount and the contracted amount.

MATCHING

___ CPT codes: **g**

___ Encounter: **a**

___ Coding: **f**

___ Midlevel provider: **b**

___ Pre-existing condition: **w**

___ ICD-9 codes: **h**

___ In-network: **x**

___ Nurse practitioner (NP): **c**

___ Out-of-network: **y**

___ Benefits package: **Aa**

___ Out-of-pocket maximum: **Ah**

___ Physician assistant (PA): **d**

___ Deductible: **z**

___ Documentation: **e**

___ Adjudication: **j**

___ Non-participating provider: **p**

___ Excluded service: **v**

___ Unprocessable: **m**

___ Secondary payer: **t**

___ Eligible: **q**

___ Modifiers: **Ab**

___ Processable: **k**

___ Place-of-service codes: **Ac**

___ Date of service: **r**

___ Payment determinition: **Ad**

___ Participating provider: **n**

___ Explanation of Benefits (EOB): **Ae**

___ Appeal: **Af**

___ Primary payer: **s**

___ Clean claim: **l**

___ Adjustment: **Ag**

___ Assignment: **o**

___ Third-party administrator (TPA): **i**

___ Covered service: **u**

LESSON 2

Commercial Insurance

OBJECTIVES

- Describe the role of commercial insurance.
- Differentiate the fundamental elements of health insurance.
- Identify the major categories of commercial insurance.
- Review the functionality of the various types of commercial insurance.

OVERVIEW OF COMMERCIAL INSURANCE

The employer-based model for purchasing healthcare insurance is the predominant model in the United States. While the United States has experienced an increase in the number of its citizens without health insurance, numbering more than 50 million at the time of this writing, the majority of employers offer healthcare insurance, and employer-based insurance is the primary source of healthcare insurance in the United States. Approximately 60 percent of people in the United States who have healthcare insurance are covered by employer-offered health insurance. This number compares to approximately 30 percent of the health insured citizenry covered by a government health insurance program, and 10 percent of the people with health insurance who have purchased an individual policy.

Economic conditions drive the number of people who have jobs and are then eligible for healthcare coverage through an employer plan. Those who find themselves out of work due to economic conditions will likely run out of affordable healthcare insurance options and become without healthcare insurance. Even the 60 percent of citizens less than age 65 covered under employer-based healthcare insurance programs have very uneven coverage benefits. The variety of benefits packages is as broad as the industries represented in hiring employees and offering coverage. Additionally the cost of coverage differs greatly from business to business and plan to plan. These cost differences are sometimes imposed by the insurance carrier based on experience rating of the employer group, and sometimes the cost of employee coverage is based on decisions made by the employer relating to how much of the cost the company is willing to pick up and how much the employer wants to pass on to the employee. Typically the employer covers most of the cost of insurance for the employee, but the cost of dependent coverage (that is, coverage for children and spouse) has transitioned away from the employer and is now largely paid by the employee.

Regardless of current payment methods, the trend is toward the employee sharing more of the cost of insurance. Those costs fluctuate from job to job. Coverage options and cost vary not only from one organization to the next but also within organizations, as a variety of coverage choices are often available. Again, these decisions are at the employer's discretion. Perhaps this lack of personal involvement relating to decision-making and purchasing accounts for the fact that few people seeking healthcare services seem to know their insurance plan benefits. No doubt the complexity of the benefits structure contributes to the confusion about coverage issues.

The work of medical office insurance staff members is further complicated because individuals are unaware of their benefits and confused by coverage criteria. Medical office insurance staff members find themselves teaching patients about healthcare insurance and plan provisions. This service delivery role makes it incumbent on medical office insurance staff to understand the elements of commercial insurance so that they can be advocates for the patients who seek services from the medical practice organizations they represent.

The cost of healthcare insurance for an individual or a family can be unpredictable and expensive. For healthy individuals who require only preventive care, the cost of healthcare services may be minimal and the entire annual out-of-pocket expense for healthcare services inconsequential. However, an unexpected illness or accident can radically change the financial impact of healthcare expenses. Without insurance, someone suffering a serious injury or a chronic health condition requiring intensive or prolonged services may face the prospect of personal bankruptcy. Healthcare insurance is intended to help share expenses related to medical treatment and to give individuals the peace of mind in knowing that they can predict the range of financial outlay they will have related to medical services each year.

TYPES OF HEALTHCARE INSURANCE

The types of healthcare insurance offered and the regulations pertaining to healthcare insurance have evolved over the years. Massive changes have occurred in healthcare insurance primarily because of the implementation of Medicare in 1965. Medicare, intended as a safety net against high healthcare cost for seniors, has proven to be the driving force behind most healthcare insurance changes affecting *all* age communities in the United States.

As insurance coverage has evolved, so too have the expectations of the American people. It is generally agreed that the current healthcare system is inadequate to meet these expectations. A little history regarding the major categories of commercial insurance, which are listed in Exhibit 2.1, and how they have evolved should help us understand how we got here.

FEE-FOR-SERVICE

Fee-for-service is an arrangement in which medical practices charge standard fees for medical services, according to a fee schedule that the practice itself has determined, with the expectation that fees will be paid as charged. Indemnity insurance is a fee-for-service insurance plan that pays 80 percent of billed fees. Healthcare insurance of the 1960s was largely indemnity insurance, which paid 80 percent of the fee-for-service charge submitted by the healthcare provider while the insured paid the remaining 20 percent of the billed charge. During that time deductibles were low, $200 or less, and patients were free to choose their own providers. Normally, with indemnity fee-for-service, insurance patients not only could choose their primary care provider but also had the flexibility to choose to see a specialist without a referral and could opt to change healthcare providers at any time.

EXHIBIT 2.1 ■ Major Categories of Commercial Insurance

Category	Definition
Fee-for-service (FFS)	Typically indemnity insurance, insurance pays 80 percent, insured pays 20 percent.
Discounted fee-for-service	Provider gives carrier discount on standard fee, discount is passed on to insured.
Managed care HMOs	Designed to provide cost savings by exerting effort to control access to services by requiring referrals and pre-certification. May require primary care gatekeeper.
Managed care PPOs	Designed to provide cost savings, emphasize in-network care. Usually no gatekeeper. Features of both FFS and HMO.
Managed care POSs	Designed to provide cost savings, emphasize in-network care. Require gatekeeper. Features of both FFS and HMO.

Source: Holt, Sarah J. 2010. *Get the Money in the Door: Physician Billing Basics.* Englewood, Colo.: Medical Group Management Association, p. 12. Reprinted with permission from Medical Group Management Association.

The closest relative to the traditional fee-for-service plan is the *discounted fee-for-service* plan. In this arrangement a health insurance carrier initiates a contracted rate with healthcare providers to provide services at a discounted percentage of their standard fee. For example, a carrier may contract with a provider to pay at 85 percent of billed charges. That gives the carrier a discount of 15 percent, which is passed on to the purchaser of the carrier's insurance plan. This may seem to be a good arrangement for all parties, because the arrangement is simple and straightforward without engaging in complex contract negotiations. However, this arrangement does not ensure predictable cost saving in purchasing healthcare services, because providers are at liberty to adjust their fee schedules to keep up with the rising cost of practicing medicine. This is particularly true with costs related to supplies and labor. In reality, traditional insurance plans lacked the ability to control costs because they were unable to dictate to a chosen group of providers where cost could be controlled. Traditional plans created an opportunity for innovations in healthcare insurance, such as networks of providers, through which insurers could exert more control.

In the 1970s the cost of medical care was increasing. The United States was beginning to see high utilization of healthcare services and was simultaneously on the brink of the explosion of technological advances in medicine. In 1973, legislation was passed to provide federal funding for the expansion of health maintenance organizations (HMOs), discussed in the next sections, to address rising costs influenced in part by the high utilization and the availability of advanced technology. What seemed then like unparalleled increases in cost made it important for insurance carriers, both government and commercial, to engage in cost containment and cost savings measures. Since the 1980s the growth of managed care has continued to increase dramatically. By the 1990s most Americans' healthcare insurance was in some form of managed care plan, and by the beginning of the 21st century only a small percentage of Americans in employee-sponsored health plans were covered by traditional indemnity fee-for-service insurance plans. Exhibit 2.2 lists the fundamental elements of health insurance.

MANAGED CARE SPECTRUM

Managed care refers to health insurance arrangements that are negotiated between insurance carriers and medical organizations to control costs. There are many managed care arrangements that are available to the American public. Because of the emphasis on cost containment, employers and individuals have welcomed the growth of managed care. Managed care plans were offered at lower costs than the indemnity fee-for-service plans and provided an opportunity to tailor healthcare benefits that better fit the needs of the insured.

Elements of managed care insurance

In contrast to fee-for-service plans, in which the insured is responsible for 20 percent of billed charges, managed care plans include many important elements that ultimately determine the out-of-pocket cost for the insured. For the insured there are several important elements of healthcare insurance — monthly premium, coinsurance, deductible, amounts insurance pays for covered services, and coinsurance. Unfortunately many insured do not

EXHIBIT 2.2 ■ **Fundamental Elements of Health Insurance**

Fundamental	How It Works
Premium	Paid monthly during contract year. Price based on contracted benefits to pay portion of insured's health services as outlined in benefits package. Paid by insured before insurance pays.
Copayment	Required payment when services are accessed. Stipulated by benefits package. Paid by insured before insurance pays.
Deductible	Self-insured portion of health insurance. Must be met before health insurance begins to pay. Re-set with each plan year. Paid by insured before insurance pays.
Insurance payment	The portion of health care services paid by insurance carrier. The amount paid is based on the benefits package purchased. Payment varies based on whether services were in-network or out-of-network.
Coinsurance	The service balance that remains after health care insurance has paid. The insured is responsible for this amount.

Source: Holt, Sarah J. 2010. *Get the Money in the Door: Physician Billing Basics.* Englewood, Colo.: Medical Group Management Association, p. 14. Reprinted with permission from Medical Group Management Association.

understand the role of each element — too many believe that because they pay a large monthly premium their healthcare services are already covered without any further financial burden to them. In fact, however, the insured is often responsible for further out-of-pocket expenses based on the other elements of their insurance.

Monthly premium

Monthly premium refers to the monthly fee paid each month by the insured to retain insurance coverage. In employee-sponsored group health plans, the monthly employee contribution is determined by the employer and assessed to the insured employee. Paying the monthly contribution, often deducted from payroll in employer-based insurance, does not ensure anything other than providing the insured with healthcare insurance. Healthcare insurance is good assurance of access to medical care provided at a discounted rate — all else is based on the benefits package.

Copay

Copay is a set charge amount that will be paid upon accessing services as designated by benefit design. Initially when copays were introduced they were small amounts in the range of $5 to $10 and were attached to physician visits, but rarely to screening or diagnostic services. Arrangements relating to copays have been altered significantly. Copays have increased several-fold, and they may be attached to both visits and tests. Some employers have opted out of copays, because the amount of money spent in copays does not contribute to meeting one's deductible.

Deductibles

Deductibles are the self-insured portion of insurance — in other words, a deductible is a set amount that the insured must pay out-of-pocket before insurance starts to cover services. Like copays, deductibles have increased considerably over time. High-deductible health plans (HDHPs) have shifted cost away from the insurance carrier and onto the insured. In some cases the employer has assumed some responsibility for a portion of the deductible by establishing health reimbursement accounts (HRAs) for employees. In any case, high-deductible plans have lowered the cost of yearly and monthly premiums for the employer and the employee. Only after the deductible has been met will insurance pay. The amount of the billed charge that insurance pays is based on the negotiated rate of the contract with the provider. That negotiated rate, known as the *allowable amount,* is the medium that ensures the insured a guaranteed discount on healthcare services. The insurance carrier starts with the negotiated allowable amount and pays a percentage of the allowable amount to the provider. The benefits package purchased by the employer dictates the percentage paid.

Coinsurance

Coinsurance is a percentage of the covered charge that the insured is required to pay to resolve the cost of the medical service. Virtually all insurance plans include a coinsurance percentage of at least 10 percent, which is paid by the insured after insurance pays its portion. Whereas a copay is a set dollar amount typically paid at the time of service, coinsurance is a percentage of the total charge paid after the service. Most plans have a maximum out-of-pocket limit after which the insured is no longer required to pay coinsurance. The coinsurance percentage can vary based on whether the healthcare provider of services is in-network or out-of-network.

Network

A *network* refers to a group of providers who have contracted with a particular insurance carrier to provide services at a negotiated cost. (One provider typically contracts with multiple insurance plans and belongs to many "networks.") *Out-of-network* refers to services provided to the insured by providers who do not have a contract with the insured's particular insurance plan. Network services have been negotiated between the insurance carrier and healthcare providers. Services provided in-network are subject to the contracted allowable amount and represent predictable costs to the insurance carrier. Network services are less costly to the insured than out-of-network services.

Out-of-network services will cost the insured more based on the terms of the benefit structure outlined by the insurance carrier. Further, because the provider is not a participating provider, under contract with the insurance carrier, the provider may not be willing to accept the allowed amount paid by the insurance carrier. As a result, the patient is responsible for the cost differential between the allowed amount and the standard fee of the provider. An important exception occurs when an insurance carrier does not have a complete network of providers available in a given geographic area. In this case, if the insured requires a service that is not available in-network within a certain distance, usually 30–60 miles, from the insured's home, an exception may be granted such that the insured receives the service out-of-network but pays the standard in-network amount.

With the complexity of insurance, particularly in managed care plans, it is understandable that insured patients are sometimes as complicated and difficult for a medical practice's insurance staff members to deal with as uninsured patients. In many cases, medical office insurance staff can provide an important service to patients by explaining the elements of their insurance and helping them identify situations, such as out-of-network exceptions, that might reduce their cost burden.

TYPES OF MANAGED CARE ORGANIZATIONS

The common types of managed care are HMOs, preferred provider organizations (PPOs), and point-of-service (POS) plans. Managed care plans provide a wide range of services and focus on reducing cost by requiring the insured to seek healthcare from network providers who have contracted with the health plan. Two other attempts at cost control are use of *utilization review,* which is designed to control the number of times a patient sees a provider, and requirement of a *referral* from a primary care provider before the patient can see a specialist.

Health maintenance organization

Traditionally HMOs focus on preventive care and can work well for healthy populations — sometimes HMOs are referred to as *well-care insurance.* HMOs can provide significant cost savings in health plan benefits for employers. HMOs usually require the insured to receive services from a network provider with whom the HMO has a contract. HMOs typically exert considerable effort to control access to services by requiring referrals for certain services and precertification for hospital admission.

Preferred provider organization

PPOs are similar to HMOs in that they are intended to provide cost saving, but they incorporate some of the features of fee-for-service insurance and they usually cost more than HMOs. In most cases PPOs do not require a *gatekeeper* (that is, a primary care provider to give a referral) but do provide lists of certain providers from whom the insured can choose. PPOs emphasize seeking care from a network provider and sometimes require written referrals before a patient can see a specialist. The coinsurance charge for the insured will be higher if the insured receives care from an out-of-network provider.

Point-of-service plan

POS plans, like PPO plans, incorporate features of both fee-for-service and HMO insurance. In fact POS plans are like PPO plans except that POS plans require a gatekeeper primary care provider who coordinates care for the insured. Because PPO and POS plans incorporate features of fee-for-service insurance, both types of managed care are more expensive than HMO plans.

CONSUMER-DIRECTED HEALTH PLANS

Although managed care plans tend to insure populations less likely to use healthcare services at the same rate of utilization as older age populations, managed care options have still not succeeded in reducing costs to acceptable rates. Dissatisfaction has given rise to consumer-directed health plans such as health savings accounts (HSAs), HRAs, and flexible spending accounts (FSAs), which are designed to offset unreimbursed medical expenses. Exhibit 2.3 displays a comparison of the self-insured plans.

Health reimbursement account

HRAs are insurance plans partially self-funded by the employer, who pays a premium up to a cap. The employer receives business expense tax savings when distributions are made. After the cap has been reached the traditional insurance policy kicks in. HRAs, also known as health reimbursement arrangements, have no health insurance requirements but normally look like traditional insurance to the insured. HRAs are largely designed at the discretion of the employer, and only employers can make contributions. While employers may seek employee input into HRA design, the employer has the discretion to make benefit design decisions. The insured typically pays physician copays, drug card copays, deductibles, and coinsurance.

Health savings account

The Medicare Prescription Drug, Improvement, and Modernization Act of 2003 provided for HSAs. HSAs are intended to provide a savings account funded with before-tax dollars that can be used for both current and future qualified medical expenses. Savings not spent within the year that the contribution is made can be carried over for use in future years. HSAs are

EXHIBIT 2.3 ■ Self-Insured Plans Benefits Comparison

Internal Revenue Service (IRS) Plan Design	Flexible Spending Account—FSA	Health Reimbursement Account—HRA	Health Savings Account—HSA
Who Qualifies?	Qualify if employer provides	Qualify if employer provides	Anyone with HDHP—including self-employed
Requires High Deductible Health Plan (HDHP)	No	No	Yes
Contribution Limits	None	None	Set yearly by IRS
When Is Money Used?	Anytime	Employer decides	Anytime
Salary Tax Status	Pre-tax allowed	Pre-tax not allowed except with HDHP offered with HRA	Allowed for pre-tax with HDHP and after tax
Carryover	No carryover for unused amounts—Use in calendar year	Permitted	Required
Medical Expenses Covered	Unreimbursed medical expenses defined by IRS Code 213(d). No insurance premiums or long-term care (LTC) services.	Unreimbursed medical expenses defined by IRS Code 214(d). Insurance premiums and LTC.	Unreimbursed medical expenses defined by IRS Code 213(d). COBRA premiums, qualified LTC, and insurance premiums while receiving unemployment benefits over age 65.
Preventive Care	Allowed	Allowed	Allowed by HDHP statute
Health Insurance Status	Not required to have insurance to participate	Employer decides	Yes, must have HDHP
Who Contributes?	Employee, employer, or both	Employee decides, employer mandatory	Employee or employer
Cash Out of Unused Amount	No	No	Permitted but with tax consequences unless 65+
Portability—job to job	No	Employer decides	Yes
Medical Expenses Year of Contribution	Yes	No	No
Annual Amount Available 1st Day of Coverage	Yes	No	No
Other Insurance Limited	No	No	Yes
Taxable Account Earnings	No	No	No, but cash-out may be taxed
Who Sets Up?	Employer	Employer	Employer

Source: Holt, Sarah J. 2010. *Get the Money in the Door: Physician Billing Basics.* Englewood, Colo.: Medical Group Management Association, p. 16. Reprinted with permission from Medical Group Management Association.

coupled with HDHPs where deductibles and out-of-pocket expenses are defined and adjusted annually and do not allow participants to be covered by secondary insurance. HSAs allow both individuals' and employers' contributions to accounts and are portable. HSAs place spending responsibility on the individual. They differ from HRAs where no separate savings account is established.

Flexible spending account

FSAs, also known as *flexible spending arrangements,* are set up by employers to allow employees the ability to use pre-tax dollars, set aside through payroll deduction, to pay for unreimbursed qualified medical expenses. While usually funded by employees, employers may also contribute. Like HRAs there is no insurance requirement for participation. Money in an FSA must be withdrawn for services provided within the calendar year in which the money is set aside. Any unused funds are forfeited to the employer, and FSAs are not portable. Prior to the Affordable Care Act of 2010, money in FSAs could be used for reimbursing over-the-counter drugs. As of January 1, 2011, that is not a qualified expense.

KEY TERMS AND DEFINITIONS

Benefits Package — The collection of services an insurance carrier has agreed to pay for under the insurance contract.

Coinsurance — The percentage of the covered charge that the insured individual is required to pay to satisfy payment for services provided. Coinsurance is paid after insurance pays its portion. The coinsurance percentage amount is established in the benefit plan purchased from the insurance carrier. The insurance deductible must be met before coinsurance is applicable.

Copayment — Required payment when services are accessed. Stipulated by benefits package. Paid by insured before insurance pays.

Deductible — The amount an insured individual must pay before insurance begins to pay for covered services. Deductibles are met at the beginning of each plan year and are defined by the insurance contract.

Discounted Fee-for-Service — Provider gives carrier discount on standard fee, discount is passed on to insured.

Fee-for-Service (FFS) — Charges for medical services based on the practice's standard fee schedule with the expectation that fees will be paid as charged. Typically indemnity insurance, insurance pays 80 percent and the insured pays 20 percent.

Flexible Spending Account (FSA) — IRS designed. Allows employees to use pre-tax dollars, set aside through payroll deduction to pay for unreimbursed qualified medical expenses. Money in FSA must be withdrawn for services provided within the calendar year for which money is set aside. Unused funds are forfeited. Not portable.

Gatekeeper — In a managed care arena, a primary care physician who manages a patient's care and makes referrals when necessary.

Health Maintenance Organization (HMO) — Managed care plan designed to provide cost saving by exerting effort to control access to services by requiring referrals and pre-certifications. May require primary care gatekeeper.

Health Reimbursement Account (HRA) — IRS designed. Employer partially reimburses participating employees for the cost of health services. Partially self-funded by employer, and employer receives business expense tax savings on distributions. Looks like traditional insurance to employees. Is portable.

Health Savings Account (HSA) — IRS designed. Allows both individuals and employers with high-deductible policies to contribute tax free to an account to pay for current and future qualified medical expenses. Is portable and places spending responsibility on individual.

High-Deductible Health Plan (HDHP) — Health plan with higher deductibles than would be expected from traditional health plans. Higher deductibles typically require lower premiums. Both HSAs and HRAs are components of an HDHP.

In-network — A provider among a group of providers that have contracted with a health plan so that its insured can access healthcare services at discounted rates.

Insurance Payment — The portion of healthcare services paid by insurance carrier. The amount is based on the benefits package purchased. Payment varies based on whether services were in-network or out-of-network.

Point-of-Service (POS) Plan — Managed care plan designed to provide cost savings, emphasize in-network care. Requires gatekeeper. Features of both FFS and HMO.

Preferred Provider Organization (PPO) — A type of healthcare plan in which a group of providers contracts with an organization at discounted rates to provide medical services. PPOs are managed care plans similar to HMO but allow employees to choose to see a provider either inside or outside of the plan. Seeing a provider who is not a plan member will cost the patient more than seeing a provider who is a plan member. Usually no gatekeeper. Incorporates features of both FFS insurance and HMOs.

Premium — Amount paid monthly during health insurance contract year to provide assurance of being eligible to receive benefits outlined in benefits package.

REVIEW OF OBJECTIVES

- **Describe the role of commercial insurance.**
  - The majority of United States citizens are covered by a policy purchased from a commercial insurance carrier.
  - Sixty percent of working citizens in the United States are covered by health insurance linked to an employer.
  - Ten percent of United States citizens are covered by health insurance individual plans.

- **Differentiate the fundamental elements of health insurance.**
  - The fundamental elements of health insurance are premium, copayment, deductible, insurance payment, and coinsurance.
  - Of the five fundamental elements the insured is required to pay four of the elements, all except the insurance payment.

- **Identify the major categories of commercial insurance.**
  - The major categories of commercial insurance, ranging from least restrictive to most restrictive, are fee-for-service, discounted fee-for-service, managed care HMO, managed care PPO, and managed care POS.

- **Review the functionality of the various types of commercial insurance.**
  - FFS is indemnity insurance, typically 80 percent/20 percent coverage.
  - Discounted FFS means the provider has given the insurance carrier a discount on standard fees.
  - HMOs are managed care, designed to control costs.
  - PPOs are the next step in managed care. Designed to control cost; emphasize in-network care.
  - POSs are more restrictive managed care designed to control cost; emphasize in-network care and require gatekeeper.
  - HRAs are self-insured and IRS designed. Employer selects and sets up participation.
  - HSAs are self-insured and IRS designed. Differ from HRAs in which no separate savings account is established.
  - FSAs are self-insured and IRS designed. Funded by payroll deductions. Use for services received in year of payroll deduction or lose money.

REVIEW EXERCISES: LESSON 2

MULTIPLE CHOICE

Please circle the best answer.

1. **In the United States most citizens have health insurance coverage linked to:**
   - **a.** Commercial insurance
   - **b.** Medicare insurance
   - **c.** Medicaid insurance

2. **Fee-for-service is insurance that:**
   - **a.** Typically insurance pays 90 percent of charge and insured pays 10 percent
   - **b.** Typically insurance pays 80 percent of charge and insured pays 20 percent
   - **c.** Typically insurance pays 70 percent of charge and insured pays 30 percent

3. **When a provider agrees with a carrier to take a discount of 15 percent on standard charges to satisfy in full payment for services, that arrangement is called:**
   - **a.** Managed care
   - **b.** Point-of-service care
   - **c.** Discounted fee-for-service

4. **The yearly deductible can be called:**
   - **a.** The self-insurance portion of health insurance
   - **b.** First-dollar coverage
   - **c.** One-time, lifetime payment

5. **The service balance that remains after insurance has paid is called:**
   - **a.** Copayment
   - **b.** Coinsurance
   - **c.** Managed care

6. **Insurance plans that have shifted the cost away from the health insurance carrier to the insured are called:**
   - **a.** High-deductible plans
   - **b.** Indemnity plans
   - **c.** FFS plans

7. **Fee-for-service plans lost attractiveness because of:**
   - **a.** Quality
   - **b.** Access
   - **c.** Cost

8. **The common types of managed care are:**
   a. HMO, PPO, POS
   b. PSO, HMO, IRA
   c. HMO, PPO, IRA

9. **Utilization review is designed to:**
   a. Control the amount of collective charges from providers by forcing providers to charge lower-level E/M codes
   b. Control the number of visits by requiring a referral from a primary care provider before seeing a specialist
   c. Control the number and billing costs of primary care providers.

10. **Discounted fee-for-service is the closest relative to:**
    a. PPO
    b. POS
    c. FFS

11. **When an insurance carrier pays for a service, the percentage of the service paid depends on:**
    a. Copay amount
    b. Deductible amount
    c. Benefits package

12. **HSAs differ from HRAs relating to:**
    a. The requirement of setting up a separate savings account
    b. The medical expenses year of contribution
    c. The annual amount available on the first day of coverage

13. **The following statement is true about commercial insurance:**
    a. Health insurance benefits structure has evolved over time
    b. Commercial insurance covers all citizens who are not insured by a government program
    c. Commercial insurance offers four different health insurance benefits packages

14. **Coinsurance percentages due by the patient to satisfy payment for services vary based on:**
    a. Copayment and deductible amounts
    b. Services in-network or out-of-network
    c. Monthly premiums

15. **Which plan prohibits carryover for unused amounts from one calendar year to the next?**
    a. HSA
    b. HRA
    c. FSA

(Answers on page 35)

CASE STUDIES

Case study 1: Jim has had several health problems this year. He has met his deductible. Now he has discovered that he has a hernia and is in need of hernia surgery. He goes to the surgeon's office for an office visit, and the woman at the front desk asks him to pay his copayment. Jim says that he has already met his deductible and doesn't owe a copayment for services. What does the front desk staff member tell Jim?

- **a.** Your copayment is required when you access services and is not linked to whether you have met your deductible or not.
- **b.** You are correct. You don't owe a copayment today.
- **c.** You are confused. As long as you pay coinsurance, you will have a copayment due.

Case study 2: Mr. Smith has called Joan in the insurance department explaining that he received a statement saying that he owes money to Always Best Medical Practice. Mr. Smith says because he has met his deductible, he doesn't owe any more money to anybody. After Joan explains the insurance process to Mr. Smith, he now says that his insurance company has paid and that the physician whom he knows very well can easily write off the coinsurance. What should Joan tell Mr. Smith?

- **a.** She will talk with the physician to see if he wants the insurance department to write off the coinsurance balance.
- **b.** The organization is unable to write off the coinsurance based on the insurance contract. In fact, if it were to write off the coinsurance after collecting the insurance portion of the charge from the insurance carrier, it would be committing insurance fraud.
- **c.** The organization is unable to write off the coinsurance based on the insurance contract. In fact, she will call the carrier and ask it for permission to write off the coinsurance amount.

Case study 3: Joan has received a personal payment on Mrs. James' balance. Mrs. James has marked the check with her account number. Joan realizes that the payment sent by Mrs. James is too much, and when she posts the payment there will be a credit balance on Mrs. James' account. Joan knows that Mrs. James' married daughter, Chris Jackson, owes the medical practice money. How should Joan handle the situation?

- **a.** Post the remaining amount of the check to Chris Jackson's account so she doesn't have to send any money back to Mrs. James.
- **b.** Post the correct payment to Mrs. James' account and create a credit balance, then follow the organization's policy for dealing with credit balances.
- **c.** Post the correct payment to Mrs. James' account and give her a call to get her permission to post the remainder of the amount to Chris Jackson's account.

(Answers on page 35)

COMPLETION QUESTIONS

1. What are the five major categories of commercial insurance?

____

2. Fee-for-service insurance is sometimes referred to as indemnity insurance. What do we mean by *indemnity insurance*?

____

3. What are the five fundamental elements of health insurance?

____

4. In 1973 legislation was passed to provide federal funding for the expansion of HMOs. Why?

____

5. Define *monthly premium*.

____

6. The deductible may be called the self-insured portion of insurance. Why?

____

7. What is the difference between *copayment* and *coinsurance*?

____

8. What does the term *in-network* mean?

____

9. What does *out-of-network* mean?

____

10. What may be the consequences of seeing an out-of-network provider to provide care?

____

11. When might an out-of-network exception occur?

____

12. Define *gatekeeper*.

____

13. When comparing the typical PPO and POS plan to HMO plans, what can we conclude?

____

14. Managed care has not succeeded in reducing cost sufficiently and as a result consumer-directed plans have been instituted. What are three kinds of plans?

____

15. What major change occurred for FSAs due to the Affordable Care Act (ACA)?

____

(Answers on page 35)

MATCHING

Please match the letter of the definition to the term.
Write the letter of the definition next to the term.

Health maintenance organization (HMO)_____	**a.** The portion of healthcare services paid by insurance carrier. The amount is based on the benefits package purchased. Payment varies based on whether services were in-network or out-of-network.
Point-of-service (POS) plan_____	**b.** In a managed care arena, a primary care physician who manages a patient's care and makes referrals when necessary.
Benefits package_____	**c.** Provider gives carrier discount on standard fee, discount is passed on to insured.
Copayment_____	**d.** IRS designed. Allows both individuals and employers with high-deductible policies to contribute tax free to an account to pay for current and future qualified medical expenses. Is portable and places spending responsibility on individual.
Insurance payment_____	**e.** Managed care plan designed to provide cost saving by exerting effort to control access to services by requiring referrals and precertifications. May require primary care gatekeeper.
Health savings account (HSA)_____	**f.** Charges for medical services based on the practice's standard fee schedule with the expectation that fees will be paid as charged. Typically indemnity insurance, insurance pays 80 percent and the insured pays 20 percent.
Fee-for-service (FFS)_____	**g.** Managed care plan designed to provide cost savings, emphasize in-network care. Usually no gatekeeper.
Flexible spending account (FSA)_____	**h.** IRS designed. Employer partially reimburses participating employees for the cost of health services. Partially self-funded by employer, and employer receives business expense tax savings on distributions. Looks like traditional insurance to employees. Is portable.
Preferred provider organization (PPO)_____	**i.** The amount an insured individual must pay before insurance begins to pay for covered services. Met at the beginning of each plan year and defined by the insurance contract.

Health reimbursement account (HRA)_____	**j.** A type of healthcare plan in which a group of providers contracts with an organization at discounted rates to provide medical services. This type of managed care plan is similar to HMO but allows employees to choose to see a provider either inside or outside of the plan. Seeing a provider who is not a plan member will cost the patient more than seeing a provider who is a plan member. Usually no gatekeeper. Incorporates features of both FFS insurance and HMOs.
In-network_____	**k.** The collection of services an insurance carrier has agreed to pay for under the insurance contract.
Coinsurance_____	**l.** A provider among a group of providers that have contracted with a health plan so that its insured can access healthcare services at discounted rates.
Gatekeeper_____	**m.** Amount paid monthly during health insurance contract year to provide assurance of being eligible to receive benefits outlined in benefits package.
Deductible_____	**n.** The service balance that remains after healthcare insurance has paid. The insured is responsible for this amount.
Premium_____	**o.** IRS designed. Allows employees to use pre-tax dollars, set aside through payroll deduction to pay for unreimbursed qualified medical expenses. Money in FSA must be withdrawn for services provided within the calendar year for which money is set aside. Unused funds are forfeited. Not portable.
Discounted fee-for-service_____	**p.** Required payment when services are accessed. Stipulated by benefits package. Paid by insured before insurance pays.
High-deductible health plan (HDHP)_____	**q.** Health plan with higher deductibles than would be expected from traditional health plans. Higher deductibles typically require lower premiums. Both HSAs and HRAs are components.

(Answers on page 36)

ANSWERS: LESSON 2

MULTIPLE CHOICE

1-a; 2-b; 3-c; 4-a; 5-b; 6-a; 7-c; 8-a; 9-b; 10-c; 11-c; 12-a; 13-a; 14-b; 15-c

CASE STUDIES

Case study 1-a; Case study 2-b; Case study 3-b

COMPLETION QUESTIONS

1. Fee-for-service (FFS), discounted fee-for-service, managed care HMOs, managed care PPOs, and managed care POSs
2. Indemnity insurance plans pay 80 percent of the fee-for-service charge submitted by the healthcare provider, and the insured pays the remaining 20 percent of the billed charge.
3. The fundamental elements of health insurance are premium, copayment, deductible, insurance payment, and coinsurance.
4. To address high costs influenced in part by the high utilization and the availability of advanced technology
5. Monthly premium is the fee paid each month by the insured in order to retain insurance coverage.
6. A deductible is a set amount that the insured must pay out-of-pocket before insurance starts to cover services.
7. Copayment is a set charge amount that will be paid upon accessing services as designated by benefit design. Coinsurance is a percentage of the covered charge that the insurance is required to pay to resolve the cost of medical services.
8. In-network means that a provider has contracted with a particular insurance carrier to provide services at a negotiated cost for services.
9. Out-of-network means that the provider does not have a contract with the insured's particular insurance plan.
10. The out-of-network provider may not be willing to accept the allowed amount paid by the insurance carrier, and the patient may be responsible for the cost differential between the allowed amount and the provider's standard fee.
11. If the carrier does not have a complete network of providers available in a given geographic area, an exception may be granted so that the insured pays the standard in-network amount.
12. In a managed care arena, a primary physician who manages a patient's care and makes referrals if necessary
13. That PPO and POS plans are likely to be more expensive because they incorporate features of fee-for-service insurance
14. HRAs, HSAs, and FSAs
15. As of January 1, 2011, FSAs can no longer be used to reimburse the cost of over-the-counter drugs.

MATCHING

__ Health maintenance organization (HMO): **e**

__ Point-of-service (POS) plan: **j**

__ Benefits package: **k**

__ Copayment: **p**

__ Insurance payment: **a**

__ Health savings account (HSA): **d**

__ Fee-for-service (FFS): **f**

__ Flexible spending account (FSA): **o**

__ Preferred provider organization (PPO): **g**

__ Health reimbursement account (HRA): **h**

__ In-network: **l**

__ Coinsurance: **n**

__ Gatekeeper: **b**

__ Deductible: **i**

__ Premium: **m**

__ Discounted fee-for-service: **c**

__ High-deductible health plan (HDHP): **q**

LESSON 3

Government Insurance

OBJECTIVES

- Review the scope of government healthcare insurance.
- Examine the importance of compliance with provisions of government health insurance programs.
- Define the provisions of the Affordable Care Act of 2010 that impact medical office insurance staff.
- Summarize Medicare Parts A through D.
- Identify the various types of government health insurance programs.

SCOPE OF GOVERNMENT HEALTHCARE INSURANCE

Medicare insurance was instituted in 1965, but the impetus for the Medicare program dates back to the original Social Security bill passed in 1935. Although Medicare is tied to the Social Security program, it has its own multiple funding streams — mandatory contributions by employers and employees, general tax revenues, beneficiaries' premiums, along with copayments and deductibles. Title XVIII of the Social Security Act designated Medicare as a complement to the traditional Social Security benefits. Persons entitled to Medicare insurance under the Social Security Act, called *beneficiaries,* include individuals who are age 65 or older, younger people with disabilities, and people with permanent kidney failure (that is, end-stage renal disease [ESRD]).

Because of the complexity of Medicare options, it is no wonder Medicare beneficiaries seek information from medical office insurance staff members who are associated with organizations they trust. While it is inappropriate for medical office insurance staff members to give advice regarding which plan to purchase, it is necessary for staff members to be knowledgeable about Medicare so that they can accurately answer questions. It is important to review the following to understand the challenges faced by potential Medicare beneficiaries.

The federal government is the largest purchaser of healthcare in the United States. The role of government in healthcare has expanded significantly since the beginning of Medicare in 1965. For three decades since the 1980s many attempts have been made to control cost and improve quality. One of the most recent in a long line of healthcare legislation is comprehensive healthcare reform (reviewed later in this lesson). Without examining the history of healthcare legislation in the United States, it is essential for medical office insurance staff to sufficiently understand the broad role of government healthcare insurance. This training manual includes an overview of various government insurances and thoroughly reviews the government programs Medicare and Medicaid.

UNDERSTANDING THE DIFFERENCE BETWEEN MEDICARE PARTS A, B, C, AND D

The following sections describe the differences between Medicare Parts A, B, C, and D.

Medicare Part A

Medicare Part A is a fee-for-service (FFS) insurance plan that pays for hospital costs including inpatient hospital services, skilled nursing facility (SNF) services, home health, and hospice care. The most comprehensive list of covered services under Part A is for *inpatient hospital services*. These services include semi-private room; meals; special diets; nursing services; lab tests; X-ray and other radiology and radiation services; operating and recovery room services; special care units; medical supplies and equipment; inpatient drugs and blood transfusions; and rehabilitation services. Patients have a 90-day hospital care stay in a benefit period and have a 60-day lifetime reserve if the 90-day stay has been exhausted.

Medicare Part B

Medicare Part B insurance pays for physician services. Part B, called Supplemental Medical Insurance, helps pay for outpatient hospital services (including ambulatory surgery centers), some home health services, and medical equipment and supplies. Part B also covers nonphysician practitioner services, diagnostic tests, ambulance transportation, and certain preventive care services. Services covered besides medical and surgical services include diagnostic tests; procedures related to treatment; radiology and pathology services; Level 1 office visit with a physician's nurse; drugs and biologicals that cannot be self-administered, such as chemotherapy; physical and occupational therapies; and speech pathology services.

Medicare Part C

Medicare Part C is known as Medicare Advantage. Part C, established by the Balanced Budget Act of 1997, is considered to be the Medicare managed care plan. Advantage plans are like health maintenance organizations (HMOs) or preferred provider organizations (PPOs). Part C offers broader coverage than the traditional Part B fee-for-service plan. If an individual is eligible for both Part A and Part B Medicare, he or she may elect to have Part C coverage instead of Parts A and B.

Medicare Part D

Medicare Part D is a voluntary drug benefit program that began in January 2006. Private insurance companies are approved by Medicare to provide Part D coverage. For a medication to be covered under Medicare, the service must be both reasonable and necessary for the diagnosis or treatment of the medical condition. Certain services are not covered, including those that have been excluded from the program as designated by the Centers for Medicare & Medicaid Services and those that have not been approved by the Food and

Drug Administration or are investigational in nature. Coverage benefits such as deductibles, premiums, and copayments depend on the plan that is chosen.

Medicare coverage eligibility

Coverage eligibility for each part of Medicare is defined by certain criteria. Patients who have questions about their Medicare eligibility can contact the Social Security Administration (800-772-1213 [TTY 800-325-0778] or www.socialsecurity.gov) for assistance.

Part A

An individual must be age 65 or older and be receiving or be eligible to receive retirement benefits from Social Security (SS) or the Railroad Retirement Board (RRB). An individual 65 or older who is *not* eligible for benefits from Social Security or RRB may be eligible to purchase Part A. Any person under age 65 must be eligible to receive disability benefits from SS or RRB for at least 24 months or be receiving dialysis or renal transplantation for ESRD.

Part B

An individual must satisfy Part A criteria and select enrollment in Part B. In most cases, Part B requires payment of a monthly premium.

Part C

An individual must be eligible for both Part A and Part B, as well as sign up during the normal enrollment period, which is usually within a seven-month window of time around his or her 65th birthday. An individual may be turned down for Part C if he or she delays enrollment beyond the window of opportunity or does not qualify because of health issues. Medicare Part C Advantage plans offer private healthcare options and are sometimes referred to as managed care plans.

Part D

An individual must be eligible for Medicare coverage and normally pays a monthly premium. A beneficiary whose income is low enough to qualify for a subsidy does not pay a monthly premium. Medicare beneficiaries should enroll in Part D when they are first eligible or they will be penalized when they decide to join. Part D is a voluntary Medicare drug benefit that began in January 2006. Private insurance companies that are approved by Medicare provide Part D coverage. Coverage benefits such as deductibles, premiums, and copays depend on the plan that is chosen.

Medicare Web site

Information regarding Medicare can be found at www.cms.hhs.gov. This Web site is massive, and the information you seek may not be easy to find. A tip for using the Web site effectively is to start at the HOME screen, then (1) click on the "Resources & Tools" section, (2) under "Sitewide Tools and Resources," click on "Frequently Asked Questions"; and (3) enter the search term for which you need information. Information in this format is often easier to understand.

MEDICAID

The Medicaid program is designed to provide medical benefits to certain low-income groups who have no or limited healthcare insurance. Medicaid does not cover all poor persons, as limited income is only one of the requirements for Medicaid coverage. The federal government establishes general guidelines for the Medicaid program, but each state is free to establish its own eligibility and benefits structure. The Medicaid program is administered by the states, and services vary by state.

Medicaid pays for medical services by sending reimbursement directly to the healthcare provider rather than sending money to the insured to pay for services. In some states, the Medicaid recipients are asked to pay a small portion of the fee for accessing services. The copayment amounts, typically $0.50 to $3.00, vary by state, as do the rules that determine income eligibility. As previously stated, income is only one of the determining criteria for Medicaid eligibility. The Federal Poverty Level Charts are used by state Medicaid agencies to help develop eligibility criteria.

Medicaid eligibility groups

Both federal and state law define Medicaid eligibility groups. Typically the *eligibility groups* are characterized as categorically needy, medically needy, or special groups. It is important to note that not all states recognize all categories.

Categorically needy

The categorically needy may not meet financial coverage thresholds but may be eligible for Medicaid because of excessive medical expenses. The *categorically needy* may be defined as:

- Families who meet the state eligibility requirements for Aid to Families with Dependent Children.
- Low-income pregnant women and children less than age six.
- Children ages 6–19 with family income below the federal poverty level.
- Legal caretakers of low-income children.
- Supplemental Security Income (SSI) recipients.
- Individuals living in medical institutions.

Medically needy

Not all states have medically needy programs; however, more than one-half of the states do. The *medically needy* include:

- Those with too much money, income, or savings to be classified as categorically needy;
- Pregnant women through a 60-day postpartum period;
- Certain newborns and children less than 18 years of age;
- Persons who are aged, blind, or disabled (SSI may serve as determining factor);

- Some groups of children younger than age 21 who meet requirements and are full-time students; or
- Individuals who would be eligible if they were not enrolled in a health maintenance organization.

Special groups

Special groups may be defined as:

- Women who have breast or cervical cancer,
- People with tuberculosis,
- Medicare beneficiaries, or
- Individuals who may have lost their Medicare coverage though they are employed but are still below the federal poverty level.

Eligibility time frame

Medicaid coverage does not necessarily start the day an individual is approved for Medicaid. Coverage may start retroactively for up to three months prior to application, depending on the eligibility condition during the retroactive period. Medicaid coverage typically stops at the end of the month in which a person's circumstances change such that eligibility is impacted.

Mandatory services

While states dictate the services they provide and the limitations of those services, certain services are mandated by federal statute. Services provided must be available to everyone in that group unless they are explicitly waived under Medicaid law. Services for the categorically needy include:

- Inpatient hospital treatment;
- Outpatient hospital treatment;
- X-ray and lab;
- State-licensed pediatric and family nurse practitioner;
- Nursing facility if age 21 and older;
- All medically necessary screening, diagnosis, and treatment if less than 21 years of age;
- Family planning;
- Physician;
- Medical and surgical dentistry;
- Home health if entitled to nursing facility;
- Nurse midwife;
- Pregnancy and complicating conditions; and
- Postpartum through 60 days.

Each state Medicaid program has unique requirements, and medical office insurance staff members should familiarize themselves with their own state's criteria. Each state has a Web site outlining its services.

IMPORTANCE OF COMPLIANCE

It is necessary for medical office insurance staff to learn as much about government health insurance programs as possible, because they are responsible to implement and abide by federal regulations in the various health insurance programs. Medical office insurance staff must understand that failure to comply with the regulations of government insurance can result in prosecution by the Office of Inspector General (OIG) under federal law, state law, and contract law. They must also understand that failure to comply with government regulations mandates prosecution in order to protect the integrity of the government programs. Committing fraud against the federal government is a crime that may result in significant fines, Civil Monetary Penalties, a prison sentence, or expulsion from participation in any federal healthcare programs. Government representatives are obligated to uphold the intent of the programs and are accountable to provide oversight assurances to the citizenry on whose behalf they work.

When government regulations are fraudulently breached, the full force of the Department of Justice (DOJ) will be used as a resource to set the violation right. Having the DOJ at its disposal, the government is willing to prosecute fraud in its programs, in contrast to commercial carriers who must hire attorneys at the expense of their profit margin. Whereas commercial carriers may prosecute breaches of contract, it is less common that conditions set forth by commercial insurance would result in prosecution unless the breaches are egregious.

PROVISIONS OF THE AFFORDABLE CARE ACT OF 2010

In 2010 Congress passed and President Obama signed into law the comprehensive healthcare reform bill, the Patient Protection and Affordable Care Act. Later in the same month the act was amended by the Healthcare and Education Reconciliation Act. The name Affordable Care Act is now used to refer to the final version of the law that includes the reform bill and the amendments to it. While there are many provisions to the comprehensive healthcare reform bill, some of the major ones that medical office insurance staff should be aware of follow. (For more details on the provisions discussed below as part of the Affordable Care Act of 2010, visit www.healthcare.gov/law/provisions.)

Young adult coverage

This provision allows young adults to be covered on the healthcare insurance policy of their parents until age 26. If a young adult can be covered under another qualified plan other than his or her parents' plan, a plan can be grandfathered to omit young adult coverage until 2014. The young adult coverage provision allows coverage on a parent's plan regardless of status relating to marriage, school enrollment, living address, or financial dependency.

Appeal of health plan decisions

For any new plan year on or after September 23, 2010, this provision allows individuals new appeal rights when coverage for healthcare services has been denied. Plans must give individuals information on how to appeal, and appeal responses are governed by law. Additionally, if the initial denial is upheld, individuals have a right to appeal to an independent reviewer working outside of the health plan.

Children's pre-existing conditions

This provision applies to job-related health plans and prohibits health plans from denying or limiting coverage to children because of pre-existing conditions.

Curbing insurance cancellations

This provision forbids health plans from cancelling coverage or rescinding benefits simply because of an honest mistake made in the application process.

Preserving physician choice and emergency care

This provision permits patients to choose any primary care physician or pediatrician in their health plan's network and permits them to see an OB/GYN physician within their health plan without referral. It also allows the right to hospital emergency care outside their network and without pre-authorization by their health plan.

Eliminating annual and lifetime limits

This provision restricts and by 2014 eliminates annual limits imposed by health plans on essential healthcare services. The lifetime limit that restricts the amount of money that a health plan will spend on an individual during that person's lifetime will be eliminated on plan coverage issued or renewing after September 23, 2010.

Patients' bill of rights

This provision is intended to put patients back in charge of their healthcare and healthcare benefits.

Preventive care

This provision requires healthcare plans to forgo copayment, coinsurance, and deductible on some preventive care so that individuals can stay healthy. Preventive services included are blood pressure, diabetes, and cholesterol tests; cancer screenings, including mammograms and colonoscopies; counseling relating to smoking cessation, weight loss, healthy eating, depression, and alcohol abuse; routine vaccinations for measles, polio, or meningitis; flu and pneumonia vaccinations; pregnancy counseling, screening, and vaccines; and well-baby and well-child visits, from birth to age 21.

OTHER GOVERNMENT HEALTHCARE INSURANCE PROGRAMS

The government offers many different insurance programs in addition to Medicare and Medicaid. They include those described in the following sections.

Children's Health Insurance Program (CHIP)

CHIP is a program that provides free or low cost health insurance to children from birth to 19 years of age. Each state designs its own program. All children get routine preventive care checkups, immunizations, hospital care, dental care, lab, and x-ray coverage under the program. Typically, coverage applies to families of four who make less than $44,000 per year, but in some states income limits are higher. Several million children are covered under this program. More information can be obtained from www.InsureKidsNow.gov.

Consolidated Omnibus Budget Reconciliation Act (COBRA)

COBRA gives employees covered by employer-sponsored health insurance who leave their employment, whether voluntarily or involuntarily, the ability, under federal law, to maintain the insurance coverage provided by their employer. COBRA dictates that employers with 20 or more employees offer continued health insurance coverage to former qualified employees or their families who wish to maintain insurance coverage. COBRA allows employers to charge the insured up to 102 percent of the monthly premium to maintain coverage. Coverage under COBRA is available in event of job loss, reduction in work hours, job transition, death, or divorce. COBRA coverage in most cases can be extended for 18 months if the employer is informed of the intent to be covered by COBRA within 60 days from the date employment was terminated and the premium is paid in full. Even employees who are not qualified to maintain health insurance under federal COBRA may be able to qualify under state law that covers an employee working for an employer with fewer employees than the federal COBRA requirement. State law will verify the state-specific requirements to qualify for small-group COBRA. More information on COBRA can be found at the Department of Labor's Web site, www.dol.gov; search COBRA.

Federal Employee Health Benefits (FEHB) Program

The FEHB Program provides health coverage to current and retired Federal employees and their survivors including members of Congress. Individuals in this program have the ability to select from a wide variety of plans. They can choose high-deductible, catastrophic plans; health savings accounts; FFS plans; PPO plans; or HMO. Plans in this program are known to provide excellent coverage.

Indian Health Services (IHS)

IHS is a program that began from legislation in 1921 to elevate the health status by providing healthcare services for American Indians and Alaska Native people. IHS is an agency within the Department of Health and Human Services. A unique government-to-government relationship exists between American Indian tribes and Alaska Native corporations that are federally recognized and the United States. This relationship allows for the provision of healthcare and other services. To learn more about this program visit www.ihs.gov.

Veterans' Benefits

Veterans' Benefits is a program that provides coverage for veterans or individuals who have served in any branch the U.S. military either in active or reserve status and were honorably discharged or released. An individual may qualify for benefits if separated from the military because of disability or health reasons; served in combat within the past five years; was a prisoner of war; was a Purple Heart recipient; or received a Veteran's Affairs pension, disability benefits, or state Medicaid. Individuals may also receive prescription drug coverage. For more information go to www.va.gov.

TRICARE

TRICARE is a healthcare program for active-duty service members, activated or non-activated National Guard or Reserve members, retirees, and their families. It is a worldwide service with military facilities that provide healthcare services for military families through a network of civilian medical professionals. To receive TRICARE benefits an individual must be registered in the Defense Enrollment Eligibility Reporting System. TRICARE recognizes both network and non-network providers. By law, non-network providers cannot charge more than 15 percent above the maximum allowable TRICARE fee schedule, and beneficiaries are not responsible for paying more than 15 percent. TRICARE may require prior authorization and some out-of-pocket costs to beneficiaries, but it will typically pay for any medical services that are considered medically necessary. TRICARE currently offers several health plan options. These options evolve as public law is amended. The most recent information regarding TIRCARE can be found online at www.tricare.mil.

WORKERS' COMPENSATION

Employees hurt in a work-related accident or illness qualify for workers' compensation insurance benefits. Workers' compensation regulations are state specific. That may mean that not all employers in a state are required to provide workers' compensation insurance for their employees. Federal law focuses on non-military federal employees and companies engaged in interstate commerce. Although state law is not bound to federal law, federal law does set the coverage standards for the states. The influence of federal law is evident in various other federal laws that pertain to broad groups of employees other than those covered by workers' compensation. These laws address requirements for companies engaged in specific types of commerce conducted broadly, particularly across state lines. Workers' compensation requires employers to pay premiums based on industry classification. The Workers' Compensation Board (WCB) administers workers' compensation insurance. The WCB is a neutral agency that resolves workers' compensation issues.

Employees who believe that they have a workers' compensation claim must notify their employer immediately. Upon notification, the employer will have the employee complete paperwork relating to the event in order to file a claim. Typically benefits covered by workers' compensation insurance require employers to be responsible for a portion — usually two-thirds — of lost wages related to the injury or illness as well as all direct cost of medical treatment. If employees collect workers' compensation benefits, generally they are giving up the right to sue their employer. Workers' compensation insurance is intended to protect employers from lawsuits if they have maintained a standardized, safe work environment. In addition to protecting employers, workers' compensation insurance also protects coworkers from liability. The key information for medical office insurance staff members relating to workers' compensation insurance is to know that the employer must verify that the workers' compensation carrier will cover medical expenses.

KEY TERMS AND DEFINITIONS

Department of Justice (DOJ) — A department of the U.S. government administered by the attorney general, who is a member of the Cabinet, a part of the executive branch. The role of the DOJ is to enforce the law fairly and impartially, providing justice to all Americans.

Federal Law — A body of law at the national level; laws enacted by Congress. Violations of federal law are tried in federal court.

Fee-for-Service (FFS) — Charges for medical services based on the practice's standard fee schedule with the expectation that fees will be paid as charged. Typically indemnity insurance, insurance pays 80 percent and the insured pays 20 percent.

Health Maintenance Organization (HMO) — Managed care plan designed to provide cost saving by exerting effort to control access to services by requiring referrals and precertifications. May require primary care gatekeeper.

Health Savings Account (HSA) — IRS designed. Allows both individuals and employers with high-deductible policies to contribute tax free to an account to pay for current and future qualified medical expenses. Is portable and places spending responsibility on individual.

Maximum Allowable — The highest amount a provider can charge for a particular service. The maximum allowable charge is set by the insurance carrier.

Office of Inspector General (OIG) — A division of the Department of Health and Human Services that protects the integrity of the Medicare and Medicaid programs by conducting audits, investigations, inspections, and other functions that may identify noncompliance.

Preferred Provider Organization (PPO) — A type of healthcare plan in which a group of providers contracts with an organization at discounted rates to provide medical services. PPOs are managed care plans similar to HMO but allow employees to choose to see a provider either inside or outside of the plan. Seeing a provider who is not a plan member will cost the patient more than seeing a provider who is a plan member. Usually no gatekeeper. Incorporates features of both FFS insurance and HMOs.

REVIEW OF OBJECTIVES

- **Review the scope of government healthcare insurance.**
  - Government is the largest purchaser of healthcare, and government decisions often influence the policy and fee structure set by private insurance companies.
  - Government insurance covers several groups of individuals, including individuals over age 65, individuals with serious medical problems, impoverished individuals, and military personnel.

- **Examine the importance of compliance with provisions of government health insurance programs.**
  - Compliance with regulations of government health insurance programs is necessary, because fraud by providers of government health insurance programs is prosecuted by the OIG in conjunction with the Department of Justice.

- **Define the provisions of the Affordable Care Act of 2010 that impact medical office insurance staff.**
  - Young Adult Coverage
  - Appeal of Health Plan Decisions
  - Children's Pre-existing Conditions

- **Summarize Medicare Parts A through D.**
  - Medicare Part A provides coverage for hospital-based services, including inpatient hospital services, SNF services, home health, and hospice care. It is typically free of charge for individuals age 65 and older who are eligible to receive retirement benefits from Social Security or the Railroad Retirement Board.
  - Medicare Part B provides coverage for outpatient medical services, including provider visits, diagnostic tests, outpatient procedures, home health services, and medical equipment. Individuals are typically required to pay monthly premiums to receive Part B.
  - Medicare Part C, also known as Medicare Advantage, is a managed care plan that may be chosen as an alternative to Parts A and B. It also requires the payment of monthly premiums.
  - Medicare Part D is the prescription drug benefit.

- **Identify the various types of government health insurance programs.**
  - Medicare
  - Medicaid
  - Children's Health Insurance Program (CHIP)
  - Consolidated Omnibus Budget Reconciliation Act (COBRA)
  - Federal Employee Health Benefits (FEHB)
  - Indian Health Services (IHS)
  - Veterans' Benefits
  - TRICARE (military health benefits)

REVIEW EXERCISES: LESSON 3

MULTIPLE CHOICE

Please circle the best answer.

1. **The largest purchaser of healthcare is:**
   - **a.** The Office of Inspector General
   - **b.** The Department of Justice
   - **c.** The federal government

2. **Failure to comply with government regulations can result in prosecution under:**
   - **a.** Federal law
   - **b.** City statutes
   - **c.** International law

3. **In 2010 Congress passed comprehensive healthcare reform referred to as:**
   - **a.** People's Choice
   - **b.** Affordable Care Act
   - **c.** Healthcare Public Option

4. **The Young Adult Coverage provision of healthcare reform allows young adults to be covered on their parents' health plan until:**
   - **a.** Age 19
   - **b.** Age 31
   - **c.** Age 26

5. **The Children's Pre-existing Conditions provision of healthcare reform prohibits health plans that cover children from:**
   - **a.** Allowing children to be covered on their parents' health plan when pre-existing conditions exist
   - **b.** Extending coverage payment to more than $5 million on pre-existing conditions
   - **c.** Denying or limiting coverage because of pre-existing conditions

6. **By 2014 the Affordable Care Act eliminates:**
   - **a.** Patients' Bill of Rights
   - **b.** Annual and lifetime limits
   - **c.** Insurance cancellations for any reason

7. **New or renewed health plans on or after September 23, 2010, are required to forgo copayment, coinsurance, and deductible on some preventive care to include:**
   - **a.** Mammograms and colonoscopies
   - **b.** CT scans and chemotherapy
   - **c.** Hysterectomy and colostomy

8. CHIP refers to:

- **a.** Comprehensive Health Insurance Plans
- **b.** Consolidated Health Insurance Plans
- **c.** Children's Health Insurance Program

9. COBRA is a government program to:

- **a.** Provide the extension of temporary health coverage to individuals whose employment circumstances have changed
- **b.** Provide the extension of temporary health coverage to individuals whose salaries have been reduced
- **c.** Provide the extension of temporary health coverage to individuals whose new health plan has reduced benefits

10. Continuation coverage may cost up to:

- **a.** 98 percent of the cost of plan coverage
- **b.** 100 percent of the cost of plan coverage
- **c.** 102 percent of the cost of plan coverage

11. FEHB is a program to provide health insurance to:

- **a.** Current and retired federal employees and their survivors
- **b.** Current members of Congress not to include their families
- **c.** Current members of the president's Cabinet

12. Indian Health Services is a program to elevate the health status of:

- **a.** American Indians and all Alaskan residents
- **b.** American Indians and Alaskan Native people
- **c.** American Indians and some Alaskan natives

13. Former prisoners of war may qualify for healthcare benefits from:

- **a.** Veterans' Benefits
- **b.** Prisoners of Foreign War Healthcare Fund
- **c.** Department of Justice

14. By law, non-network providers cannot charge TRICARE members more than:

- **a.** 20 percent above the maximum allowable
- **b.** 15 percent above the maximum allowable
- **c.** 25 percent above the maximum allowable

15. TRICARE is a healthcare program for:

- **a.** U.S. military
- **b.** U.S. Congress
- **c.** U.S. teachers

(Answers on page 54)

CASE STUDIES

Case study 1: Mary works in the insurance department for XYZ Medical Group. The organization has a contract with Best Benefits Commercial Insurance, which has been in existence for 20 years. The terms of the contract prohibit XYZ from collecting deductibles from patients before services. The administrator has asked Best Benefits to renegotiate the contract to no avail, so the administrator at XYZ has put a process in place that requires a portion of the deductible to be collected from patients before surgery is scheduled. A patient has complained to Best Benefits, and the insurance carrier's representative has spoken to Mary on the telephone about the situation. The representative has told Mary that Best Benefits will take action if XYZ continues that practice. How should Mary handle the situation?

- **a.** Tell the administrator that Best Benefits will prosecute XYZ under federal law.
- **b.** Tell the administrator that Best Benefits has threatened to void the contract and prosecute under federal law.
- **c.** Tell the administrator about the call and ask the administrator to call the Best Benefits representative.

Case study 2: Mike Smith served in the military for a short period of time and received a Purple Heart for his service, but he was separated from the military because of health reasons. Mr. Smith is a patient of XYZ Medical Group but has no insurance and has asked for help from the insurance department. Mary has been asked to talk with him and has learned of his situation. Mary can tell Mr. Smith that he may be eligible for health benefits from:

- **a.** Consolidated Omnibus Budget Reconciliation Act
- **b.** Federal Employee Health Benefits
- **c.** Veterans' Benefits

Case study 3: Jane works in the insurance department for a radiology group that performs mammography. The radiology group collects a $30 copayment on every mammogram if a patient doesn't know if she has a mammogram copayment. Jane has learned that mammography is covered as a preventive service under the Affordable Care Act. What should Jane do in this situation?

- **a.** Let the group continue to collect copayments, even if the copayment creates a credit balance on the account.
- **b.** Realize that the organization's policies are not her business because she only works in the insurance department.
- **c.** Look up the information relating to preventive care under the Affordable Care Act and make the supervisor aware of the provision.

(Answers on page 54)

COMPLETION QUESTIONS

Please fill in the blank.

1. Providers of healthcare services must comply with Medicare regulations; willful non-compliance is fraud. Providers who commit fraud may expect to be prosecuted. Who prosecutes providers who commit fraud?

   ____

2. List the main categories of services that are covered by Medicare Part A.

   ____

3. List the main categories of services that are covered by Medicare Part B.

   ____

4. What other parts of Medicare will not be purchased if Medicare Part C, known as Medicare Advantage, is purchased?

   ____

5. List the various types of government health insurance programs noted in this lesson.

   ____

6. What is workers' compensation insurance intended to do?

   ____

7. Workers' compensation is federally mandated for certain groups conducting commerce. What kind of commerce?

   ____

8. States involved with workers' compensation are bound to coverage standards set by whom?

   ____

9. Define what is meant by the term *fee-for-service*.

   ____

10. What purpose does COBRA serve?

    ____

11. What population group does CHIP serve?

____

12. What coverage options are allowed to persons participating in the health insurance program Federal Employee Health Benefits?

____

13. Medicaid distinguishes three categories of need. What are they?

____

14. What services are included in the Medicaid coverage requirements for the categorically needy that states must meet as mandated by federal statute?

____

15. What persons may be included to qualify for Medicaid under the medically needy category?

____

(Answers on pages 54–55)

MATCHING

Please match the letter of the definition to the term.
Write the letter of the definition next to the term.

Department of Justice (DOJ) _____	**a.** A division of the Department of Health and Human Services that protects the integrity of the Medicare and Medicaid programs by conducting audits, investigations, inspections, and other functions that may identify noncompliance.
Federal law _____	**b.** The highest amount a provider can charge for a particular service. The maximum allowable charge is set by the insurance carrier.
Preferred provider organization (PPO) _____	**c.** Charges for medical services based on the practice's standard fee schedule with the expectation that fees will be paid as charged. Typically indemnity insurance, insurance pays 80 percent and the insured pays 20 percent.
Office of Inspector General (OIG) _____	**d.** IRS designed. Allows both individuals and employers with high-deductible policies to contribute tax free to an account to pay for current and future qualified medical expenses. Is portable and places spending responsibility on individual.
Health savings account (HSA) _____	**e.** Managed care plan designed to provide cost saving by exerting effort to control access to services by requiring referrals and precertifications. May require primary care gatekeeper.
Health maintenance organization (HMO)_____	**f.** A type of healthcare plan in which a group of providers contracts with an organization at discounted rates to provide medical services. PPOs are managed care plans similar to HMOs but allow employees to choose to see a provider either in or outside of the plan. Seeing a provider who is not a plan member will cost the patient more than seeing a provider who is a plan member.
Fee-for-service (FFS) _____	**g.** A body of law at the national level; laws enacted by Congress. Violations of federal law are tried in federal court.
Maximum allowable _____	**h.** A department of the U.S. government administered by the attorney general, who is a member of the Cabinet, a part of the executive branch that enforces the law fairly and impartially, providing justice to all Americans.

(Answers on page 55)

ANSWERS: LESSON 3

MULTIPLE CHOICE

1-c; 2-a; 3-b; 4-c; 5-c; 6-b; 7-a; 8-c; 9-a; 10-c; 11-a; 12-b; 13-a; 14-b; 15-a

CASE STUDIES

Case study 1-c; Case study 2-c; Case study 3-c

COMPLETION QUESTIONS

1. Providers that commit fraud of government health insurance programs are prosecuted by the Office of Inspector General in conjunction with the Department of Justice.
2. Medicare Part A covers inpatient hospital services, SNF services, home health, and hospice care.
3. Medicare Part B provides coverage for outpatient medical services, including provider visits, diagnostic tests, outpatient procedures, home health services, and medical equipment.
4. Medicare Parts A and B
5. The various programs reviewed are Medicare, Medicaid, Children's Health Insurance Program (CHIP), Consolidated Omnibus Budget Reconciliation Act (COBRA), Federal Employee Health Benefits (FEHB), Indian Health Services (IHS), Veterans' Benefits, and TRICARE (military health benefits).
6. Workers' compensation insurance provides health insurance coverage for employees hurt in a work-related accident or illness.
7. Federal workers' compensation laws address requirements for companies engaged in specific types of commerce conducted broadly, particularly across state lines.
8. Although state law is not bound to federal law, federal law does set the coverage standards for the states.
9. Fee-for-service (FFS) means that charges for medical services are based on the practice's standard fee schedule with the expectation that fees will be paid as charged.
10. The Consolidated Omnibus Budget Reconciliation Act (COBRA) gives employees covered by employer-sponsored health insurance who leave their employment, whether voluntarily or involuntarily, the ability, under federal law, to maintain the insurance coverage provided by their employer.
11. The Children's Health Insurance Program (CHIP) provides free or low-cost health insurance to children from birth to 19 years of age.
12. They can choose high-deductible, catastrophic plans; health savings accounts; fee-for-service (FFS) plans; preferred provider organization (PPO) plans; or health maintenance organizations (HMOs).

13. The three categories are the categorically needy, medically needy, and special groups.

14. Categorically needy requirements are to cover inpatient hospital treatment; outpatient hospital treatment; x-ray and lab; state-licensed pediatric and family nurse practitioner; nursing facility if age 21 and older; all medically necessary screening, diagnosis, and treatment if less than 21 years of age; family planning; physician; medical and surgical dentistry; home health if entitled to nursing facility; nurse midwife; pregnancy and complicating conditions; and postpartum care through 60 days.

15. Those individuals with too much money, income, or savings to be classified as categorically needy; pregnant women through a 60-day postpartum period; certain newborns and children less than age 18; persons who are aged, blind, or disabled (SSI may serve as determining factor); some groups of children less than age 21 who meet requirements and are full-time students; or individuals who would be eligible if they were not enrolled in a health maintenance organization.

MATCHING

__ Department of Justice (DOJ): **h**

__ Federal law: **g**

__ Preferred provider organization (PPO): **f**

__ Office of Inspector General (OIG): **a**

__ Health savings account (HSA): **d**

__ Health maintenance organization (HMO): **e**

__ Fee-for-service (FFS): **c**

__ Maximum allowable: **b**

LESSON 4

Medicare Overview and Medicare Part A

OBJECTIVES

- Describe the hierarchy of the Medicare program.
- Explain the informational elements of the Medicare card, including the Medicare Claim Number.
- Identify Part A Medicare payment criteria.

WHAT IS MEDICARE?

The Social Security Act signed into law in 1935 set the stage for the Medicare program. Medicare is a federal program established by Congress and regulated at the federal level. Medicare insurance was instituted in 1965 to provide a safety net for the elderly in the nation who were finding themselves without healthcare coverage. Medicare seeks to ensure that individuals covered by health insurance under Medicare programs will receive high-quality, effective, and up-to-date healthcare coverage.

Medicare has multiple funding streams. First, there are mandatory contributions from employees and employers. Employees' contributions consist of 1.45 percent on all wages earned, with a matching 1.45 percent contributed by employers. There is no maximum contribution; rather, the total 2.9 percent applies on all wages earned. Second, general tax revenues are used to fund Medicare. Third, beneficiaries help fund Medicare through premiums, copayments, and deductibles. The beneficiaries entitled to Medicare insurance include those individuals who are 65 years of age or older, younger individuals with disabilities, and individuals with end-stage renal disease (ESRD).

Title XVIII of the Social Security Act designated Medicare as a complement to traditional Social Security benefits. Individuals who are eligible for retirement benefits from Social Security or the Railroad Retirement Board (RRB) are entitled to get some Medicare benefits premium free, but charges will apply for some benefits. The Medicare benefit structure consists of Parts A, B, C, and D. Complete information on each is presented as you progress through the lessons in this training manual.

WHO IS IN CHARGE OF MEDICARE?

The Medicare program is massive, requiring a large multipart organizational structure. The Centers for Medicare & Medicaid Services (CMS) organizational structure chart in Exhibit 4.1 on the next page displays the complicated nature of the leadership authority.

EXHIBIT 4.1 ■ CMS Organizational Chart

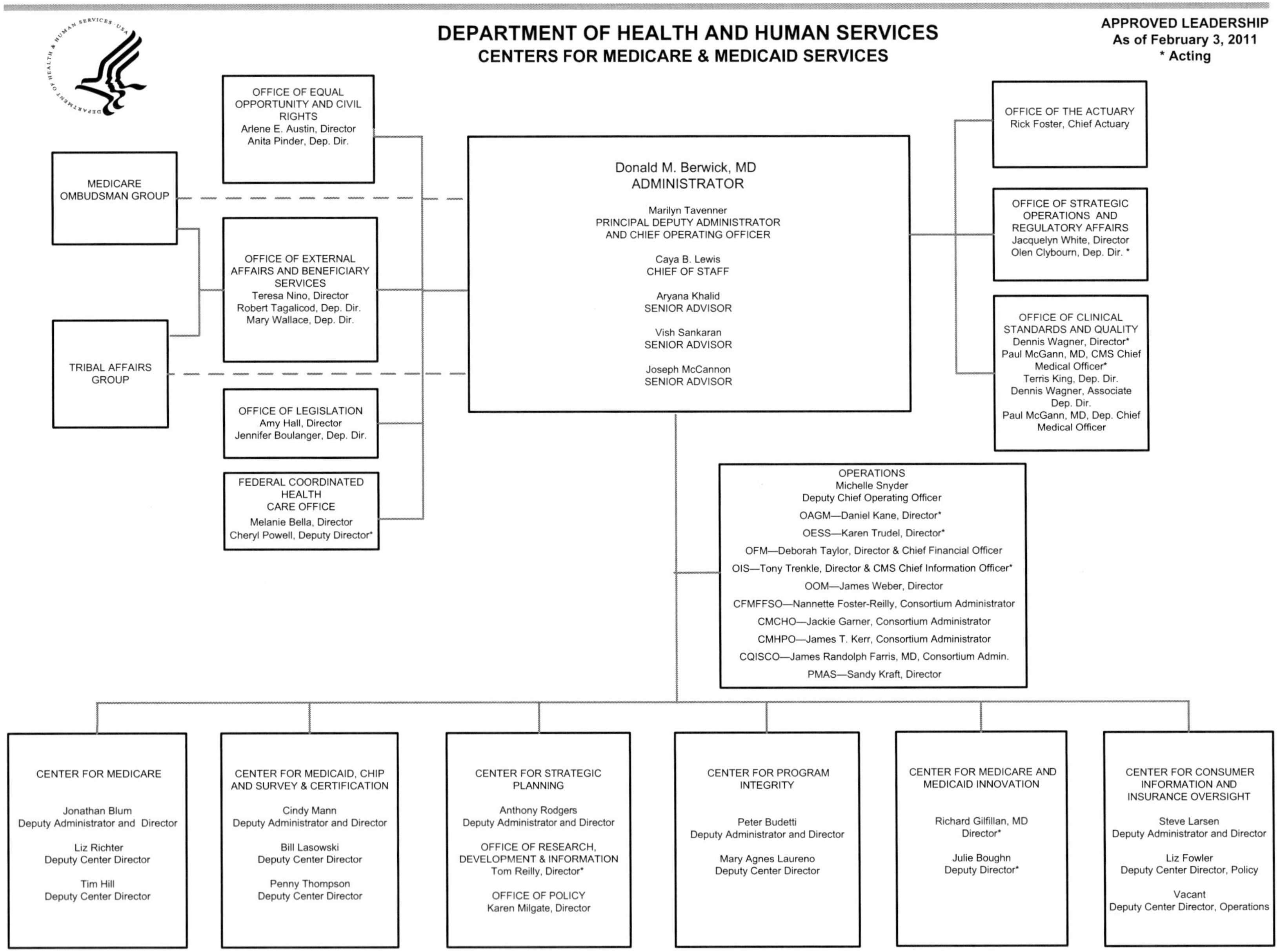

Source: www.cms.gov/CMSLeadership/Downloads/CMS_Organizational_Chart.pdf. (Accessed 7/27/11.)

While the leadership chart is instructive, it is more important for medical office insurance staff to understand the hierarchy of the Medicare program so they know which agencies regulate and administer the program. A simplified approach assists medical office insurance staff in understanding the major players in the Medicare program. Those players are the federal government's legislative branch, the CMS administrative agencies, and the non-governmental agencies contracted with Medicare to assist in administering the program. (See Exhibit 4.2.)

EXHIBIT 4.2 ■ Major Players in the Medicare Program

The federal government	The legislative branch of the federal government mandates Medicare program rules and regulations. The legislative branch appropriates money to run the Medicare program and governs the funding mechanism.
Medicare's administrative agencies	In 2001, the administrative agency's name was changed from Health Care Financing Administration to Centers for Medicare & Medicaid Services. This organization is part of the Department of Health and Human Services (HHS). CMS has 10 Regional Offices (ROs). They are located in Boston, New York, Philadelphia, Atlanta, Chicago, Dallas, Kansas City, Denver, San Francisco, and Seattle. The ROs are further reorganized into a consortia structure based on key business lines. The four consortia are: ➢ Consortium for Medicare Health Plans Operations (CMHPO) ➢ Consortium for Financial Management and Fee for Service Operations (CFMFFSO) ➢ Consortium for Medicaid and Children's Health Operations (CMCHO) ➢ Consortium for Quality Improvement and Survey & Certification Operations (CQISCO)
Non-governmental agencies	Agencies contract with CMS to administer the Medicare program for all providers at a local, state, or regional level. The private contracting agencies administering for all parts of Medicare are called Medicare Administrative Contractors (MACs).

CMS and its ROs share mission, vision, and objectives as stated below.

Mission: To ensure effective, up-to-date healthcare coverage and to promote quality care for beneficiaries.

Vision: To achieve a transformed and modernized healthcare system. CMS will accomplish our mission by continuing to transform and modernize America's healthcare system.

Objectives:

- Skilled, committed, and highly motivated workforce;
- Affordable healthcare system;
- High-value health care;
- Confident, informed consumers; and
- Collaborative partnerships.

WHAT DOES THE MEDICARE CARD LOOK LIKE, AND WHAT DOES IT MEAN?

The Medicare card is a red, white, and blue card that includes valuable information about the beneficiary, including his or her name, gender, insurance benefits entitled, and effective date of each benefit. (See Exhibit 4.3.) Staff should pay special attention to the effective date, because entitlement dates may be different. For example, the beneficiary may be entitled to benefits from Part A for hospital insurance before he or she elects to enroll for Part B medical insurance.

EXHIBIT 4.3 ■ **Sample Medicare Card**

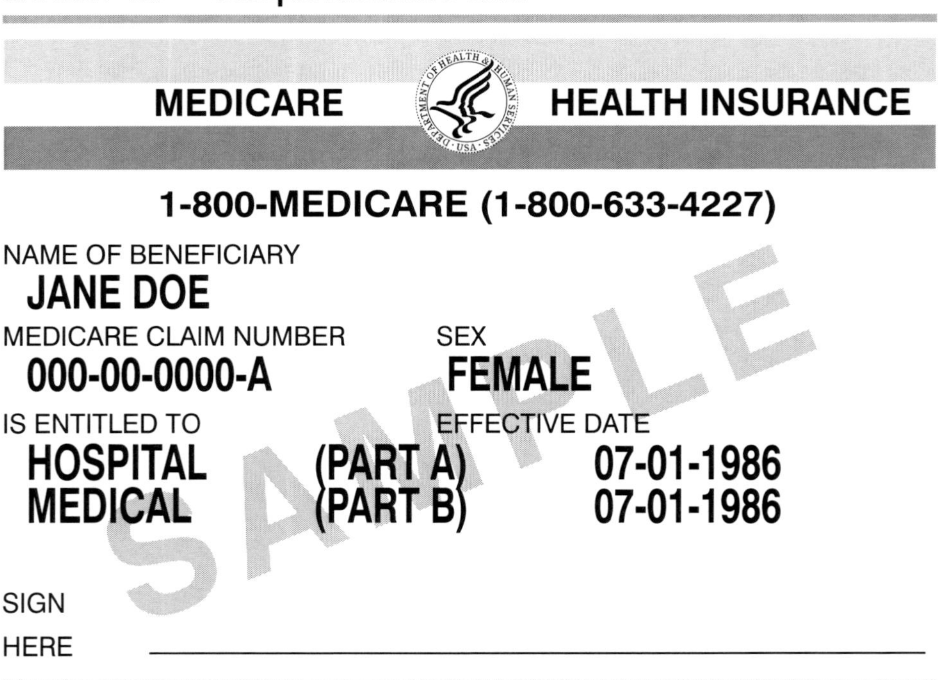

The Medicare Claim Number, also known as the Health Insurance Claim (HIC) number, on the card is extremely important. The first part of the HIC number is a six- to nine-digit number, which is typically the nine-digit Social Security Number (SSN) or the six-digit RRB number of the retired wage earner. The second part is one to two digits (one letter that may be followed by a number) that indicate the beneficiary's relationship to the retired wage earner. For example, if a wife were receiving benefits based on the wage earning of her husband, her Medicare Claim Number would consist of her husband's SSN followed by a suffix indicating that she is the wife of the retired wage earner. Note that a quick generalized guide to the suffixes as shown in Exhibit 4.4 can be informative for insurance staff members.

EXHIBIT 4.4 ■ Generalized Guide to the Suffixes

- **Suffix A:** Denotes the beneficiary is the wage earner, retired worker older age 65, or disabled worker.
- **Suffixes beginning with B:** Denote marital status. For instance, B denotes the wife of the wage earner, and B1 denotes the husband of the wage earner.
- **Suffixes beginning with C:** Denote children, including disabled children or students. The suffixes are assigned by age, with C1 being the youngest child, C2 being the second-youngest child, and so on.
- **Suffixes beginning with D:** Denote deceased spouse status (for example, widow).
- **Suffixes beginning with E:** Denote widowed mother status.
- **Suffixes beginning with F:** Denote parent category for aged dependents.
- **Suffixes beginning with J and K:** Denote beneficiaries entitled based on quarters of Social Security–qualified employment, some of whom are entitled to Part A. Others are not entitled to Part A but may purchase it.
- **Suffixes beginning with M:** Denote Part B coverage but not entitled or not enrolled in Part A.
- **Suffix T:** Denotes an individual entitled to Part A based on chronic renal disease.
- **Suffixes beginning with W:** Denote disabled deceased spouse status.

On the Medicare Explanation of Benefits, the Medicare Claim Number is referred to as the HIC number. *The claim number must be duplicated on the claim exactly as it appears on the card for the claim to be paid by Medicare.*

RRB beneficiaries' Medicare cards carry prefixes. For example, prefix A denotes a retired railroad worker, and prefix H denotes a retired worker on a pension. These examples are not all inclusive of the prefixes used by the Railroad Retirement Board.

MEDICARE PART A

As described in Lesson 3, Medicare is divided into four parts, A, B, C, and D, each of which governs different aspects of coverage. This lesson describes Medicare Part A in more detail, and Lesson 5 focuses on Medicare Part B.

Medicare Part A is a fee-for-service plan that pays for hospital services including inpatient hospital services, skilled nursing facility services, home healthcare, and hospice care. Medicare Part A is designed for an individual 65 years of age or older who is receiving or is eligible to receive retirement benefits from Social Security or the RRB. Any person less than age 65 must be eligible to receive disability benefits from Social Security or the RRB for at least 24 months or be receiving dialysis or renal transplantation for ESRD. Individuals less than 65 years of age and disabled will automatically receive Medicare Part A and Part B after they receive Social Security or RRB disability benefits for 24 months. Individuals older than age 65 who are not eligible to receive benefits from Social Security or the RRB may still be able to purchase coverage through Medicare. These individuals should contact the Social Security Administration for more information regarding eligibility. Exhibit 4.5 details the Part A covered services.

EXHIBIT 4.5 ■ Part A Covered Services Detailed

Inpatient hospital stays ➤ Acute care hospital ➤ Critical access hospital ➤ Inpatient rehabilitation facility ➤ Long-term care hospital ➤ Qualifying clinical research study ➤ Mental healthcare	**Includes:** Semi-private room, meals, general nursing, drugs related to inpatient treatment. **Does not include:** Private room (unless medically necessary), private-duty nursing, charges for a television or telephone in room, personal care items. The maximum benefit period consists of 60 full days of hospitalization plus 30 coinsurance days, totaling 90 days per benefit period. The benefit period is renewed when a beneficiary has not been in a hospital or SNF for 60 days. Beneficiaries have a 60-day lifetime reserve, if the 90-day stay has been exhausted. The count for a day begins at midnight and ends 24 hours later. Days are charged in units of full days for hospital and skilled nursing facility. Even if a different definition of a day is used for statistical reporting, benefit period days are counted as described.
Blood	If a hospital must purchase blood for a patient rather than acquire it from a blood bank, the patient must pay for the first three units of blood that are received in a calendar year, unless another individual donates replacement blood on behalf of the patient.
SNF care	After a three-day minimum inpatient hospital stay for the same episode of care, coverage includes a semi-private room, meals, skilled nursing, rehabilitative services, and other medically necessary services and supplies. A physician must certify that daily skilled care is required.
Home health services	Medically necessary part-time skilled nursing, physical therapy, speech pathology, or occupational therapy. A healthcare provider enrolled in Medicare must order care, and a Medicare-certified home health agency must provide care. May include medical social services, part-time home health aide services, and medical supplies. Individuals qualifying for care must meet criteria that leaving home is a major effort or, in other words, be homebound.

Hospice care	Individuals must be terminally ill with a life expectancy of six months or less. Includes drugs to relieve pain and manage symptoms; medical care, nursing care, and social services; spiritual and grief counseling; and certain durable medical equipment. Services provided by Medicare-approved hospice in home or other facility such as nursing home. Hospice teams may determine that short-term inpatient stays are necessary, if treatment cannot be managed successfully at home. These stays must be in a Medicare-approved facility — hospice facility, hospital, SNF. Respite care can be approved up to five days, so that the usual caregiver can rest. Care unrelated to the terminal illness will be paid by Medicare while hospice care continues, if medical director or hospice physician recertifies terminal illness.
Inpatient care in religious non-medical healthcare institution	For individuals whose religious beliefs are incompatible with medical care, Medicare covers room and board in a religious institution for people who qualify for hospital or SNF care. Medicare will cover non-medical services, such as wound dressing or items such as a walker, but will not cover religious aspects of care.

Adapted from CMS publication: *Medicare & You, 2011*. www.medicare.gov/publications/pubs/pdf/10050.pdf. (Accessed 7/29/11.)

Additionally, services furnished in the following entities are covered by Part A.

- Federally qualified health centers,
- Histocompatibility laboratories,
- Indian Health Services facilities,
- Multiple hospital components in a medical complex,
- Organ procurement organizations,
- Rural health clinics, and
- Program for all-inclusive care for the elderly providers.

What is the difference between Medicare Part A inpatient and outpatient?

The individual's status as an inpatient or outpatient make a difference in what Medicare pays and what the patient pays for services such as x-ray, drugs, and lab tests, as well as whether an individual will be covered in an SNF facility.

An inpatient admission requires a physician's order. Admission occurs based on the date the physician's order is written. Inpatient status starts the date the order is written; the day before a patient is discharged is the last inpatient day. A patient getting emergency services, observation services, lab tests, or x-rays or even experiencing an overnight stay is considered to be receiving outpatient services, unless a physician has written an admission order. Medicare will only cover SNF care if an individual has spent at least three days in a row at a qualifying hospital as an inpatient.

All observation services, including overnight in-hospital observation, are considered outpatient services. Generally, Medicare Part B covers outpatient hospital and physician services. This may require a copayment for each outpatient hospital service. For Part A–only beneficiaries, services received in a hospital emergency room, an outpatient surgery, or overnight observation status stays will not be paid by Medicare.

Insurance staff should be aware that some procedures are inpatient-only procedures. CMS has determined that certain procedures require 24 hours of postoperative care due to the severity of the procedure or medical condition. In these cases the inpatient procedure will be paid only if the patient was an inpatient with a written order prior to the time the procedure was performed. Some patients are scheduled as outpatients for procedures that are permitted as outpatient surgeries. If the patient's condition changes during surgery requiring the surgeon to change the status to inpatient, the admit order must be written immediately following surgery.

KEY TERMS AND DEFINITIONS

Centers for Medicare & Medicaid Services (CMS) — The administrative agency is in HHS.

ESRD — End-stage renal disease.

Inpatient — A patient's status for whom a physician has written an admission order. Services for patients with inpatient status are paid by Medicare Part A.

Medicare Claim Number — The identifying number on a beneficiary's Medicare card; it must be on every Medicare claim exactly as it appears on the card.

Outpatient — A patient's status for whom a physician has not written an admission order, regardless of hospital services received. Services for outpatients are paid by Medicare Part B.

ROs — Regional offices of CMS. Ten offices are designated across the nation. ROs share the mission, vision, and objectives of CMS.

RRB — The Railroad Retirement Board was created by the U.S. government in the 1930s to provide retirement benefits for railroad workers. Administers healthcare benefits.

Title XVIII of the Social Security Act — Designated Medicare as a complement of traditional Social Security benefits.

REVIEW OF OBJECTIVES

- **Describe the hierarchy of the Medicare program.**
  - Medicare is a large multipart organization with a complex structure.
  - A simplified hierarchy structure is:
    - Legislative branch of the federal government
    - CMS and its Regional Offices
    - MACs, which are private contracting agencies that administer Medicare benefits

- **Explain the informational elements of the Medicare card, including the Medicare Claim Number.**
  - The Medicare card is red, white, and blue.
  - The card contains the name of the beneficiary, the Medicare Claim Number, the gender of the beneficiary, the Medicare parts to which the beneficiary is entitled, the effective date for each part, and the beneficiary's signature.
  - The Medicare Claim Number, also known as the HIC number, contains a number (usually SSN or RRB number) that identifies the wage earner and a suffix that explains the patient's status in relation to the wage earner.
  - Railroad Retirement Medicare cards start with a prefix that explains the patient's status.

- **Identify Part A Medicare payment criteria.**
  - Part A is a fee-for-service plan for individuals age 65 or older and must be receiving or eligible to receive retirement benefits from Social Security or Railroad Retirement Board.
  - Part A includes payment for services such as inpatient hospital, SNF, home health, and hospice care.
  - To receive benefits for hospital services under Part A, patients must be admitted as inpatients by a physician's order.
  - Patients are eligible to receive benefits under Part A for SNF services after an inpatient stay of three days or more.
  - Hospice care is covered under Part A for terminally ill individuals with a life expectancy of six months or less.

REVIEW EXERCISES: LESSON 4

MULTIPLE CHOICE

Please circle the best answer.

1. **Medicare is funded by multiple funding streams including:**
   - **a.** Mandatory wage contributions, local property taxes, and beneficiaries' contributions
   - **b.** Mandatory wage contributions, general tax revenues, and beneficiaries' contributions
   - **c.** Mandatory wage contributions, state real estate taxes, and beneficiaries' contributions

2. **The federal government mandates Medicare program rules and regulations from which branch?**
   - **a.** Judicial
   - **b.** Executive
   - **c.** Legislative

3. **CMS has Regional Offices involved in administering Medicare. There are:**
   - **a.** 20 ROs
   - **b.** 10 ROs
   - **c.** 15 ROs

4. **Which of the following identifying elements is found on the front of the Medicare card?**
   - **a.** Birth date
   - **b.** Address
   - **c.** Claim number

5. **Non-governmental agencies that contract to help administer the Medicare program are called:**
   - **a.** COBs
   - **b.** MACs
   - **c.** ASCs

6. **Suffix A on the Medicare card denotes:**
   - **a.** The beneficiary is the wage earner
   - **b.** Marital status of the beneficiary
   - **c.** The individual has chronic renal disease

7. **Medicare Part A pays for which of the following services?**
   - **a.** Inpatient hospital services
   - **b.** Outpatient hospital services
   - **c.** Ambulance services

8. **Medicare Part A pays for SNF services after:**
   a. A two-day minimum inpatient hospital stay
   b. A three-day minimum inpatient hospital stay
   c. A four-day minimum inpatient hospital stay

9. **Hospice care coverage requires individuals must be terminally ill with a life expectancy of:**
   a. One year
   b. Nine months
   c. Six months

10. **Medicare will pay for blood if:**
    a. A hospital acquires blood from a blood bank
    b. A hospital must purchase blood and after a replacement donor has donated three units on the patient's behalf
    c. A hospital receives blood from the Red Cross

11. **Home health services can be paid for when which of the following conditions are met?**
    a. Care must be ordered by a Medicare provider and provided by a Medicare-certified agency
    b. Care must be ordered by a licensed provider and provided by a Medicare-certified agency
    c. Care must be ordered by a licensed provider and provided by an agency owned by the hospital

12. **The maximum total mandatory contribution on earned wages to fund Medicare is:**
    a. 7.65 percent
    b. 2.9 percent
    c. 3.5 percent

13. **Medicare beneficiaries may be younger than 65 years of age if:**
    a. They are disabled or have ESRD
    b. They are on Medicaid
    c. They have retired at age 55

14. **If you are less than 65 years of age, disabled, and have received Social Security or RRB disability benefits, you will automatically receive Medicare Part A and Part B after:**
    a. 12 months
    b. 18 months
    c. 24 months

15. **Medicare Part A is a:**
    a. Managed care plan
    b. Fee-for-service plan
    c. Health maintenance plan

(Answers on page 72)

CASE STUDIES

Case study 1: Marge went to the emergency room to receive services; she has only Medicare Part A coverage. The emergency room physician called in a specialist who admitted Marge to the hospital to watch her condition. Marge was subsequently released without having any surgery. She is asking the insurance department personnel at her specialist's office who will pay her hospital charges. What should they tell her?

- **a.** Her hospital charges are her responsibility.
- **b.** Her inpatient hospital charges will be paid by Part A.
- **c.** She can sign up for Medicaid to pay her charges.

Case study 2: Frank's surgeon scheduled him to have outpatient surgery at the hospital. Frank had the surgery without complication, but his blood pressure was elevated and the surgeon was uncomfortable about discharging him after surgery. The surgeon asked to keep Frank in the hospital overnight to monitor his blood pressure, but Frank was not admitted to the hospital. Medicare will pay for his hospital stay under:

- **a.** Part A
- **b.** Part B
- **c.** Part D

Case study 3: Harry went to the emergency room to be admitted for inpatient services. He received services and had several tests. Harry asked to be admitted because he only has Medicare Part A coverage. Harry was in the hospital for a two-night stay. Medicare Part A is denying coverage on the hospital charges. Why would it deny charges?

- **a.** The physician never wrote an admission order, and Harry was in observation status.
- **b.** The physician found out Harry only had Medicare Part A and knew his services wouldn't be paid.
- **c.** Harry was an inpatient because he asked for that status and Medicare paid incorrectly.

(Answers on page 72)

COMPLETION QUESTIONS

1. What are the Medicare funding streams?

2. Who is eligible for Medicare benefits?

3. What major agencies are actors in regulating and administering the Medicare program?

4. Where are the 10 Regional Offices of CMS?

5. What is the role of the CMS Medicare Administrative Contractors (MACs)?

6. What is the HIC number?

7. How many days are included as maximum in a benefit period?

8. When does a benefit period renew?

9. What happens if a beneficiary needs to be hospitalized longer than the maximum days in a benefit period?

____

____

10. When is SNF care utilized?

____

____

11. What services does Medicare Part A include for inpatients?

____

12. What services does Medicare Part A not cover for inpatients?

____

____

13. What services are included for SNF care?

____

____

14. May any Medicare beneficiary receive SNF services?

____

15. When can a Medicare beneficiary receive home health services?

____

16. Which individuals qualify for home health services?

____

17. Which individuals qualify for hospice care?

____

18. What is required for a beneficiary to obtain inpatient status?

____

19. What is the status of an observation service, including a patient's overnight in-hospital observation?

____

20. What is the status of a patient getting emergency services, observation services, lab tests, or x-rays?

____

(Answers on pages 72–73)

MATCHING

Please match the letter of the definition to the term.
Write the letter of the definition next to the term.

ESRD _____	**a.** Designated Medicare as a complement of traditional Social Security benefits.
Medicare Claim Number _____	**b.** Regional Offices of CMS. Ten offices are designated across the nation. ROs share the mission, vision, and objectives of CMS.
Outpatient _____	**c.** A patient's status for whom a physician has written an admission order. Services for patients with inpatient status are paid by Medicare Part A.
CMS _____	**d.** The identifying number on a beneficiary's Medicare card; it must be on every Medicare claim exactly as it appears on the card.
RRB _____	**e.** A patient's status for whom a physician has not written an admission order, regardless of hospital services received. Services for outpatients are paid by Medicare Part B.
Inpatient _____	**f.** The Railroad Retirement Board was created by the U.S. government in the 1930s to provide retirement benefits for railroad workers. Administers healthcare benefits.
ROs _____	**g.** End-stage renal disease.
Title XVIII of the Social Security Act _____	**h.** Centers for Medicare & Medicaid Services; the administrative agency is in HHS.

(Answers on page 73)

ANSWERS: LESSON 4

MULTIPLE CHOICE

1-b; 2-c; 3-b; 4-c; 5-b; 6-a; 7-a; 8-b; 9-c; 10-b; 11-a; 12-b; 13-a; 14-c; 15-b

CASE STUDIES

Case study 1-b; Case study 2-b; Case study 3-a

COMPLETION QUESTIONS

1. The funding streams are first, mandatory contributions from employers, 1.45 percent, and from employees, 1.45 percent; second, general tax revenues; and third, beneficiaries' premiums, copayments, and deductibles.
2. Individuals who are eligible for retirement benefits from Social Security or the the Railroad Retirement Board are typically eligible for Medicare.
3. The major players are the legislative branch of the federal government, CMS, and non-governmental MACs.
4. Boston, New York, Philadelphia, Atlanta, Chicago, Dallas, Kansas City, Denver, San Francisco, and Seattle
5. The role of the MACs is to administer the Medicare program for all providers at a local, state, or regional level.
6. The Medicare Claim Number found on the Medicare card
7. 90 days
8. A benefit period renews when a beneficiary has not been in a hospital or an SNF for 60 days.
9. A beneficiary has a 60-day lifetime reserve after the 90-day benefit period has been exhausted.
10. When a beneficiary has been an inpatient for three days, he or she may be transferred to an SNF for the same episode of care.
11. Semi-private room, meals, general nursing, drugs related to inpatient treatment
12. Private room (unless medically necessary), private-duty nursing, charges for a television or telephone in room, and personal care items
13. Semi-private room, meals, skilled nursing, rehabilitative services, and other medically necessary services and supplies.
14. No, a physician must certify that daily skilled care is required.
15. After a provider enrolled in Medicare has ordered care
16. Those who meet the criteria that leaving home is a major effort or those who are homebound

17. Those individuals who are terminally ill with a life expectancy of six months or less

18. An inpatient admission requires a physician's order.

19. Outpatient

20. Outpatient

MATCHING

__ ESRD: **g**

__ Medicare Claim Number: **d**

__ Outpatient: **e**

__ CMS: **h**

__ RRB: **f**

__ Inpatient: **c**

__ ROs: **b**

__ Title XVIII of the Social Security Act: **a**

LESSON 5

Medicare Part B

OBJECTIVES

- Explain the importance of the role of Medicare Part B to medical office insurance staff.
- Outline the process and rationale for providers to participate in Medicare Part B.
- Appreciate the scope of services provided by Medicare Part B.
- Describe the purpose for Medigap (supplemental insurance) policies.
- Characterize the distinction between Medicare as a primary or secondary payer.
- Define the legal requirements for providers participating in Medicare, including Advance Beneficiary Notice, mandatory filing, and timely filing.

UNDERSTANDING MEDICARE PART B

Knowledge about Medicare Part B is essential for medical office insurance staff members for three reasons. First, Medicare Part B is the medical insurance that helps pay for physician office services, outpatient services, and services in ambulatory surgery centers (ASCs) as well as many other services. Because medical office insurance staff members are likely working with Part B every day, they must have a strong working knowledge of the Medicare Part B program.

Second, medical practices play an important role in delivering services to patients. Although medical office insurance staff members are not clinical staff, they serve as the liaison among the practice, the patient, and the patient's insurance carrier. Insurance coverage is complex — too complex for patients to understand because they do not deal with health insurance every day. Medical office insurance staff members have an obligation to provide customer service to patients in the practice when they seek help. Medicare Part B is important to understand because it is the government program that pays for physicians' services. Moreover, it serves as the model for commercial carriers to follow in making their own regulations. While it is inappropriate to say that *all* insurance carriers model Medicare, it is true that Medicare influences other carriers.

Third, insurance staff must understand that committing fraud against the Medicare program is a federal crime. Convictions of a crime against the U.S. government may carry a prison sentence, entail significant monetary fines, or result in exclusion from Medicare or other federal programs. Exclusion may be temporary or permanent, and in some states healthcare providers and organizations may lose their licenses.

VIOLATIONS

Violations of Medicare regulations may be subject to Civil Monetary Penalties (CMPs). Amounts vary, but the CMP may be up to $10,000 per violation. Exclusion from the Medicare program may also apply. CMP categories may include violations of Medicare assignment provisions, Medicare physician agreements, anti-kickback statutes, Stark law, submitting false or misleading information relating to decision to discharge; unbundling hospital outpatient surgery costs; and dumping beneficiaries who lack resources and cannot pay. When overpayments are made, CMS has the authority to withhold payments that are due and may use those payments to recoup money that was overpaid. Outright suspension of payments may occur when fraud or willful misrepresentation is evident. It may also occur if reliable information comes to light relating to incorrect or overpayments.

To reiterate, Medicare coverage is a government health insurance program that covers people who are 65 years of age or older, people younger than age 65 who have certain disabilities, and people of any age with end-stage renal disease (ESRD). (ESRD is the result of permanent kidney failure and requires dialysis or kidney transplant.) Medicare Part A is typically thought of as hospital insurance, whereas Part B is thought of as physician insurance. Part C is the managed care plan, and Part D is prescription drug coverage.

All individuals who are eligible for Medicare Part A, which is a premium free benefit, are eligible to enroll in Medicare Part B. Unlike Medicare Part A, if an individual elects to have Medicare Part B, a monthly premium is required. A standard premium applies to most individuals eligible for Medicare Part B, but some people pay more based on their income as reported from the individual's Internal Revenue Service (IRS) tax return two years prior. The cost and coverage of Medicare Part B can change yearly.

BENEFICIARY SIGN-UP PERIOD

Individuals who receive Social Security or Railroad Retirement Board (RRB) benefits automatically receive Medicare Parts A and B starting in the month they turn 65. Those who do not get Social Security or RRB benefits must sign up for Medicare. The initial enrollment for those individuals who are eligible is a seven-month period. Sign-up may take place three months before an individual turns 65 to ensure that coverage begins the month the individual turns 65. If the individual signs up the month of the 65th birthday or in the following three months after the birthday month, coverage benefits will be delayed. If individuals delay sign-up because they are still working and covered by a group health plan, different sign-up criteria apply. Sign-up may occur after employment or employment coverage ends for the next eight-month period. This period of time is considered a special enrollment period.

In addition to Medicare Part B, individuals may want to sign up for Medigap coverage. Medigap, known as Medicare Supplemental Insurance, is provided by private insurance carriers to fill the cost gaps that Medicare Part B does not cover. For example, Medicare Part B pays 80 percent of the Medicare allowed amount, and the insured is responsible for the rest. Medigap coverage assists with the 20 percent not paid by Part B. Individuals have six months after they sign up for Medicare Part B to participate in the Medigap enrollment period, when individuals are guaranteed the right to purchase a Medigap policy. Within the first six months of electing Part B coverage, each beneficiary is provided an initial preventive physical exam, a "Welcome to Medicare," brochure (www.medicare.gov/welcometomedicare/visit.html), and screening for diabetes and heart disease. If sign-up for Medicare Part B occurs late, there is an enrollment penalty of up to 10 percent for each year that the individual was eligible for Part B but did not participate. This penalty is ongoing as long as the individual has Medicare. It should be noted that individuals who sign up for Medicare Advantage Part C do not need to purchase Medigap, Medicare Supplemental Insurance. Medicare Part C eliminates the need for the Medicare fee-for-service products Part A and Part B, and Part C also typically includes a prescription drug benefit (Part D).

In addition to the initial enrollment period, there are several other enrollment periods when benefits may be elected and/or changed. Enrollment periods are listed in Exhibit 5.1

EXHIBIT 5.1 ■ Benefit Enrollment Periods

Initial Coverage Election Period (IEP)	Seven-month period around the individual's 65th birthday (three months before through three months after the birthday month)
Annual Coordination Election Period (AEP)	November 15–December 31
Special Enrollment Period (SEP)	Applies for certain circumstances
Transfer Enrollment Period	Beneficiary enrolled in Medicare Part C may enroll in premium Part A

NATIONAL PROVIDER IDENTIFIER

The Health Insurance Portability and Accountability Act (HIPAA) of 1996 requires each healthcare provider to have a National Provider Identifier (NPI) to be used on all standard claims transactions. This unique identifier replaces all other identifying numbers for providers and is broadly recognized by health plans. The 10-digit NPI follows the provider throughout his or her career, even if the individual moves from state to state. While a provider must obtain a state license in each state in which he or she practices, the NPI number remains the same. NPI numbers must be used for submitting claims for payment as adopted by HIPAA.

The Centers for Medicare & Medicaid Services (CMS) developed the National Plan and Provider Enumeration System (NPPES) for the purpose of assigning the unique numbers to healthcare providers. Providers may apply for an NPI number by one of several methods (see Exhibit 5.2), the fastest of which is to apply online.

EXHIBIT 5.2 ■ Methods by Which to Apply for NPI Number

Apply online from Web site	https://nppes.cms.hhs.gov/NPPES/Welcome.do
Apply by sending an e-mail	customerservice@npienumerator.com
Apply by telephone	1.800.465.3203
Apply by sending a letter	NPI Enumerator PO Box 6059 Fargo, ND 58108-6059

PROVIDER ENROLLMENT IN MEDICARE

Providers wishing to enroll with Medicare must submit application forms appropriate for the services they will be providing to Medicare beneficiaries. An NPI must be obtained before enrolling with Medicare. Signatures on application forms must be original; stamped signatures are not accepted by Medicare.

Enrollment ensures that a provider meets the criteria to participate in the Medicare program. The appropriate form to complete depends on the type of provider or supplier. The following paragraphs provide brief reference information on enrollment; complete information on enrollment can be found at www.cms.hhs.gov/MedicareProvider/SupEnroll. Exhibit 5.3 lists the traditional Medicare enrollment application paper forms.

EXHIBIT 5.3 ■ Traditional Medicare Enrollment Application Paper Forms

Form CMS-855A	Institutional providers
Form CMS-855B	Clinics/group practices
Form CMS-855I	Physicians and nonphysician practitioners
Form CMS-855R	Reassignment of Medicare benefits
Form CMS-855S	Suppliers of durable medical equipment, prosthetics, orthotics, and supplies

In lieu of the CMS-855 series of forms, providers may use the Internet-based Provider Enrollment, Chain and Ownership System (PECOS) to enroll. PECOS is not only faster for initial applications — 45-day processing as opposed to paper 60-day processing — but it also allows for ease in tracking, viewing, changing information, or reassignment in and withdrawal from the Medicare program. Before beginning to use PECOS, the "Basics of Internet-based Provider Enrollment, Chain and Ownership System for Provider and Supplier

Organizations" fact sheet should be reviewed. For complete information go to www.cms.gov/MLNProducts/downloads/MedEnroll_Provider.Sup_FactSheet_ICN903767.

PECOS should be used to create new enrollment records, make changes to existing enrollment, reactivate enrollment, or voluntarily withdraw from Medicare. PECOS allows for an authorized official (AO) to keep enrollment information up to date; a medical office insurance staff person may be asked to fulfill the AO role for a provider. Using the PECOS site requires IDs and passwords. Individuals acting on behalf of providers will go to https://pecos.cms.hhs.gov to register and create a user ID and password. Physicians may use PECOS with the ID and password established when the NPI was obtained from NPPES. Enrollment changes must be reported within 90 days.

Additionally, forms CMS-460 and CMS-588 are submitted with Medicare enrollment. Providers or suppliers wishing to participate complete Form CMS-460 and Form CMS-588/EFT for electronic funds transfer.

MEDICARE PARTICIPATION

It is beneficial for any physician intending to see Medicare patients to sign a participation agreement. Providers participating with Medicare receive higher allowances than non-participating providers. Any provider seeing Medicare beneficiaries as patients is required to bill Medicare's limiting charge, unless the provider is a participating provider. The fee schedule for a non-participating provider is 95 percent of the fee schedule for a participating provider. In addition to receiving lower reimbursement, non-participating providers must collect payment from the Medicare beneficiary rather than directly from Medicare. Claims filed by non-participating providers are referred to as *non-assigned claims,* and payment does not go directly to the provider.

Participating physicians accept assignment on all claims and can expect payment in 14 days from Medicare. Medicare pays participating physicians 80 percent of the Medicare allowable; 20 percent is collected from the patient. Once a physician has signed a Participating Physician or Supplier Agreement, the agreement renews automatically each year unless either the provider notifies Medicare in writing that he or she wishes to terminate or the physician violates the agreement and is terminated. Noncompliance with Medicare rules and regulations may incur civil and criminal penalties. Most medical practices providing services to large numbers of Medicare patients become participating providers to take advantage of the benefits of participation. Participating physicians are included in the *Physician and Other Healthcare Professional Directory*.

Non-participating provider

If a provider does not accept assignment on a claim and the services provided will likely cost more than $500, the provider must give the Medicare beneficiary an estimate of the charges in written form prior to providing the service. The written information advises the beneficiary of the estimated charges that are likely to be the beneficiary's responsibility. If this estimate is not provided, any money collected from the beneficiary must be refunded. If the refund is not made, CMPs and exclusion from the Medicare program may apply. Providers may opt to accept assignment on a per claim basis. If assignment is not accepted, providers must collect payment for services from the beneficiary on non-assigned claims.

Limiting charges of 95 percent of the participating providers' fee schedule will apply to non-participating providers, regardless of who provides services to Medicare beneficiaries.

Opt-out

In addition to making the decision not to participate with Medicare, providers may opt out of Medicare and contract with Medicare beneficiaries privately. A broad group of providers may opt out. When opt-out status is chosen, the opt-out period is two years but can be terminated early if the provider fails to maintain the opt-out status. Opt-out status requires the status to be maintained for all beneficiaries and on all services except for urgent need of care. Claims for urgent care may be filed with Medicare but require the HCPCS modifier GJ denoting that the emergency service was provided by a provider who was an opt-out status provider.

FEE-FOR-SERVICE

Fee-for-service, or traditional Parts A and B, Medicare allows beneficiaries to go to their choice of physician or hospital. The beneficiary is financially responsible to the provider for coinsurance, deductible, any non-covered service, or services included in a written advance notice. Fee-for-service beneficiaries may also have Medicaid and Medigap insurance to help pay for services. To qualify for Medicaid coverage, certain financial requirements must be met, and not all beneficiaries will qualify for Medicaid. On the other hand, Medigap is a supplemental insurance policy designed for any beneficiary who wishes to purchase a policy to help cover the expense of coinsurance that the beneficiary would otherwise be responsible for as an out-of-pocket expense.

MANAGED CARE PLAN

Managed care plans, or Part C Medicare, typically require beneficiaries to receive their healthcare from providers and hospitals identified by the managed care plan. Beneficiaries who qualify for Part A and Part B may participate in a Medicare Advantage (MA) plan. Private insurance carriers administer Advantage plans. If a beneficiary chooses to participate in an Advantage plan, the beneficiary must enroll in one that provides service where the beneficiary lives. In other words, a beneficiary cannot choose to be covered by a plan if the community where he or she lives is not in its service area.

Individuals selecting Medicare Part C instead of choosing the traditional fee-for-service plans, Part A and Part B, may also have Medicare Part D benefits for drugs included in the Medicare Advantage plan, Part C, if they wish to take advantage of prescription drug benefits. As with other Medicare programs, beneficiaries may leave or join Medicare Advantage plans in specified ways, including:

- IEP — the seven-month period,
- AEP — November 15–December 31,
- SEP — applies for certain circumstances, and
- OEP — January 1–March 31 for transfer to another MA.

The OEP is an opportunity for Part C beneficiaries to transfer to another MA plan of the same type, if the plan they wish to transfer to is accepting new members.

Medical office insurance staff should be aware that Medicare Advantage plans may be health maintenance organization (HMO) plans, preferred provider organization (PPO) plans, private fee-for-service plans, or special needs plans. These plans follow the Medicare rules, but services covered may differ.

Part B covered services

Part B covers medical services that are medically necessary. For a service to meet the criteria of medical necessity in general, the service must (1) have reasonable beneficial effect on the patient, (2) be proven to be effective, and (3) be appropriate for a specific diagnosis. Medicare Part B covers services such as office visits, surgical procedures, and many diagnostic and therapeutic services. Physician services may be provided in a variety of authorized settings, including:

- Physicians' office,
- Hospital,
- ASC,
- Skilled nursing facility,
- Post-acute care setting,
- Hospice,
- Outpatient dialysis facility,
- Clinical lab, and
- Beneficiary home care.

In addition to covering physician services, Part B covers medical services that are medically necessary when provided by limited license practitioners such as:

- Nurse practitioner (NP),
- Physician assistant (PA),
- Audiologist,
- Certified registered nurse anesthetist,
- Clinical nurse specialist (CNS),
- Clinical psychologist (PhD-level),
- Clinical social worker (master of social work degree),
- Occupational therapist, and
- Physical therapist.

See Exhibit 5.4 on the next page for a more comprehensive list of Medicare Part B–covered services.

EXHIBIT 5.4 ■ List of Medicare Part B–Covered Services

Physician/doctor	Beneficiary typically pays 20 percent.
Outpatient: medical and surgical services **Outpatient: supplies related to services**	Part B deductible applies.
Ambulatory surgical centers	Beneficiary pays 20 percent facility and physician fees.
Ambulance services	Beneficiary pays 20 percent of allowable.
Durable medical equipment (DME)	Walkers, wheelchairs, oxygen, hospital beds, etc.
Blood	From blood bank — no charge, if purchased. Beneficiary pays for first three units, or donor replaces.
Clinical laboratory services	No charge. Beneficiary may pay 20 percent of visit charge.
Emergency department	Urgent care — no charge for facility. Beneficiary may pay 20 percent for physician visit.
Surgical second opinions	Beneficiary may pay 20 percent of allowable.
Surgical dressing services	Surgically treated wound — Beneficiary pays 20 percent of physician services fee.
Diagnostic tests	X-ray; magnetic resonance imaging, computed tomography, and electrocardiogram (EKG) scans; etc. — Beneficiary pays 20 percent of allowable.
EKG initial screening	Beneficiary pays 20 percent of physician allowable.
Hearing and balance exam	Beneficiary pays 20 percent of provider allowable.
Kidney dialysis services and supplies	Beneficiary with ESRD pays 20 percent of allowable.
Kidney disease education services	Kidney disease, six sessions — Beneficiary pays 20 percent of allowable applies.
Home health services: for homebound	Part-time or intermittent skilled nursing care, physical therapy, speech/language pathology, occupational therapy, certified medical social services, home health aide, DME, and medical supplies.
Occupational therapy: to return to usual activity	Beneficiary pays 20 percent of allowable.
Outpatient mental healthcare	Payment depends on diagnosis and condition.
Cardiac rehabilitation	Exercise, education, and counseling — 20 percent of allowable if in physicians' office; if in hospital, outpatient hospital copay.

Implantable automatic defibrillator	Beneficiary pays 20 percent of physician allowable.
Diabetes supplies	Blood sugar testing monitors and test strips, lancets and devices, blood sugar control solution, possible therapeutic shoes, insulin for external insulin pump. Beneficiary pays 20 percent of allowable.
Foot exam and treatment	Diabetes-related nerve damage. Beneficiary pays 20 percent of allowable.
Prosthetic/Orthotic	Artificial limbs and replacement parts (items include arm, leg, back, and neck braces; artificial eyes; artificial breast prostheses after mastectomy; internal prosthetic devices). Beneficiary pays 20 percent of allowable.
Limited eyeglasses	One pair standard frames after cataract surgery with implants. Beneficiary pays 20 percent of allowable.
Physical therapy	Treatment to restore functionality. Beneficiary pays 20 percent of allowable.
Pulmonary rehabilitation	For severe chronic obstructive pulmonary disease, beneficiary pays 20 percent of allowable.
Speech/language pathology services	Treatment to restore cognitive and swallowing speech and language skills. Beneficiary pays 20 percent of allowable.
Nonphysician services	PA, NP, psychologist, social workers, physical therapists. Beneficiary pays 20 percent of allowable.
Rural health clinic services	Primary care services. Beneficiary pays 20 percent of allowable.
Chiropractic services	Manipulation of spine when out of position. Beneficiary pays 20 percent of allowable.
Clinical research studies	Qualifying for studies, physician visits and tests. Beneficiary pays 20 percent of allowable.
Federally qualified health center services	Includes services through community-based organizations. Beneficiary typically pays 20 percent of allowable.
Transplants and immunosuppressive drugs	Transplants: Physician services for lung, heart, kidney, pancreas, intestine, and liver. Immunosuppressive drugs associated with transplants.
Telehealth	Available in some rural areas if conditions are met; beneficiary pays 20 percent of allowable.
Limited prescription drugs	Oral cancer drugs, drugs for nebulizers and external infusion pumps. Beneficiary pays 20 percent of allowable.

Adapted from Centers for Medicare & Medicaid Services. *Medicare & You*, 2011. www.medicare.gov/publications/pubs/pdf/10050.pdf. (Accessed 7/29/11.)

Medigap policies

Exhibit 5.4 points out some cases where Part B Medicare beneficiaries are required to pay a coinsurance amount of 20 percent of the Medicare allowable. Medicare beneficiaries who have Part A and Part B are allowed to purchase Medicare supplement insurance called *Medigap* to help pay the gaps in coverage of Medicare fee-for-service. These standardized plans, designed to protect beneficiaries from out-of-pocket expenses, were introduced by the Omnibus Budget Reconciliation Act of 1990 (OBRA 1990). Before 1990, Medigap policies were not standardized. Medigap policies are purchased from private insurance companies and, like any other insurance policy, require a premium. These policies are regulated by federal and state laws so that beneficiaries are protected. Standardized Medigap policies are identified by letters such as A, B, C, D, E, F, G, H, I, J, K, L, M, and N. All states except Massachusetts, Minnesota, and Wisconsin, which have state waivers, standardize their policies in the same way. Medigap policies help pay for copayments, coinsurance, and deductibles not covered by traditional Medicare fee-for-service. It is most advantageous to purchase a Medigap policy upon enrollment in the Medicare program. Each beneficiary interested in coverage of the 20 percent unpaid by Medicare must purchase a personal Medigap policy. Medigap policies are divided into three categories Medical office insurance staff should be aware of the three Medigap policy categories:

- Pre-standard plans,
- OBRA 1990 standard plans, and
- Waiver state standard plans.

Medigap plans were revised beginning June 1, 2010. Plans M and N are the new Medigap plans. Plans E, H, I, and J are no longer sold to new beneficiaries, but beneficiaries who already had those plans may keep the plan coverage. While plans are regulated, insurance carriers may charge different premium amounts for the same coverage. It is a good idea to shop more than one company when purchasing Medigap coverage. Some states offer a Medigap plan called Medicare SELECT, which requires beneficiaries to use certain hospitals or physicians. Beneficiaries who purchase Medicare SELECT have the opportunity to reconsider their selection within 12 months and purchase a standard Medigap policy. Persons who have Medicare Advantage do not need a Medigap plan, and it is illegal for anyone to sell a Medicare Advantage beneficiary a Medigap policy. Beneficiaries may have a Medicare drug plan and have prescription drug coverage in their Medigap policy.

Preventive services covered by Medicare Part B

Beginning January 1, 2011, many preventive services are available to Medicare Part B beneficiaries at no cost to the beneficiary, if the care is provided by a participating provider. However, a cost for coinsurance may apply for the office visit. For some services, one or more risk factors must be present for the testing to be covered. See Exhibit 5.5 for a list of preventive services as outlined by CMS.

EXHIBIT 5.5 ■ Preventive Services Outlined by CMS

Abdominal aortic aneurysm screening	An exam for an individual new to Medicare who is at risk and has a referral from a provider. A one-time screening.
Bone density test	For a beneficiary who is at risk of osteoporosis. Covered once every 24 months.
Cardiovascular screening for heart attack and stroke	Blood test of cholesterol, lipid, and triglyceride levels. Covered every 5 years. 20 percent coinsurance applies
Colorectal cancer screening for precancerous polyps and early cancer detection	➢ Fecal occult blood test — age 50+ every 12 months ➢ Flexible sigmoidoscopy — age 50+ every 48 months high risk, otherwise every 10 years ➢ Colonoscopy — high risk every 24 months, otherwise every 10 years. ➢ Barium enema — high risk every 24 months, age 50+ every 48 months 20 percent coinsurance applies
Diabetes screening	Risk factors: high blood pressure, history of high cholesterol, triglyceride, obesity, high blood sugar, or family history of diabetes.
Diabetes self-management training	With diabetes with physician order. 20 percent coinsurance and deductible apply.
Flu shots	Seasonal flu and H1N1.
Glaucoma test	Every 12 months. Risk factors: diabetes, family history of glaucoma; African American age 50+; Hispanic age 65+. 20 percent coinsurance and deductible apply.
Hepatitis B shots	High- or medium-risk factors: hemophilia, ESRD, or as indicated by physician.
HIV screening	Every 12 months if desired. Up to three during pregnancy. 20 percent coinsurance applies.
Mammogram screening (x-ray for breast cancer)	Every 12 months age 40+ with one baseline age 35–39.
Medical nutrition therapy services	Risk factors: diabetes, kidney disease or kidney transplant in last 36 months.
Pap test and pelvic exam	High risk for cervical or vaginal cancer, every 12 months. Otherwise, every 24 months. Also includes clinical breast exam for breast cancer.
Physical exam	Within first 12 months on Medicare; then once per year.
Pneumococcal shot	Pneumonia prevention.
Prostate cancer screening	PSA every 12 months age 50+.
Smoking cessation counseling	Complications, risk factors due to smoking; 8 visits in 12-month period.

Adapted from Centers for Medicare & Medicaid Services. *Medicare & You,* 2011. www.medicare.gov/publications/pubs/pdf/10050.pdf. (Accessed 7/29/11.)

Services not covered by Medicare

Some services are not covered by Medicare. When a provider provides services to Medicare beneficiaries for services not covered by Medicare, the provider will not be reimbursed unless the beneficiary signs an Advance Beneficiary Notice (ABN), which is described in more detail in the following section, before services are delivered. See Exhibit 5.6 for a sample list of non-covered services by category.

EXHIBIT 5.6 ■ Sample List of Non-covered Services by Category

Not medically necessary	➢ Services provided in inappropriate location ➢ Services exceeding approved length of stay ➢ Evaluation management services that exceed appropriate level ➢ Services in excess of usage limits ➢ Services not warranted by diagnosis
Bundled services	➢ Fragmented services already covered ➢ Indirect prolonged care ➢ Physician standby services ➢ Case management services, such as phone calls ➢ Supplies included in allowable, such as surgical tray
Other excluded services	➢ Acupuncture ➢ Cosmetic surgery ➢ Custodial care in home or nursing home ➢ Most dental services ➢ Routine eye care ➢ In most cases care provided outside the United States

Adapted from Centers for Medicare & Medicaid Services. *Medicare & You*, 2011. www.medicare.gov/publications/pubs/pdf/10050.pdf. (Accessed 7/29/11.)

Advance beneficiary notice

If a provider believes that Medicare may deny payment because Medicare standards may consider the service medically unnecessary, the provider must provide written notification to the Medicare beneficiary in advance of the service. If the provider intends for the patient to be responsible for the bill, an ABN must be signed indicating that the patient is aware of his or her financial responsibility. When filing the insurance claim on a service that the physician believes will be denied, a "GA" modifier should be added to the billed service. A "GA" modifier on the claim form signals to CMS that the provider has provided the Medicare beneficiary with an ABN to notify that the service will not likely be covered. A "GY" modifier should be used to indicate that a service is not a Medicare benefit — it is non-covered. A "GZ" modifier indicates that the provider has not had the beneficiary sign an ABN but expects that Medicare will deny the service as not reasonable or necessary. An ABN form, a sample of which appears in Exhibit 5.7, may be downloaded at www.cms.hhs.gov/BNI/01 overview.asp.

EXHIBIT 5.7 ■ **Sample ABN Form**

***(A)* Notifier(s): Name of Organization**

***(B)* Patient Name:** ***(C)* Identification Number:**

ADVANCE BENEFICIARY NOTICE OF NONCOVERAGE (ABN)

NOTE: If Medicare doesn't pay for ***(D)*** surgery below, you may have to pay.

Medicare does not pay for everything, even some care that you or your health care provider have good reason to think you need. We expect Medicare may not pay for the ***(D)*** surgery below.

(D) Reference Source	***(E)* Reason Medicare May Not Pay:**	***(F)* Estimated Cost:**

WHAT YOU NEED TO DO NOW:

- Read this notice, so you can make an informed decision about your care.
- Ask us any questions that you may have after you finish reading.
- Choose an option below about whether to receive the ***(D)*** surgery listed above.

  Note: If you choose Option 1 or 2, we may help you to use any other insurance that you might have, but Medicare cannot require us to do this.

***(G)* OPTIONS:** **Check only one box. We cannot choose a box for you.**
❑ **OPTION 1.** I want the ***(D)*** procedure listed above. You may ask to be paid now, but I also want Medicare billed for an official decision on payment, which is sent to me on a Medicare Summary Notice (MSN). I understand that if Medicare doesn't pay, I am responsible for payment, but **I can appeal to Medicare** by following the directions on the MSN. If Medicare does pay, you will refund any payments I made to you, less co-pays or deductibles.
❑ **OPTION 2.** I want the ***(D)*** procedure listed above, but do not bill Medicare. You may ask to be paid now as I am responsible for payment. **I cannot appeal if Medicare is not billed**.
❑ **OPTION 3.** I don't want the ***(D)*** procedure listed above. I understand with this choice I am not responsible for payment, and I cannot appeal to see if Medicare would pay.

***(H)* Additional Information:**

This notice gives our opinion, not an official Medicare decision. If you have other questions on this notice or Medicare billing, call **1-800-MEDICARE** (1-800-633-4227/**TTY**: 1-877-486-2048).

Signing below means that you have received and understand this notice. You also receive a copy.

***(I)* Signature:**	***(J)* Date:**

According to the Paperwork Reduction Act of 1995, no persons are required to respond to a collection of information unless it displays a valid OMB control number. The valid OMB control number for this information collection is 0938-0566. The time required to complete this information collection is estimated to average 7 minutes per response, including the time to review instructions, search existing data resources, gather the data needed, and complete and review the information collection. If you have comments concerning the accuracy of the time estimate or suggestions for improving this form, please write to: CMS, 7500 Security Boulevard, Attn: PRA Reports Clearance Officer, Baltimore, Maryland 21244-1850.

Form CMS-R-131 (03/08) Form Approved OMB No. 0938-0566

COLLECTING DEDUCTIBLES, COINSURANCE, AND COPAYMENTS

Physician office insurance staff must be aware that Medicare providers and suppliers are required to collect from beneficiaries their unmet deductibles, coinsurance, and copayments. To reiterate, *the deductible must be paid by the beneficiary before Medicare pays for covered services*. The coinsurance is the 20 percent of the Medicare allowable in the fee-for-service Medicare Part B program. If the beneficiary has a Medigap supplemental insurance policy that will pay for the deductible and coinsurance, providers should collect those amounts from the Medigap policy before asking the beneficiary for payment. Some Medicare plans require a copayment when each service is accessed.

Collection of deductibles, coinsurance, and copayment is required for all patients, Medicare and non-Medicare beneficiaries alike. When these items are not collectable, the medical practice should have documentation substantiating practical attempts to collect. If a medical practice consistently waives deductibles, coinsurance, and copayments, that behavior will be considered unacceptable and perhaps even abuse of the program.

PRIMARY AND SECONDARY PAYERS

Medicare requires that providers establish and verify if Medicare is the primary or secondary payer. When a beneficiary has two or more payers that may have financial responsibility, providers determine responsibility. This process, called coordination of benefits, clarifies the respective financial responsibility for claim payment. Beneficiaries cannot be billed if the provider sends a claim to Medicare, but the claim is denied because Medicare is not the primary payer. Medical office insurance staff should use the coordination of benefits contractor (COBC), who can help make payment management determinations. COBC does not process claims — Medicare contractors are responsible for processing — but COBC investigates and reports insurance coverage. COBC is responsible for the crossover process of Medicare claims to state Medicaid programs.

Medicare normally pays as the *primary insurance* in the absence of other insurance. Medicare may be the *secondary payer* if there are other insurances. These may include group health plan insurance, no-fault or liability insurance, workers' compensation, COBRA continuation coverage, the Federal Black Lung Program, or military insurance from the Veteran's Administration or TRICARE. There are several situations that result in Medicare as the secondary payer. One common one is when a beneficiary or spouse is working and covered under an employer group health plan; in this case, Medicare is secondary insurance. In addition, when an individual is entitled to Medicare because of ESRD, Medicare is often the secondary insurance. Medicare Secondary Payer (MSP) information can be found in the Auxiliary File of the Common Working File from the CMS Web site.

The Medicare-provided COBC can identify a beneficiary's benefits that would put Medicare in a position to be the secondary payer. The COBC's role is to make sure that payments are coordinated, so that no payment mistakes occur. The COBC (800-999-1118; TTY 800-318-8782) will answer general questions regarding MSP, such as those related to the following situations:

- If a patient has Medicare insurance but is covered by a group health plan, and the employer has fewer than 20 employees, Medicare is the primary payer and the group health plan is the secondary payer.

- If a patient has Medicare insurance but is covered by a group health plan, and the employer has 20 or more employees, the group health plan is the primary payer and Medicare is the secondary payer.
- If a patient has Medicare and an employer retirement plan or is disabled, Medicare is the primary payer and the retiree coverage pays secondary.
- If a patient is a disabled Medicare beneficiary and is covered by a large group health plan of fewer than 100 employees, Medicare is the primary payer and the large group health plan pays as secondary.
- If a patient is a disabled Medicare beneficiary and is covered by a large group health plan of 100 or more employees, the large group health plan pays as primary and Medicare is the secondary payer.
- If a patient has ESRD and a group health plan and is in the first 30 months of Medicare eligibility, the group health plan pays as primary and Medicare pays as as secondary.
- If a patient has ESRD and a group health plan and has been entitled to Medicare for 30 months or longer, Medicare pays as primary and the group health plan pays as secondary.
- If a patient has ESRD and COBRA coverage and is in the first 30 months of Medicare eligibility, COBRA pays as primary and Medicare pays as secondary.
- If a patient has ESRD and COBRA and has been entitled to Medicare for 30 months or longer, Medicare pays as primary and COBRA pays as secondary.
- If a patient is covered by workers' compensation due to a job-related mishap and the patient is entitled to Medicare, workers' compensation pays as primary and Medicare pays as secondary.
- If a patient has been involved in a situation covered by no-fault or liability insurance and is entitled to Medicare, no-fault or liability insurance pays as primary and Medicare pays as secondary. (Examples from "Medicare Secondary Payer Fact Sheet," Table 1. List of Common Situations When Medicare May Pay First or Second can be found at www.cms.hhs.gov/MLNProducts/downloads/msp_fact_sheet.pdf.)

It is the provider organization's responsibility to determine whether Medicare is the primary payer or if there is another insurance that should pay before Medicare. The medical practice's front office staff should make this determination during patient registration; otherwise, the insurance claim may be filed to the wrong carrier. If Medicare pays as primary when another carrier should have done so, then Medicare will recover the payment.

MANDATORY FILING

Providers and suppliers are required to file Medicare claims for beneficiaries when providing covered services. Claims must be filed in a timely manner. As of January 1, 2010, claims must be filed within 12 months from the date of service to be considered timely filing. Claims filed beyond the timely filing deadline will be denied. Beneficiaries are not held responsible for payment for timely filing violations or for mandatory claims filing costs. If providers fail to meet mandatory filing requirement or try to charge beneficiaries for that service, they may face a Civil Monetary Penalty as high as $10,000 per violation. In those cases where Medicare is the secondary payer and the primary payer made payment directly to the beneficiary, the provider is not required to file with Medicare for the secondary claim. In addition, providers or suppliers are not required to comply with the mandatory filing policy when excluded services are provided or when the provider has opted out of Medicare. A good rule of thumb is for medical office insurance staff to automatically file a claim requesting payment when services are provided to a Medicare beneficiary.

KEY TERMS AND DEFINITIONS

Advance Beneficiary Notice (ABN) — A written notice given to a Medicare beneficiary before services are provided notifying the beneficiary that the services about to be provided may not be covered by Medicare and that the beneficiary may be personally responsible for paying for the services identified on the form. The beneficiary may decide not to receive services as outlined on the form.

Civil Monetary Penalties — Fines imposed for violations of regulations in the Medicare program.

Coordination of Benefits Contractor (COBC) — A contractor responsible for making payment determinations about financial responsibility for payment of claims.

Initial Coverage Election Period (IEP) — The three months prior, the month of, and the three months after an individual is 65 years of age. This is the period in which individuals should enroll for Medicare coverage. Enrollment after that period may require payment of a late enrollment penalty.

Mandatory Filing — The requirement that Medicare claims for beneficiaries be filed by providers at no cost to the beneficiary when the beneficiary is receiving covered services.

Medicare Advantage (MA) plan — Medicare Part C, the managed care part of Medicare.

Medicare Timely Filing — The requirement that Medicare claims be filed within a certain period after the date of service. As of January 1, 2010, claims must be filed within 12 months from the date of service to be considered timely.

Medigap Policy — The Medicare supplemental insurance that protects beneficiaries from out-of-pocket expenses.

National Provider Identifier (NPI) — The unique 10-digit number assigned to healthcare providers that is required by HIPAA to be used on all standard claims transactions.

Opt-Out — Status chosen by providers who wish to contract with Medicare beneficiaries privately.

Participating Provider — A medical services provider who has voluntarily agreed to accept assignment on all claims benefits considered a covered service for Medicare beneficiaries.

PECOS — Internet system used by providers to enroll, change information, reactivate status, or withdraw from Medicare.

Primary Insurance — The insurance that has responsibility to pay first on a claim for services when a beneficiary has two or more payers.

Secondary Payer — The carrier that will pay after the primary insurance on a claim for services when a beneficiary has two or more payers.

REVIEW OF OBJECTIVES

- **Explain the importance of the role of Medicare Part B to medical office insurance staff.**
  - Part B pays for physician services.
  - Insurance staff members serve as liaison between practice, patient, and insurance.
  - Violating Medicare regulations may result in prosecution for federal crime or in payment of Civil Monetary Penalties.

- **Outline the process and rationale for providers to participate in Medicare Part B.**
  - Provider participation requires National Provider Identification (NPI) number.
  - Providers enroll using of standard paper forms or online using PECOS.
  - Participation is advantageous for providers seeing Medicare beneficiaries, in part because the fee schedule for non-participating providers is 95 percent of the fee schedule for participating providers.
  - Providers have the opportunity to be non-participating providers or to opt out of the Medicare program.

- **Appreciate the scope of services covered by Medicare Part B.**
  - Part B pays for medically necessary non-inpatient services such as office visits, surgical procedures, and many diagnostic and therapeutic services.
  - Services may be provided in various locations, including physicians' offices, hospitals, clinical laboratories, ambulatory surgery centers, skilled nursing facilities, and other post-acute care facilities.
  - Multiple types of care providers may bill under Part B, including physicians, nurse practitioners, physician assistants, psychologists, social workers, occupational therapists, and physical therapists (please see full list in text).
  - Beginning January 1, 2011, many preventive services are available to Medicare Part B beneficiaries at no cost to the beneficiary if the care is provided by a participating provider.
  - Some services are paid as covered services, some are paid as preventive services, and others are excluded from payment.

- **Describe the purpose for Medigap (supplemental insurance) policies.**
  - Individuals eligible for Medicare may also enroll in a Medigap, or supplemental insurance, policy to cover costs not paid by Medicare.
  - Policies are designed to protect beneficiaries from out-of-pocket expenses.
  - Policies are standardized by OBRA 1990.

- **Characterize the distinction between Medicare as a primary or secondary payer.**
  - When a beneficiary is covered by Medicare and one or more other insurance policies, Medicare may be the primary or secondary payer.
  - Medical office staff members are responsible for determining in which cases Medicare should be billed as the primary or secondary payer. The rules to determine whether Medicare is primary or secondary are reviewed in the lesson. Also, Medicare provides a coordination of benefits contractor, who can assist in making these determinations.
  - If Medicare is billed as a primary payer but should be a secondary payer, the claim will be denied.

- **Define the legal requirements for providers participating in Medicare, including Advance Beneficiary Notice, mandatory filing, and timely filing.**
  - If services are provided to a Medicare beneficiary that are not likely to be covered by Medicare (for example, cosmetic procedures), the provider must ask the beneficiary to sign an Advance Beneficiary Notice (ABN) explaining that the service is not likely to be covered by Medicare and the beneficiary will be responsible for the cost. If an ABN is not signed *in advance of the service,* the beneficiary is not responsible for the cost.
  - Medicare requires that providers file claims for services provided to beneficiaries at no cost to the beneficiary. If providers fail to meet this mandatory filing requirement or charge beneficiaries for services without filing a Medicare claim, Civil Monetary Penalties may be assessed.
  - It is also inappropriate to bill Medicare for a service and then write off the coinsurance for which the beneficiary is responsible. This practice is considered abuse.
  - Medicare claims must be filed in a timely manner. As of January 1, 2010, this is defined as within 12 months of the date of service. Claims not filed by this time will be denied for not meeting timely filing requirements.

REVIEW EXERCISES: LESSON 5

MULTIPLE CHOICE

Please circle the best answer.

1. **Medical office insurance staff must be very familiar with Medicare Part B because:**
   - **a.** Violations of regulations may be subject to CMP
   - **b.** They serve as a liaison between the practice, the patient, and the patient's insurance
   - **c.** Both a and b

2. **It can be said that Medicare Part B beneficiaries:**
   - **a.** Pay a premium
   - **b.** Pay a deductible
   - **c.** Both a and b

3. **Medicare Part B beneficiaries may sign up:**
   - **a.** During three months before, the month of, or three months after the 65th birthday
   - **b.** Only during the initial coverage election period
   - **c.** Both a and b

4. **Providers are required to have an NPI by:**
   - **a.** CMS 855B
   - **b.** NPPES
   - **c.** HIPAA

5. **The online system designed for providers to create new enrollment records, make changes to existing enrollment, reactivate enrollment, or voluntarily withdraw from Medicare is:**
   - **a.** HIPAA
   - **b.** PECOS
   - **c.** NPPES

6. **Participating providers can expect payment from Medicare Part B within:**
   - **a.** 7 days
   - **b.** 14 days
   - **c.** 28 days

7. **Medicare Part B pays providers:**
   - **a.** 60 percent of the allowable
   - **b.** 70 percent of the allowable
   - **c.** 80 percent of the allowable

8. **Non-participating providers must provide Medicare beneficiaries written information about charges if the cost of charges is:**
   a. More than $250
   b. More than $500
   c. More than $750

9. **Opt-out of Medicare means:**
   a. Providers make a decision to participate with Medicare as non-participating providers
   b. Contracting with Medicare beneficiaries privately
   c. Medicare beneficiaries cannot get emergency services

10. **Beneficiaries of Part A and Part B Medicare can opt to purchase a:**
   a. Medicare Advantage plan
   b. Medigap plan
   c. Both a and b

11. **Part B Medicare covers services in authorized settings such as:**
   a. Dental offices
   b. Physician offices
   c. Hospitals outside the United States

12. **Part B Medicare covers services in authorized settings such as:**
   a. Ambulatory surgery centers
   b. Skilled nursing facilities
   c. Both a and b

13. **Part B Medicare covers services provided by limited license practitioners such as:**
   a. Nurse practitioners
   b. Physician assistants
   c. Both a and b

14. **As of January 1, 2011, many preventive services are available to Part B beneficiaries including:**
   a. Prostate cancer screening
   b. Smoking cessation counseling
   c. Both a and b

15. **Consistently waiving deductibles, coinsurance, and copayment is:**
   a. Permitted by the Medicare program
   b. Considered abuse of the Medicare program
   c. Neither a nor b

(Answers on page 101)

CASE STUDIES

Please select the best answer.

Case study 1: Joan works in the insurance department of Always Best Service medical practice. She just received a call from Mrs. Thompson, who said that when she came into the practice for physician services, the front desk person insisted that she pay her Medicare Part B deductible before she received services, even though she presented the Medigap policy information and explained that the Medigap policy would pay her deductible. Joan verified the correctness of Mrs. Thompson's information while on the phone with her. How should Joan handle this situation?

- **a.** Explain to the patient that she will make sure that she receives a refund promptly for the amount she paid.
- **b.** Tell the patient that the provider has the right to collect the money from the patient.
- **c.** Tell the patient that she will refund Medicare immediately.

Case study 2: Dr. Smith has a big heart and is very empathetic. After he heard about the front desk personnel collecting deductibles from Medicare Part B patients, he told Joan, who works in the insurance department, that he wants to waive all deductibles, coinsurance, and copayments on Medicare Part B patients. Dr. Smith thinks that will not only be kind to patients but will encourage more individuals to use him as their doctor. How should Joan handle this situation?

- **a.** Joan should follow Dr. Smith's directive and make sure that Medicare Part B patients don't ever get a statement.
- **b.** Explain to Dr. Smith that consistently waiving deductibles, coinsurance, and copayments for Medicare beneficiaries or non-beneficiaries may be considered abuse of the Medicare program.
- **c.** Explain to Dr. Smith that he can only omit collecting deductibles, coinsurance, and copayments for Medicare Advantage beneficiaries.

Case study 3: Mrs. Kurt received services at Always Best Service from Dr. Jones. Medicare Part B denied payment on services as a non-covered service. Pat, the insurance supervisor, told Joan to bill Mrs. Kurt for the services. Joan asked if Mrs. Kurt signed an ABN and was told that she did not. Joan researched the situation and confirmed that Mrs. Kurt did not sign an ABN in advance of receiving the service. How should Joan handle the situation?

- **a.** Send a statement for services to Mrs. Kurt.
- **b.** Explain to Pat that no ABN was signed and that they can't hold Mrs. Kurt responsible for charges.
- **c.** Explain that they can have Mrs. Kurt sign an ABN when she comes in again and then bill Mrs. Kurt for services.

Case study 4: Dr. Jones is a participating provider with Medicare Part B. He has become discouraged with participation because of the rising practice cost and low reimbursement. Dr. Jones told the insurance staff to post a sign in the waiting room to inform patients that Always Best Service medical practice will no longer file claims for Medicare beneficiaries because Medicare pays so poorly. Dr. Jones told Joan that if patients ask, she can tell them he will see them but will not spend money filing claims. How should Joan handle this situation?

a. Joan should inform Dr. Jones of mandatory filing requirements.

b. Joan should tell the front desk to start collecting for services provided at the time of service.

c. Joan is aware of the opt-out option and should start contracting privately with beneficiaries.

(Answers on page 101)

COMPLETION QUESTIONS

Please fill in the blanks.

1. Name three of the large categories of Medicare Part B services provided.

2. Violations of Medicare regulations are serious. Name two consequences that may happen if violations occur.

3. What are the categories of violations that may occur?

4. While a standard premium applies to most individuals eligible for Medicare Part B, all beneficiaries do not pay the same premium amount. Explain.

5. The initial enrollment period for Medicare Part B is seven months. Explain.

6. If an individual 65 years of age continues working and is covered by a group health plan, when does he or she sign up? What is the period called?

7. What is Medigap?

8. What is the National Provider Identifier (NPI)?

9. CMS has developed a system to assign and maintain all NPI numbers. What is the name of the system?

10. Where is the NPI used?

____

11. What does the NPI replace?

____

12. What is the name of the Internet-based provider enrollment system for providers to enroll in the Medicare program?

____

13. What is the Medicare fee schedule for non-participating providers compared to participating providers?

____

14. Other than the fee schedule, name another benefit of Medicare participation.

____

____

15. Providers who are not accepting assignment on a claim must provide Medicare beneficiaries with an estimate of the charge in written form if the charge is over a certain amount. What is that amount?

____

16. What are the criteria to meet the requirement for medically necessary?

____

____

17. What are the three categories of Medigap policies?

____

18. Name the three states that have state waivers to standardize their policies differently from the other states.

____

19. Some states offer a Medigap policy plan called Medicare SELECT. How does it differ from others?

____

20. What is the situation relating to Medigap for persons who have Medicare Advantage, Part C?

____

21. When is an ABN used?

22. What are the three modifiers that may be used relating to an ABN, and what do they indicate?

23. Medicare requires providers and suppliers to collect unmet deductibles, copayments, and coinsurance from supplemental insurance policies or from beneficiaries. Does that apply only to Medicare beneficiaries?

24. If a patient has Medicare insurance but is covered by a group health plan, and the employer has 20 or more employees, who is the primary payer, and who is the secondary payer?

25. What does *mandatory filing* mean?

(Answers on page 101–102)

MATCHING

Please match the letter of the definition to the term.
Write the letter of the definition next to the term.

Medigap policy _____	**a.** The three months prior, the month of, and the three months after an individual is 65 years of age. This is the period in which individuals should enroll for Medicare coverage. Enrollment after that period may require payment of a late enrollment penalty.
Civil Monetary Penalties _____	**b.** The Medicare supplemental insurance that protects beneficiaries from out-of-pocket expenses.
Initial coverage election period (IEP) _____	**c.** The unique 10-digit number assigned to healthcare providers that is required by HIPAA to be used on all standard claims transactions.
PECOS _____	**d.** A medical services provider who has voluntarily agreed to accept assignment on all claims benefits considered a covered service for Medicare beneficiaries.
Opt-out _____	**e.** A contractor responsible for making payment determinations about financial responsibility for payment of claims.
Advanced Beneficiary Notice (ABN) _____	**f.** The insurance that has responsibility to pay first on a claim for services when a beneficiary has two or more payers.
Coordination of benefits contractor (COBC) _____	**g.** A written notice given to a Medicare beneficiary before services are provided notifying the beneficiary that the services about to be provided may not be covered by Medicare and that the beneficiary may be personally responsible for paying for the services identified on the form. The beneficiary may decide not to receive services as outlined on the form.
Primary insurance _____	**h.** The requirement that Medicare claims for beneficiaries be filed by providers at no cost to the beneficiary when the beneficiary is receiving covered services.
Medicare timely filing _____	**i.** The carrier that will pay after the primary insurance on a claim for services when a beneficiary has two or more payers.
Mandatory filing _____	**j.** The requirement that Medicare claims be filed within a certain period after the date of service. As of January 1, 2010, claims must be filed within 12 months from the date of service to be considered timely.
Secondary payer _____	**k.** Medicare Part C, the managed care part of Medicare.
Medicare Advantage (MA) plan _____	**l.** Status chosen by providers who wish to contract with Medicare beneficiaries privately.
Participating provider _____	**m.** Internet system used by providers to enroll, change information, reactivate status, or withdraw from Medicare.
National Provider Identifier (NPI) _____	**n.** Fines imposed for violations of regulations in the Medicare program.

(Answers on page 102)

ANSWERS: LESSON 5

MULTIPLE CHOICE

1-c; 2-c; 3-a; 4-c; 5-b; 6-b; 7-c; 8-b; 9-b; 10-c; 11-b; 12-c; 13-c; 14-c; 15-b

CASE STUDIES

Case study 1-a; Case study 2-b; Case study 3-b; Case study 4-a

COMPLETION QUESTIONS

1. Medicare Part B helps pay for services in physician office services, outpatient services, and services at ambulatory surgical centers (ASCs).
2. Civil Monetary Penalties (CMPs) and exclusion from the Medicare program may apply.
3. Violations of the Medicare assignment provision, Medicare physician agreement, anti-kickback statutes, Stark laws, submitting false or misleading information relating to decision to discharge, hospital outpatient surgery unbundling costs, and dumping beneficiaries who lack resources and cannot pay.
4. Some people pay more based on their income as reported from the individual's IRS tax return two years prior.
5. An individual may sign up during the three months before the month he or she turns 65, the month of the 65th birthday, or during the three months following the 65th birthday month.
6. Those individuals may sign up during the next eight-month period after employment coverage ends, and the period is called a *special enrollment period*.
7. Medigap, known as Medicare supplement insurance, is provided by private insurance carriers to fill the cost gap, that is, the 20 percent that Medicare Part B does not cover.
8. A 10-digit number assigned to healthcare providers that is unique to a specific provider and will follow him or her throughout his or her career even if the individual moves from state to state
9. National Plan and Provider Enumeration System (NPPES)
10. On all standard claims transactions
11. NPI replaces all other identifying numbers for providers.
12. Provider Enrollment, Chain and Ownership System (PECOS)
13. Non-participating providers receive 95 percent of the fee schedule for a participating provider.
14. Payment goes directly to the provider rather than the provider being required to collect the payment from the Medicare beneficiary.
15. $500

16. (1) The service must have reasonable beneficial effect on the patient. (2) The service provided is proven to be effective. (3) The procedure that is performed is appropriate for a specific diagnosis.

17. (1) Pre-standard plans, (2) OBRA 1990 standard plans, and (3) waiver state standard plans.

18. Massachusetts, Minnesota, and Wisconsin.

19. Medicare SELECT requires beneficiaries to use certain hospitals or providers.

20. Persons who have Medicare Advantage do not need a Medigap plan. It is illegal for anyone to sell a Medicare Advantage beneficiary a Medigap policy.

21. When a provider believes that Medicare may deny payment because Medicare standards may consider the service medically unnecessary, the provider provides written notification to the Medicare beneficiary in advance of the service for the beneficiary's signature to ensure the patient's financial responsibility for the service.

22. "GA" indicates that the beneficiary has signed an ABN, "GY" indicates the service is not a Medicare benefit, and "GZ" indicates that the beneficiary has not signed an ABN.

23. No, unmet deductibles, copayments, and coinsurance are required for all patients, Medicare and non-Medicare beneficiaries alike. Consistently waving deductibles, copayments, and coinsurance is unacceptable and may be considered abuse of the Medicare program.

24. The group health plan is the primary payer and Medicare is the secondary payer.

25. Mandatory filing means that providers are required to file Medicare claims for beneficiaries at no cost to the beneficiary when providing covered services.

MATCHING

__ Medigap policy: **b**

__ Civil Monetary Penalties: **n**

__ Initial coverage election period (IEP): **a**

__ PECOS: **m**

__ Opt-out: **l**

__ Advanced Beneficiary Notice (ABN): **g**

__ Coordination of benefits contractor (COBC): **e**

__ Primary insurance: **f**

__ Medicare timely filing: **j**

__ Mandatory filing: **h**

__ Secondary payer: **i**

__ Medicare Advantage (MA) plan: **k**

__ Participating provider: **d**

__ National Provider Identifier (NPI): **c**

LESSON 6

Understanding the Revenue Cycle — Pre-visit

OBJECTIVES

- Identify the elements of the pre-visit phase of the revenue cycle.
- Identify the items needed for physician credentialing.
- Describe the scheduler's role in the pre-visit phase.
- Describe how the pre-visit phase impacts insurance staff.

REVENUE CYCLE

Revenue cycle is a term used to describe the complex process by which providers are paid for services rendered. In most industries, the revenue cycle is straightforward: a product is made, sold, billed, and paid for. In healthcare, however, the revenue cycle is much more complex. It begins far in advance of the patient visit and may not end until several months after the patient visit — even after final payment is collected. The revenue cycle is divided into three distinct phases: the pre-visit, the visit, and the post-visit. The insurance department is primarily charged with the post-visit phase, but the other two phases directly impact the work that the insurance department does. Poor execution of processes in the pre-visit phase and visit phase multiplies the insurance department staff members' work and hampers their chances to get claims paid successfully. The best possibility for success in the revenue cycle starts with hiring the right people for the right job in the organization.

Practices that maximize the revenue cycle have done so by making everyone in the organization understand his or her various roles in creating the financial success. High-functioning organizations hold the individuals in those various roles accountable. The organization's financial viability depends on a well-managed revenue cycle. Processes in every stage of the revenue cycle must be well defined and followed consistently. Because of the volume and complexity of the revenue cycle, it is important to automate as many tasks as possible. Many medical practices do not have adequate practice management software to support efficiency. On the other hand, some organizations have superior practice management software but underutilize the system's features. It is important to share common values and attitudes across the organization. Part of the common purpose is having all the supports in place that work toward perfecting the revenue cycle. These organization-wide activities and the work of improving the revenue cycle functions include maximal utilization of the organization's technology; the work is ongoing, and insurance staff in busy practices are never caught up.

PRE-VISIT PHASE

The billing process starts before the patient makes an appointment. As illustrated in Exhibit 6.1, the pre-visit phase includes negotiating with insurance companies; provider credentialing; educating staff and patients; and setting up technology, in particular the computer system, to best facilitate the work of the office staff.

EXHIBIT 6.1 ■ The Pre-visit Phase

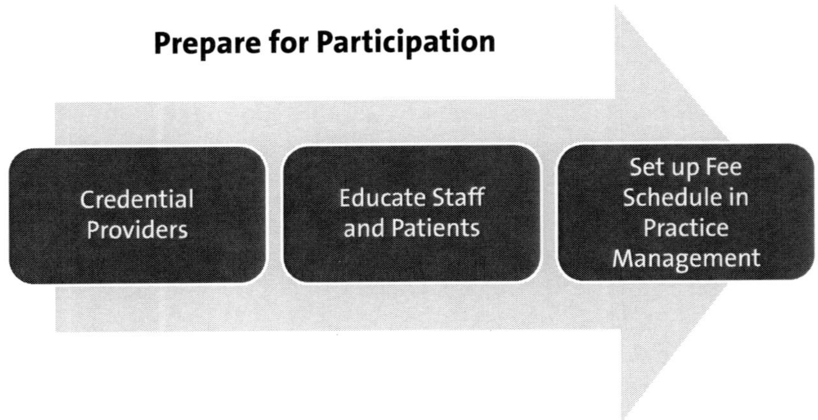

Contract negotiations

Contract negotiations between providers and insurance carriers begin in what might be called "behind the scenes" work that starts the billing process. Medical office insurance staff members are rarely involved in this aspect of the revenue cycle, but they witness the impact of contract negotiations every day in the course of their work when they are making adjustments between the standard charge and the contracted rate.

The medical practice has a standard fee schedule and negotiates with carriers starting from that fee schedule. Carriers expect discounted rates, and the contract can occur when both parties agree to a fee schedule that is unique to that carrier.

A tool that summarizes the fee schedules for each insurance carrier, such as the contracting spreadsheet in Exhibit 6.2, allows insurance staff to understand and set a clear expectation about the amount that can be collected from carriers based on the rate contracted with the organization. To share this kind of information with insurance staff members puts staff in a position to accept accountability for working insurance by payer.

Additionally, decisions relating to financial policies within the organization must be set in the pre-visit phase. Written policies that are clear, well communicated, and adhered to are particularly helpful in supporting the work of insurance staff.

EXHIBIT 6.2 ■ Sample Contracting Spreadsheet

Top CPT Codes	Standard Charges	Medicare Allowable	Payer Name	Payer % of Medicare Allowable	Repeat with Top 5 or 6 Payers
47565	$3,000.00	$710.30			

Setting up fee scheduling

Additional setup work in practice management that may fall to the insurance department includes setting up the fee schedules for the major insurance payers in the practice management system (PMS) and credentialing providers. Both of these are labor intensive, but necessary, tasks. Some practices chose to forgo the investment of staff time for loading in fee schedules. Those practices pay a greater price day after day when payments are posted and inappropriate payment amounts are not caught as having paid incorrectly. Expected payment amounts on the computer screen serve as a visual reminder of correct payment. When this information is lacking, an insurance staff member is likely to move through payment posting without regard for whether the payment received is correct.

Educating staff and patients

The pre-visit phase is also a time when patients may be invited to find out more about the practice via visiting its Web site. The practice may also send out patient packets that contain items such as a welcome letter, a brochure about the practice, educational brochures as appropriate, insurance and financial information, and contact information for patients to use as a resource for questions to be answered. The brochure may highlight the physicians' training and experience along with the breadth of services offered. The pre-visit sets the tone for the patient as to what to expect from the practice. This opportunity should be taken seriously and used well.

Physician credentialing

Before a physician can participate with an insurance carrier, he or she must be credentialed with the carrier. This time-consuming process, often taking up to six months to complete, must be well thought through in the organization. Physicians and management must understand that this lengthy process requires the submission of extensive information, which must be supplied by the physician who is being credentialed to the organization doing the credentialing. If not enough time is allowed, the physician will not be a participating provider when he or she begins work. The resulting non-participation status may affect the relationship between patients and the physician going forward if the situation is not handled carefully by the organization. This kind of situation must be dealt with within the organization. The best plan is to ensure that the physician is credentialed with the organization's health plans before the physician's effective employment date.

The medical organization should have a standard list of items that a newly hired physician must provide to the practice so that credentialing can take place. See Exhibit 6.3 for a sample physician credentialing checklist. Often physicians do not understand the significant amount of information required or the steps in the process. It is important that the organization help the physician understand that the employment start date with the organization may be altered if the information is not submitted to the practice in a timely manner.

Of the many items on the standard list, the primary need is for a valid medical license issued by the state in which the provider will be providing services. Acquiring a state license itself may take several months. The medical organization should print a specific state license application for the new provider to complete, so that the practice will have complete and correct information, particularly if the practice is applying for state licensure for the provider. Items needed on a state license application may include:

- Social Security Number
- Date of birth
- Name (exactly as it is to appear on license)
- Mailing address
- Daytime telephone
- E-mail address
- Name as it appears on degree or other credential(s)
- Citizenship information
- Personal conduct information such as:
  - Found or pleaded guilty, no contest, or nolo contendere to any felony or misdemeanor or pending court charges;
  - Any disciplinary action by a medical licensing authority;
  - Professional misconduct; and
  - Restricted privileges information.

EXHIBIT 6.3 ■ Physician Credentialing Checklist

Item	Date Requested	Date Received	Date Sent	Sent To
1. Name				
2. CAQH password				
3. Current state licenses—copy				
4. DEA—copy (with address of new location)				
5. BNDD—copy (with address of new location)				
6. CV—current				
7. Date of birth				
8. Social Security Number				
9. Practice address: location 1				
10. Practice address: location 2				
11. Practice tax ID number				
12. Practice phone number				
13. Practice fax number				
14. Practice contact — each location				
15. Physician NPI number				
16. All education (month and year of attendance, address for each institution, name of program director)				
17. All training (month and year of attendance, address for each institution, name of program director)				
18. Hospital affiliations (past, present, and pending)				
19. Practice specialty (board certification/affiliation)				
20. Work history (10 years since completion of training)				
21. Professional certificates (license numbers: include all state licenses current and past)				
22. Professional liability insurance (past 10 years: agent, address, policy number, and group name)				
23. Professional liability insurance (copy of current insurance with name, amount of coverage, expiration date; if name not on certificate, attach list of physicians covered by policy)				
24. Malpractice claims history				
25. Hospital privileges (sheet including education needed, proctoring requirements, and recent education completed)				
26. CME documents				
27. Peer references (same degree and specialty notes with fax number)				
NOTES				

Note: See Key Terms and Definitions at the end of this lesson for definition of acronyms.

- School information (beginning with high school to include post-secondary education, medical education, and a chronology of all experience or activities since beginning medical school)
  - Name of schools attended
  - Locations
  - Years attended
  - Entrance and leaving dates
  - Title of diploma or degree (if conferred); if not conferred, credits earned
- Information about where the physician will practice
- Gender and ethnicity
- Financial obligations
  - Loans
  - Child support
- Permission for the licensing authority to research education
- Photo
- Signed and notarized affidavit of truthfulness of the information provided

Issuing controlled substances: Other necessary items for credentialing include current certificates from the Bureau of Narcotics and Dangerous Drugs (BNDD) and the U.S. Department of Justice's Drug Enforcement Administration (DEA). The BNDD is issued by the state. States are required to maintain a registry of persons who are authorized to prescribe and dispense controlled substances. Applications for BNDD certification can be found for each state on its department of health Web site.

The DEA is a federal government registration entity. The DEA credential cannot be issued until the applicant has shown proof that he or she has completed all the state requirements for conducting business and received licensure in the state in which he or she intends to provide care. A DEA certificate will not be issued if the applicant cannot obtain state licensure. Likewise, if state licensure is revoked, then DEA certification must be relinquished, and the state authority will also be revoked. Drugs are listed in schedules of controlled substances, and each application must be clear about which schedules of controlled substances the provider is asking to be authorized to prescribe or dispense. Every three years providers must renew the DEA registration. If a provider has more than one principal business location from which he or she will be dispensing controlled substances, then an additional registration will be required for each location. Along those same lines, when a provider changes business addresses, the DEA must be updated to reflect the new address. Address change request forms, as well as complete DEA information, may be found at www.DEAdiversion.usdoj.gov.

Curriculum vitae: The curriculum vitae is also a necessary part of licensure and credentialing. The curriculum vitae contains the general identifying information relating to an applicant. It also contains the complete education and training history of the applicant, which includes not only addresses but also contact names within institutions (for example, the name of the program director).

It is important that the information contained on each submitted document be verifiable by the information on other documents. The education and work history reported on each document should match that information with every other document submitted. If not, each step in completing the process may be held up. Work history should include all affiliations with hospitals where the provider has held privileges, including pending as well as past and present privileges. In addition to hospital affiliations, the provider must provide all professional associations, with months and years noted, since the completion of training or at least for the past 10 years. As noted earlier, any chronological gap must be explained. All current and past state licenses, professional certificates, and practice specialty information such as board certification should be accessible to use for licensure and credentialing application.

Professional liability insurance information, along with a malpractice claims history with complete history on each claim, will be necessary. Claims history may be sent as an attachment with each claim's history outlined in detail. Even if there are no claims, the claims report must be completed by noting that there are no claims. Current medical liability information, such as coverage dates and limits, must be submitted. A certificate showing that the provider will have medical liability insurance with the group, including the names of the other providers covered under the policy, may be required. Information relating to the practice that is credentialing the provider is required (for example, practice address, tax identification number, telephone and fax numbers), as well as a contact name and telephone number in the practice where information can be clarified when questions arise. The provider's continuing medical education (CME) documentation may also be required.

The insurance credentialing and re-credentialing process is an important issue in the insurance department of medical practices. The credentialing issue has been so time consuming in the past for insurance departments that some states have agreed to mandate and accept a standardized credentialing form rather than allowing each insurance carrier to dictate the format of the information used to do credentialing in their individual organization. Additionally, there are many organizations that offer credentialing services online for providers to relieve the credentialing burden. Some organizations offering services are for-profit organizations. On the other hand, the Council for Affordable Quality Healthcare (CAQH) is a nonprofit alliance founded by many of the nation's large health plans and trade associations offering a simplified approach to credentialing through its Universal Provider Datasource. CAQH credentialing services are free to providers in all 50 states and in the District of Columbia and provide an accepted format for credentialing with hundreds of health plans. CAQH uses a standard online form where information can be revised and authorized for release to health plans as designated by providers. After authorization is received to access information from the secure CAQH database, payers download the credentialing information to credential and re-credential providers. The CAQH Web site is www.caqh.org. Even with the improvements made by using CAQH, credentialing is an additional chore that must be attended to on a regular basis.

INFORMATION COLLECTION

Collecting information from the patient during the pre-visit phase serves two very important functions. First, it provides accurate information about how to contact the patient who may need to be contacted for medical reasons or financial purposes. Second, information that is gathered during pre-visit must be correct so that insurance can be billed correctly.

SCHEDULING AND FRONT DESK

Competent work by the front desk staff members is essential in supporting the insurance office staff's work. It is ideal if organizations can collect patient information at the time the appointment is made or at least during the pre-visit phase of the revenue cycle. Obviously, if the organization has referring physicians' offices making appointments for patients, the medical practice must be sensitive to the time of the referring physicians' office staff. Organizations should systematically gather the essential information from the referring physician's office and secure the remainder of the information from the patient.

Schedulers or front desk personnel making appointments must have an appropriate appointment template. For example, some providers may see 10 patients in a half-day segment, while others may see 30 patients in a half-day segment. It is typically the role of the administrative or clinical staff to set the appointment template. Regardless, the template must be appropriate to the provider, so that patients are not forced to experience wait time in the medical practice. Patients who have excessive wait times are less inclined to want to make sure that the provider gets paid promptly.

Standardized appointment types are an important part of the scheduling template. The organization must determine in advance what type of patients they have and in what order and in what time interval those patients are to be seen. For example, the provider may want to start with seeing established patients while new patients are being processed through the organizations system. The schedule should be set so that the provider's time is maximized.

The information that the front desk is responsible for collecting can be thought of as completing boxes 1–11d on the Centers for Medicare & Medicaid Services (CMS) 1500 form, which is the standard paper format for filing insurance claims (see Exhibit 6.4).

While most insurance claims — 90 percent or greater — are filed electronically, the paper claim form creates a good visual of the information that is necessary to file the claim. The boxes on the paper claim relate to fields of the electronic claim, as follows:

- Box 1 — Type of insurance
- Box 1a — Insured's (or subscriber's) ID number
- Box 2 — Patient's name (as on card)
- Box 3 — Patient date of birth and sex
- Box 4 — Insured's name (same as or different from box 2)
- Box 5 — Patient's address
- Box 6 — Patient relationship to insured (patient, spouse, parent, other)
- Box 7 — Insured's address (patient or different from box 5)
- Box 8 — Patient status (single, married, other)
- Box 9 — Other insured's name (for secondary insurance)
- Box 9a — Other insured's policy/group number

EXHIBIT 6.4 ■ CMS 1500 Form

1500

HEALTH INSURANCE CLAIM FORM

APPROVED BY NATIONAL UNIFORM CLAIM COMMITTEE 08/05

PICA — PICA — CARRIER

1. MEDICARE (Medicare #) MEDICAID (Medicaid #) TRICARE CHAMPUS (Sponsor's SSN) CHAMPVA (Member ID#) GROUP HEALTH PLAN (SSN or ID) FECA BLK LUNG (SSN) OTHER (ID)

1a. INSURED'S I.D. NUMBER (For Program in Item 1)

2. PATIENT'S NAME (Last Name, First Name, Middle Initial)

3. PATIENT'S BIRTH DATE MM DD YY SEX M F

4. INSURED'S NAME (Last Name, First Name, Middle Initial)

5. PATIENT'S ADDRESS (No., Street)

6. PATIENT RELATIONSHIP TO INSURED Self Spouse Child Other

7. INSURED'S ADDRESS (No., Street)

CITY STATE

8. PATIENT STATUS Single Married Other

CITY STATE

ZIP CODE TELEPHONE (Include Area Code) ( )

Employed Full-Time Student Part-Time Student

ZIP CODE TELEPHONE (Include Area Code) ( )

9. OTHER INSURED'S NAME (Last Name, First Name, Middle Initial)

10. IS PATIENT'S CONDITION RELATED TO:

11. INSURED'S POLICY GROUP OR FECA NUMBER

a. OTHER INSURED'S POLICY OR GROUP NUMBER

a. EMPLOYMENT? (Current or Previous) YES NO

a. INSURED'S DATE OF BIRTH MM DD YY SEX M F

b. OTHER INSURED'S DATE OF BIRTH MM DD YY SEX M F

b. AUTO ACCIDENT? PLACE (State) YES NO

b. EMPLOYER'S NAME OR SCHOOL NAME

c. EMPLOYER'S NAME OR SCHOOL NAME

c. OTHER ACCIDENT? YES NO

c. INSURANCE PLAN NAME OR PROGRAM NAME

d. INSURANCE PLAN NAME OR PROGRAM NAME

10d. RESERVED FOR LOCAL USE

d. IS THERE ANOTHER HEALTH BENEFIT PLAN? YES NO *If yes*, return to and complete item 9 a-d.

READ BACK OF FORM BEFORE COMPLETING & SIGNING THIS FORM.

12. PATIENT'S OR AUTHORIZED PERSON'S SIGNATURE I authorize the release of any medical or other information necessary to process this claim. I also request payment of government benefits either to myself or to the party who accepts assignment below.

SIGNED DATE

13. INSURED'S OR AUTHORIZED PERSON'S SIGNATURE I authorize payment of medical benefits to the undersigned physician or supplier for services described below.

SIGNED

PATIENT AND INSURED INFORMATION

14. DATE OF CURRENT: MM DD YY ILLNESS (First symptom) OR INJURY (Accident) OR PREGNANCY(LMP)

15. IF PATIENT HAS HAD SAME OR SIMILAR ILLNESS. GIVE FIRST DATE MM DD YY

16. DATES PATIENT UNABLE TO WORK IN CURRENT OCCUPATION MM DD YY FROM TO

17. NAME OF REFERRING PROVIDER OR OTHER SOURCE 17a. 17b. NPI

18. HOSPITALIZATION DATES RELATED TO CURRENT SERVICES MM DD YY FROM TO

19. RESERVED FOR LOCAL USE

20. OUTSIDE LAB? YES NO $ CHARGES

21. DIAGNOSIS OR NATURE OF ILLNESS OR INJURY (Relate Items 1, 2, 3 or 4 to Item 24E by Line)

1. ___ . ___ 3. ___ . ___

2. ___ . ___ 4. ___ . ___

22. MEDICAID RESUBMISSION CODE ORIGINAL REF. NO.

23. PRIOR AUTHORIZATION NUMBER

	24. A. DATE(S) OF SERVICE From MM DD YY To MM DD YY	B. PLACE OF SERVICE	C. EMG	D. PROCEDURES, SERVICES, OR SUPPLIES (Explain Unusual Circumstances) CPT/HCPCS MODIFIER	E. DIAGNOSIS POINTER	F. $ CHARGES	G. DAYS OR UNITS	H. EPSDT Family Plan	I. ID. QUAL.	J. RENDERING PROVIDER ID. #
1									NPI	
2									NPI	
3									NPI	
4									NPI	
5									NPI	
6									NPI	

25. FEDERAL TAX I.D. NUMBER SSN EIN

26. PATIENT'S ACCOUNT NO.

27. ACCEPT ASSIGNMENT? (For govt. claims, see back) YES NO

28. TOTAL CHARGE $

29. AMOUNT PAID $

30. BALANCE DUE $

31. SIGNATURE OF PHYSICIAN OR SUPPLIER INCLUDING DEGREES OR CREDENTIALS (I certify that the statements on the reverse apply to this bill and are made a part thereof.)

SIGNED DATE

32. SERVICE FACILITY LOCATION INFORMATION a. b.

33. BILLING PROVIDER INFO & PH # ( ) a. b.

PHYSICIAN OR SUPPLIER INFORMATION

NUCC Instruction Manual available at: www.nucc.org *PLEASE PRINT OR TYPE* APPROVED OMB-0938-0999 FORM CMS-1500 (08-05)

SAMPLE

- Box 9b — Other insured's date of birth and sex
- Box 9c — Employer or school name
- Box 9d — Insurance plan name
- Box 10 — Is patient's condition related to employment? Auto accident? Other accident?
- Box 11 — Insured's policy group or Federal Employee's Compensation Act number
- Box 11a — Insured's date of birth and sex
- Box 11b — Employer's name or school name
- Box 11c — Insurance plan name or program name
- Box 11d — Is there another health benefit plan?

The organization should be very deliberate in training appointment schedulers and front desk personnel. Schedulers should use a friendly tone with patients. They have the opportunity to create an impression of competency and fairness that will lead to developing an excellent relationship between the patient and the organization. Schedulers and front desk personnel should always communicate with patients well and appropriately.

It is extremely important to the efficiency of the organization that appointments in a provider's schedule fit the type of practice and scope of services that the provider is prepared to deliver to patients. Organizations should have a list of service offerings as part of their education and training for schedulers and front desk staff.

Successful organizations create scripts for schedulers to use when they are talking with patients. These scripts quickly become second nature and ensure that schedulers convey all the necessary information to the patient. Some of the elements that should be included in the scheduler's script include the following:

1. The scheduler should establish the patient's insurance status.
   - The scheduler should review with the patient the organizational requirements relating to the insurance status.
   - The scheduler should explain the financial requirements of the organization in a straightforward manner without being shy.
   - The scheduler should disclose financial policy relating to collecting at time of service relating to copays, deductible payment, and so on.
   - The scheduler should offer payment options based on particular circumstances of patient and organization — credit cards accepted, charity care, financial counseling, and so on.
2. The scheduler should ask the patient to have the insurance card in hand to provide accurate information.
   - The scheduler directs the patient where to locate the information on the card.
   - The scheduler collects information as required to complete box 1–9d on the CMS 1500 form.

It is incumbent on the scheduling and front desk staff to be educated in various insurance plan types:

- Government (for example, Medicare, Medicaid, TRICARE)
- Commercial (for example, fee-for-service, discounted fee-for-service, health maintenance organization, preferred provider organization, point of service)
- Self-insured benefits (for example, flexible spending account, health reimbursement account, health savings account)

The schedulers and front desk staff must be capable of answering insurance participation questions and articulate clearly the ramifications of non-participation.

AVOID CLAIM DENIALS

The most frequent reasons claims are denied are related to functions that can be handled at the front desk including non-covered services, ineligible for benefits, claims lacking information, and prior authorization required. Attention to each of the steps outlined in the pre-visit phase can reduce these common denials.

Appointment schedulers and front desk personnel have the responsibility of verifying insurance eligibility. It must be verified that the patient has insurance and that the patient's conditions meet the payer's requirements as a covered service. The organization must make eligibility verification decisions based on the practice's circumstances. Once the process for determining eligibility is made, all personnel must adhere to the process so that all staff knows what to expect in relationship to eligibility verification. For example, if the organizational process is that all patients' insurance with Always Best Payer will be verified, then the insurance staff can proceed with confidence that verification has occurred and that the patient was eligible to receive services covered by insurance on the date that services were received.

Online insurance verification is always preferred. Staff should avoid telephone verification when possible. It is time consuming and may not be as accurate as online eligibility verification. When online verification is used, ensure that staff knows how to interpret information on screen so that verification is accurate.

Medicaid eligibility should be verified at each visit. Medicaid coverage changes often. In addition, coverage is complicated by certain services being covered with some patients while with others it is not. In some cases, a *spend down* (a monthly amount of money that a patient must pay out-of-pocket before Medicaid will cover services) may apply.

If a carrier requires written confirmation — pre-determination — before services are provided, staff must do this to improve the chances of payment for the service provided. For some tests, surgical procedures, and hospitalizations, the patient's insurance may require a pre-authorization or precertification stating that the care to be provided is medically necessary based on the carrier's protocol prior to treatment. Staff must contact the patient's insurance to ensure that each of these requirements — pre-determination, pre-authorization, precertification — are met, if required, so that the claim will not be denied.

The terms *pre-determination*, *precertification*, and *pre-authorization* may be used slightly differently in different contexts and by different carriers. Generally, *pre-determination* is an advance request *in writing* to determine coverage for a specific service or procedure. Approval of a pre-determination request is a *guarantee of payment*. *Pre-authorizations* are requests made for tests and procedures with the purpose of ensuring that the medical necessity requirements have been met. Pre-authorizations may be done over the telephone, online, by fax, or in writing. In contrast to pre-determinations, approval of a pre-authorization does *not* guarantee payment. *Precertification* is very similar to pre-authorization, and the terms are sometimes used interchangeably. Precertifications generally cover requests for hospital admission or surgical procedures.

Pre-determination: Pre-determinations typically require a letter, such as the sample in Exhibit 6.5, sent to the health insurer to request that a patient's coverage pay for a specific service or procedure. Some procedures require pre-determination letters to ensure payment, while other procedures do not. Likewise, some carriers may require pre-determinations to avoid denials, while others do not. If a letter must be submitted, it should substantiate medical necessity for the service or procedure. The pre-determination letter should provide all the relevant information relating to the patient and provider as well as the history of the patient's illness including all findings from tests, examinations, and previous treatment. The medical practice should have processes in place that ensure the patient is well informed about any requirements for pre-determination and kept up to date on the information from the carrier.

Pre-authorization/precertification: The terms *pre-authorization* and *precertification* are sometimes used interchangeably. The purpose of both is for the insurance carrier to attempt to control costs by ensuring that their insured has met the medical necessity requirement for certain diagnostic tests and surgical procedures. Carriers may allow telephone, fax form, or online pre-authorization and precertification. The practice should use the method that is most efficient and effective with the carrier. When obtaining pre-authorization or precertification the health insurance carrier will want the following information:

Relating to patient:

- Patient name
- Patient date of birth
- Insurance ID number
- Member group name/number

Relating to provider:

- Physician name
- Tax ID
- Provider ID with carrier
- Provider telephone/fax

EXHIBIT 6.5 ■ Sample Pre-determination Letter

Always Best Practice
600 Practice Place
Anywhere, State Zip Code

Date ________________

ATTN: Pre-determination Department
Insurance Provider Company Name
Address
City, State Zip Code

RE: Pre-determination

Patient Name: ____________________

Patient DOB: ____________________

ID Number: ____________________

Group Number: ____________________

Insured's Member's Name (if other than patient): ____________________

Dear Health Insurer Representative:

This letter is to request a pre-determination for payment in advance of service for *(patient's name)* for *(CPT code, service description, ICD-9-CM code)*. The information for the provider providing this service is:

Physician Name: ____________________

Tax ID: ____________________

Insurance Provider PIN: ____________________

(Patient name) has been under the care of *(physician name, MD)* since *(mm/dd/yyyy)*. If approved, this service will take place at *(place of service)* on *(mm/dd/yyyy)*. Attached is supporting documentation for the requested pre-determination:

Patient history pertaining to illness
Physician documentation (medical records)
Physician documentation (progress notes)
Test results

After review please forward a determination to:

Attn: Appropriate Name
Always Best Practice
600 Practice Place
Anywhere, State Zip Code

Sincerely,

Physician or appropriate name,
Department

Relating to service:

- Date
- Type of service
- Place of service
- Current Procedural Terminology code or description of service
- Diagnosis
- History of present illness

In most instances the staff member can obtain both pre-authorization and precertification from the carrier by calling the number on the back of the insurance card. If you do not have a copy of the card in hand, you many need to direct the patient where to look for the number. While insurance cards vary, the information is usually titled "Eligibility and Benefits Information" with a telephone number listed. If much of your patient population is insured with certain carriers, it may be worthwhile to create for staff a reference sheet with the oft-needed numbers and information for those carriers. Some carriers require certain service providers for in-network benefits. To best direct patients, staff doing pre-authorization or precertification should have this information at hand. Exhibit 6.6 is a template for such a tool.

EXHIBIT 6.6 ■ Template for Pre-authorization Information Tool

PLAN INFORMATION	PLAN TELEPHONE NUMBER	PRE-CERT REQUIREMENTS	CONTRACTED HOSPITALS	CONTRACTED LABS

As many tools as possible should be automated from the PMS. If tools are used from spreadsheet or word processing programs, information should be entered, saved, and stored in a systematic way throughout the organization. Keeping track of pre-authorization and precertification requests and information received from those requests is important for use of the claim and for future reference by the insurance staff. The tool, such as the sample in Exhibit 6.7, can be set up for quick reference by date requested or patient name based on practice preference.

EXHIBIT 6.7 ■ Template for Tracking Authorization Requests by Patients

DATE REQUESTED: BY:	PATIENT NAME	PRACTICE ACCT. #	SCHEDULED DATE	PRE-CERT REFERENCE NUMBER	CARRIER APPROVED BY

Some carriers have online pre-authorization. When online processes are available, they should be utilized. Some carriers require fax forms to be completed and sent, particularly for inpatient hospital admissions. If carriers prefer faxed forms, those should be obtained by the carrier. Obtaining pre-authorization or precertification does not ensure payment. The benefits depend on the patient's eligibility at the time of service and are subject to benefit limitations. The request is granted based on the system information on the day of the request but does not guarantee that once the claim is filed with the services received that insurance will pay.

KEY TERMS AND DEFINITIONS

Appointment Template — A prearranged setup in the appointment schedule denoting what patient types may be seen and in what intervals those patients are to be seen.

Bureau of Narcotics and Dangerous Drugs (BNDD) — A state agency that issues certificates to providers authorized to prescribe and dispense controlled substances. Maintains a state registry of those persons it has authorized.

Council for Affordable Quality Healthcare (CAQH) — An organization that offers free credentialing services to providers in all 50 states and in Washington, D.C., that uses an accepted format for credentialing and re-credentialing providers with health plans.

Curriculum Vitae (CV) — Contains the general identifying information relating to an applicant such as education and training history, similar to a resume.

Drug Enforcement Administration (DEA) — A federal agency within the U.S. Department of Justice that provides federal government registration of each location from which a provider has certification to prescribe or dispense controlled substances.

Financial Policy — An organizational policy outlining the financial expectations of the organization toward patients relating to collecting for services provided. Each practice should develop how it intends to handle those practices.

Physician Credentialing — A process for submitting relevant information about a physician and the physician's practice that must occur before a physician can participate with an insurance carrier.

Pre-determination — Established by written approval from a carrier that payment for a particular service is guaranteed.

Prior Authorization — An insurance requirement to review and approve the expected delivery of medical services before services are provided to ensure that they are necessary and appropriate. Prior authorization, also called precertification, is used as an attempt to reduce utilization and control the health plan's cost.

Professional Liability Insurance — Malpractice insurance to cover providers when allegations of inappropriate or wrongful care are made.

Revenue Cycle — A term used to describe the complex process by which providers are paid for services rendered.

Spend down — A monthly amount of money that a patient must pay out-of-pocket before Medicaid will cover services.

State License Application — Paperwork requiring extensive information to be completed before a provider can obtain a legal license to provide services in a state.

REVIEW OF OBJECTIVES

- **Identify the elements of the pre-visit phase of the revenue cycle.**
  - Contracting with insurance carriers
  - Payer's fee schedule loaded in PMS
  - Provider credentialing
  - Educate staff and patients of organizational expectations
  - Create sensible appointment templates
  - Determine registration type — full or abbreviated
  - Process for determining eligibility requirements
  - Pre-authorization requirements
  - Referral requirements
- **Identify the items needed for physician credentialing.**
  - Name
  - Current state licenses
  - DEA
  - BNDD
  - Social Security Number
  - Date of birth
  - Practice address

- Practice tax ID
- Practice telephone
- Physician National Provider Identifier
- All education
- All training
- Hospital affiliations
- Practice specialty
- Work history
- Professional certificates
- Professional liability insurance (history and certificate of coverage)
- Continuing medical education documents
- Peer references

➤ **Describe the scheduler's role in the pre-visit phase.**

- Scheduler makes appointment and gathers patient information.
- Scheduler establishes patient's insurance status.
- Scheduler explains financial requirements.
- Scheduler enters accurate insurance information in PMS.

➤ **Describe how the pre-visit phase impacts insurance staff.**

- Incorrect information in PMS will result in denied claims.
- Lack of verifying eligibility, obtaining pre-authorizations, or obtaining referrals will result in denied claims.
- Inaccurate or incomplete information for claims filing results in insurance staff having to spend time to fix issues.

REVIEW EXERCISES: LESSON 6

MULTIPLE CHOICE

Please circle the best answer.

1. **The schedulers and front desk personnel support the work of the insurance staff by recording in the PMS accurate:**
   a. Insurance information
   b. Immunization record
   c. Vitals

2. **Physician credentialing requires certain information including:**
   a. State license, DEA, BNDD
   b. Practice location address
   c. Both a and b

3. **It is important that every stage of the revenue cycle be:**
   a. Designed to make less work for the front desk personnel
   b. Well defined and followed consistently
   c. Designed to minimize work for the clinical staff

4. **The pre-visit may be the time to send informational packets to the patient. They may contain:**
   a. Educational brochures
   b. Insurance and financial information
   c. Both a and b

5. **State license applications may include:**
   a. Gender and ethnicity
   b. Financial obligations such as loans and child support
   c. Both a and b

6. **Physician credentialing may include:**
   a. Gender and ethnicity
   b. Financial obligations such as loans and child support
   c. Neither a nor b

7. **A scheduling template should be set for each physician. It should:**
   a. Be realistic based on the number of patients that a physician can see
   b. All be the same
   c. Neither a nor b

8. **The information that the front desk is responsible for collecting can be thought of as completing:**
   a. Boxes 1–11d of the CMS 1500
   b. Boxes 1–33 of the CMS 1500
   c. Boxes 14–33 of the CMS 1500
9. **The scheduler should:**
   a. Record the patient's Social Security Number
   b. Review with the patient the organizational requirements relating to the patient's insurance
   c. Advise patients that the physician typically runs late
10. **The scheduling and front desk personnel:**
   a. Don't need to know about insurance plan types
   b. Should be educated about insurance plan types
   c. Neither a nor b
11. **The type of insurance verification that is recommended is:**
   a. Telephone
   b. Manual
   c. Online
12. **Pre-determinations:**
   a. Typically require a letter
   b. Typically require a telephone call
   c. Typically take 90 days
13. **Pre-authorizations:**
   a. Typically require a letter
   b. Typically require a telephone call
   c. Typically take 90 days
14. **Organizations should develop and utilize a tool for tracking:**
   a. Pre-authorizations
   b. Precertifications
   c. Both a and b
15. **The following may be said about pre-authorization and precertification:**
   a. Payment is guaranteed by the authorization number obtained
   b. Payment is not guaranteed by the authorization number obtained
   c. Neither a nor b

(Answers on page 127)

CASE STUDIES

Please select the best answer.

Case study 1: Mary works in the insurance department for the Anywhere Best Service medical practice. The organization made a conscious decision to conduct full registrations when appointments are made and hired two extra staff to accommodate that effort. Jill is one of the new schedulers. Mary has noted in working denied claims that Jill is not entering full registration information at the time the appointment is made. How should Mary handle this situation?

- **a.** Speak to Jill about what information is required when making an appointment.
- **b.** Speak to her supervisor to suggest more training for Jill about the information required for full registrations.
- **c.** Both a and b.

Case study 2: Mary is responsible for credentialing new physicians. Her organization has hired a physician who is scheduled to start in one month. Mary has been in touch with the physician asking for the information required to do credentialing. After several attempts, she still does not have the information she needs to move forward. How should Mary handle this situation?

- **a.** Understand that the physician is busy and he will get the information to her when he has time.
- **b.** Inform her supervisor that she is unable to get the information needed and that if the physician is not credentialed when he starts work, the organization will not get paid.
- **c.** Send the physician one more letter.

(Answers on page 127)

COMPLETION QUESTIONS

Please fill in the blank.

1. What set of provider's paperwork must be completed that may require reporting financial obligations such as loans and child support?

____

2. Both the state and the federal government have agencies that issue certificates that authorize the prescribing and dispensing of controlled substances. Which is issued by the state? Which is issued by a federal agency?

____

3. How often must DEA registration occur?

____

4. What are the most frequent reasons that claims are denied?

____

____

5. What personnel in the medical practice typically have responsibility for verifying insurance eligibility?

____

6. What is the recommended form of insurance verification?

____

7. What purpose does a pre-determination letter serve?

____

8. How are pre-authorizations and precertifications obtained in most instances?

____

9. Does pre-authorization or precertification ensure payment?

____

10. When obtaining pre-authorization or precertification the health insurance carrier will want information in three categories. To what do the categories relate?

____

11. What pre-authorization or precertification information may be required about the patient?

____

12. What pre-authorization or precertification information may be required about the provider?

____

13. What pre-authorization or precertification information may be required about the service?

____

____

14. Why is it necessary to keep track of pre-authorization and precertification requests?

____

15. What is the name of the organization that provides a free service for credentialing providers for health plans?

____

(Answers on page 127)

MATCHING

Please match the letter of the definition to the term.
Write the letter of the definition next to the term.

State license application _____	**a.** A state agency that issues certificates to providers authorized to prescribe and dispense controlled substances. Maintains a state registry of those persons it has authorized.
Drug Enforcement Administration (DEA) _____	**b.** A process for submitting relevant information about a physician and the physician's practice that must occur before a physician can participate with an insurance carrier.
Curriculum vitae _____	**c.** Paperwork requiring extensive information to be completed before a provider can obtain a legal license to provide services in a state.
Professional liability insurance _____	**d.** An organizational policy outlining the financial expectations of the organization toward patients relating to collecting for services provided. Each practice should develop how it intends to handle those practices.
Appointment template _____	**e.** An insurance requirement to review and approve the expected delivery of medical services before services are provided to ensure that they are necessary and appropriate. Prior authorization, also called precertification, is used as an attempt to reduce utilization and control the health plan's cost.
Financial policy _____	**f.** An organization that offers free credentialing services to providers in all 50 states and in Washington, D.C., that uses an accepted format for credentialing and re-credentialing providers with health plans.
Revenue cycle _____	**g.** A prearranged setup in the appointment schedule denoting what patient types may be seen and in what intervals those patients are to be seen.
Spend down _____	**h.** A federal agency within the U.S. Department of Justice that provides federal government registration of each location from which a provider has certification to prescribe or dispense controlled substances.
Bureau of Narcotics and Dangerous Drugs (BNDD) _____	**i.** Established by written approval from a carrier that payment for a particular service is guaranteed.
Pre-determination _____	**j.** Malpractice insurance to cover providers when allegations of inappropriate or wrongful care are made.

Prior authorization_____	**k.** A monthly amount of money that a patient must pay out-of-pocket before Medicaid will cover services.
Council for Affordable Quality Healthcare (CAQH)_____	**l.** A term used to describe the complex process by which providers are paid for services rendered.
Physician credentialing_____	**m.** Contains the general identifying information relating to an applicant such as education and training history, similar to a resume.

(Answers on page 128)

ANSWERS: LESSON 6

MULTIPLE CHOICE

1-a; 2-c; 3-b; 4-c; 5-c; 6-c; 7-a; 8-a; 9-b; 10-b; 11-c; 12-a; 13-b; 14-c; 15-b

CASE STUDIES

Case study 1-c; Case study 2-b

COMPLETION QUESTIONS

1. An application for state license
2. The BNDD certificate is issued by the state, and the DEA certificate is issued by the federal government.
3. Every three years
4. Non-covered services, ineligible for benefits, claims lacking information, and prior authorization required
5. Appointment schedulers or front desk personnel
6. Online
7. It is an advance request in writing to determine coverage for a specific service or procedure to ensure payment.
8. By a telephone call, fax form, or online
9. No
10. Patient, provider, and service
11. Patient name, date of birth, insurance ID number, and member group name/number
12. Physician's name, tax ID, provider ID with carrier, and provider telephone/fax
13. Date of service, type of service, place of service, CPT code or description of service, diagnosis, and history of present illness
14. For future reference for insurance staff when the claims are being worked
15. Council for Affordable Quality Healthcare (CAQH)

MATCHING

__ State license application: **c**

__ Drug Enforcement Administration (DEA): **h**

__ Curriculum vitae: **m**

__ Professional liability insurance: **j**

__ Appointment template: **g**

__ Financial policy: **d**

__ Revenue cycle: **l**

__ Spend down: **k**

__ Bureau of Narcotics and Dangerous Drugs (BNDD): **a**

__ Pre-determination: **i**

__ Prior authorization: **e**

__ Council for Affordable Quality Healthcare (CAQH): **f**

__ Physician credentialing: **b**

LESSON 7

Understanding the Revenue Cycle — Visit Phase

OBJECTIVES

- Identify the elements of the visit phase of the revenue cycle.
- Describe the information collected during the check-in process.
- Describe the importance of charge capture and charge entry during the visit.
- Identify the essential aspects of the check-out process.

VISIT

The visit phase of the revenue cycle is critical to the long-term relationship between the patient and the provider. Several important aspects of the visit impact the revenue cycle.

First, everything in the practice should create a unified image that the organization wishes to project to patients. The image is created beginning with how patients are greeted and treated when they walk through the front door. Patients should be met by friendly, competent staff members who know their role in the revenue cycle and consistently carry out their supportive duties.

Second, staff members must enter accurate and complete information in the practice management system (PMS), distribute the financial policy, and make patients aware of how the financial policy applies to them. Any verifications or authorizations not handled in the pre-visit phase of the revenue cycle must be handled now, before service is provided.

Third, in addition to the staff's friendliness and competency, the professional look and feel of the waiting room influence patients' image of the organization. All signage should support the financial expectations of the organization, and the wait time before seeing the medical provider should be kept to a minimum.

INFORMATION COLLECTION

Personal and insurance information that was not obtained prior to the visit must be collected during the visit portion of the revenue cycle. Any information that is in the PMS must be verified when the patient arrives for the visit. Paperwork completed at the visit must be accurate and complete. It is a good idea to have a second staff person verify the information entered into the PMS. Verifying the information entered allows the organization to be sure when insurance is filed, preferably the day after the visit, that the claim will go out to the right carrier with all the correct information. When there are mistakes in inputting the information, the individual who entered the information initially should make the corrections during a less-hectic part of that day.

The staff member verifying the information should be careful not to nitpick the work of the front desk staff. Rather, he or she should be charged with ensuring that the claim goes out correctly, so that revenue from the carrier can be turned around as quickly as possible. Requiring staff members to correct their own mistakes is not punitive; it is a teaching moment. When individuals are required to correct their own mistakes, they learn what to pay attention to and quickly learn to take a few seconds longer to input information into the computer system correctly. Those extra seconds save time in the long run and improve the percentage of clean claims that go out of the practice. One the other hand, staff members who are not aware of the mistakes they make tend to repeat those mistakes. Although verifying information input in the PMS may be time consuming, it does give the organization a better chance to capture revenue more quickly.

The front desk staff performs essential tasks at check-in, but it is not necessary to try to do everything at the front desk. Processes may be implemented so that other functions are not done at the busy front desk. These may include informing patients about additional fees, such as record-copying fees or having patients sign an Advance Beneficiary Notice form if there is a possibility that Medicare may not cover the service that is about to be provided.

The organization should create front desk check-in processes that follow good business principles and support time-of-service collections. These processes include daily posting of all receipts, daily computer balancing, and daily bank deposits. In general, front desk functions in organizations should:

- Use automated processes whenever possible.
- Gather and accurately record patient information, if it was not gathered prior to the visit. If it was obtained prior to the visit, the front desk personnel should verify the content with the patient.
- Ensure that front desk personnel have the skills, ability, and personal characteristics to effectively perform the duties required.
- Establish follow-up processes that monitor and ensure that the intended functions of front desk personnel are being carried out (for example, tracking copayment collections).
- Provide continuing education and training to staff.

CHECK-IN

The visit phase of the revenue cycle begins with *check-in* — the initial face-to-face interaction with the patient. This phase should occur precisely in the same order with each patient. Although some organizations manage to perform check-in processes during the pre-visit stage of the revenue cycle, most organizations still have processes they must conduct during check-in. The check-in patient touch points are:

- **Greet the patient:** Immediately look up to acknowledge the patient and verify the appointment in a friendly manner.
- **Ask to see the following documents at every visit:** patient's insurance card and driver's license.
- **Look at the patient:** Verify that the photo on the driver's license is that of the patient.
- **Scan the insurance card:** front and back, each visit. Store in the PMS.
- **Scan the driver's license:** Keep it on file; store in the PMS.

Insurance cards

The first element of patient paperwork is the insurance card. The medical office staff, usually the front desk employees, must have access to the patient's insurance card and be able to interpret the information on the card correctly. It is necessary to accurately input that information into the medical practice's computer system, so that an insurance claim can be filed. Insurance cards should be scanned or copied, front and back, at every visit. Only if the information is processed correctly does the possibility exist for the physician to be paid correctly by the insurance carrier. If the carrier pays properly, the patient should pay the remaining balance or *coinsurance,* the portion of the fee for which the patient is responsible. However, if the insurance information is not processed correctly, the insurance carrier will not issue correct payment to the physician, and in some cases, the patient may be held responsible for the services.

Patient identification

Medical practices have an obligation to ensure that the persons they treat are, in fact, who they say they are. Staff can verify a patient's identity by scanning an official identification card such as a driver's license and taking a picture of the patient, which is retained in the medical record. Electronic health records provide a perfect format for housing this important identification. Verifying patient identity promotes patient safety and serves as a valuable reimbursement tool in trying to collect for services.

Signature on file

Medical practices are well served to have the patient sign a document that assigns benefits and creates a financial agreement between the patient and the practice upon presenting for treatment at the first office visit. These multipurpose agreements are often titled *signature on file, assignment of benefits,* and *financial agreement.* The rationale of this document is to ask patients to sign one document that can be retained by the medical practice so that the medical practice can satisfy several objectives. For example, the signature on file provides the authorization for the release of information. Additionally, the medical practice needs the patient's cooperation in agreeing to allow his or her insurance carriers to send payment directly to the physician (assignment of benefits) and in agreeing to accept financial responsibility for services if insurance does not cover the service (financial agreement or insurance coverage waiver).

The initial purpose of the document is to ensure that the medical practice is paid directly by the insurance carrier. The form also authorizes the medical practice to release information to the carrier so that a determination for payment of benefits can be made. The form may refer specifically to item 9 of CMS 1500 form for payment and designate Medicare as the primary carrier and Medigap as the secondary insurance policy. Typically the form explains to the patient that he or she is financially responsible for payment of services rendered and, if signed, constitutes an acknowledgment of financial responsibility on his or her part. This form must use language that causes the patient, by signing the form, to agree to be financially responsible for the copay, deductible, coinsurance, and services that are not covered by his or her benefits package. Language should be clear that, if the medical practice does not have a contract with the patient's insurance carrier, the patient accepts full financial responsibility for charges and will sign over to the practice any payment from an insurance carrier that is made to the patient rather than to the practice.

Another important component of this multipurpose form is *release of information*. This not only guarantees payment from the patient but also allows for medical information to be released to another healthcare provider for the continuation of care for the patient. The form may also address release of information for medical, educational, and scientific purposes relating to medical advancement and medical research. When an organization has a need to take medical photographs, the form should contain a section that grants permission for photographs. The medical practice should be specific in disclosing the purpose of the photograph and whether the patient will be identifiable from the photograph. Some forms also contain *informed consent for treatment* sections. Neither the photograph section nor the informed consent section of the multipurpose form is particularly relevant to medical office insurance staff, but other aspects of the form are. The patient's signature on this form serves as a contract between the patient and the practice that is invaluable for the medical office insurance staff members to refer to when trying to resolve the patient's account. See Exhibit 7.1 for a sample of a multipurpose form.

Insurance verification

Patients often have both primary and secondary insurance, and it can be difficult to determine which is which. Patients themselves often do not know. Medicare provides rules that determine when Medicare is primary or secondary. It is the responsibility of the physician's office, specifically medical office insurance staff members acting on the physicians' behalf, to determine whether Medicare is primary or secondary. For example, a Medicare patient may have Medicare as the primary insurance. However, if that patient seeks services for injuries resulting from an auto accident, Medicare will not be primary if there is auto insurance that will cover the medical expenses. In this case, the auto insurance is the primary insurance and Medicare is the secondary payer. In this and many other situations, knowledge of Medicare regulations is required to file insurance claims correctly.

The insurance card is often helpful to staff in determining primary and secondary benefits, but not always. Ideally, an insurance card contains several additional pieces of information that assist in proper claim filing: the name of the insured, the name of the holder of the card seeking payment of healthcare services when different than the insured, and the relationship of the person seeking healthcare services to the insured. A card should have a policy or group number clearly visible and an eligibility period for coverage benefits.

EXHIBIT 7.1 ■ Multipurpose Form

Always Best Medical Practice

1. Authorization for Release of Information

____

I authorize Always Best Medical Practice to release all medical information (including, but not limited to, information on psychiatric conditions, sickle cell anemia, alcohol and drug abuse, and HIV or communicable diseases) requested by my health insurance carrier, Medicare, or any other third-party payers. I authorize Always Best Medical Practice to release all medical information to my referring physician and my primary (family) physician. I authorize Always Best Medical Practice to contact my insurance company or health plan administrator and obtain all pertinent financial information concerning coverage and payments under my policy. I direct the insurance company or health plan administrator to release such information to Always Best Medical Practice.

I agree that these provisions will remain in effect until I provide written revocation to Always Best Medical Practice.

Signature of Patient/Legal Guardian: ______________________________

Date: ______________________________

2. Assignment of Benefits

____

I hereby assign to Always Best Medical Practice any insurance or other third-party benefits available for healthcare services provided to me. I understand that Always Best Medical Practice has the right to refuse or accept assignment of such benefits. If these benefits are not assigned to Always Best Medical Practice, I agree to forward to Always Best Medical Practice all health insurance and other third-party payments that I receive for surgical services rendered to me immediately upon receipt.

Signature of Patient/Legal Guardian: ______________________________

Date: ______________________________

3. Insurance Coverage Waiver

I understand that my eligibility for coverage by (name of insurance company) ____________________ ____________________cannot be confirmed at this time. I wish to receive medical service from an Always Best Medical Practice's physician. If it is determined that I am not eligible for coverage, I understand that I will be responsible for payment of all services provided.

Signature of Patient/Legal Guardian: ______________________________

Date: ______________________________

PLEASE BE ADVISED:

Your account will be turned over to a collection agency, if you do not pay on your personal balance every 30 days.

Information relating to the insurance plan *copay* (the amount of required payment from the patient at time of service) and *deductible* (the amount of money the insured patient must pay before insurance benefits begin) are important. A toll-free telephone number and the paying entity's address should be obvious on the card.

No standardized format for insurance cards has been mandated in the United States. Some bear all the required information; others do not. Some cards are imprinted with the policyholder's name, or the insured name, or both. Other insurance cards are not imprinted at all. Rather, these are generic cards that have an individual's name handwritten or typed on the card. Medical office staff members in receipt of such cards may be unsure who is insured, whether it is the bearer of the card, or if not, what is the cardholder's relationship to the insured. Insurance cards differ greatly from carrier to carrier, network to network, and third-party payer to third-party payer. Cards even differ from policy to policy when issued by a single carrier. A single carrier may use an unlimited number of card styles, each style bearing different information.

Whenever electronic verification of insurance is possible, medical practices should take advantage of that opportunity. Often front desk personnel feel that they do not have time to verify insurance. If this is the case, managers should support adding personnel to provide that function or assign that task to existing personnel. The added effort to verify insurance coverage will pay off financially for the medical practice. At a minimum, the organization should disclose to the patient that insurance coverage has not been verified and that the he or she will be responsible for payment if the insurance carrier does not cover the charges for the service. Disclosure gives the patient an opportunity to sign an "addition to form" for the signature on file, assignment of benefits, and financial agreement indicating that he or she understands the situation.

Check-in includes:

- A time to set the tone for a positive impression
- Face sheet — personal and demographic information (see Exhibit 7.2 for a sample sheet)
  - Each practice will decide what information is important to collect on the face sheet (for example, some practices may think it more important to have the patient provide an e-mail address than redundantly write insurance information since staff has already scanned the card front and back)
- If pre-visit functions were not carried out, perform now
  - Verify insurance coverage
  - Verify benefits eligibility
  - Receive financial policy (give opportunity to discuss with collector to understand or clarify)
  - Obtain referral or authorizations, if required
- Check-in paperwork for patient to sign:
  - Authorization for release of information — permission to release information for insurance purposes, signature on file on insurance claim
  - Assignment of benefits — allows carrier to send payment directly to medical practice

EXHIBIT 7.2 ■ Sample Face Sheet

Patient Information Form

Always Best Medical Practice

Thank you for choosing Always Best Medical Practice.
Please completely fill out this form to ensure the fastest and best healthcare service.

Patient name: ____________________ (Last, first, and middle initial) Maiden name (if applies): ____________	Social Security Number (last four digits): What year was your last appointment here?
Date of birth: _______ Current age: ________ Sex: M F Martial status: M S D W Referring physician: ________________	Address: Street ________________ City ________________ State & Zip ________________
Home phone:	Employer:
Mobile phone or pager:	Work phone:
Personal e-mail address:	Occupation:
Insurance company name and policy number/ primary (see your insurance card): ____________________ Effective date: ____________	Insurance company name and policy number/ secondary (see your insurance card) ____________________ Effective date: ____________

Primary care physician: ________________________________

Name of spouse (if married) or parent (if child): ________________________

Spouse or parent contact numbers: ____________________________

Emergency contact: Name ____________________ Phone ________________

If you are covered under the policy of a spouse, partner, parent, or legal guardian, please tell us about him or her:

Information on spouse, parent, etc.

Name:	Social Security number (last four digits):
Date of birth:	Address:
Home and mobile phone numbers:	Work phone:
Employer:	Occupation:
Employer:	Occupation:

- Insurance coverage waiver — patient agrees to be responsible for payment for services if insurance carrier determines patient is not eligible for coverage
- Scan and retain all paperwork for insurance and collection purposes

Patients who owe money on a prior balance should expect to pay at the time of their next visit. The appointment scheduler should remind the patient of the prior balance when the appointment is made, and the front desk personnel should make sure that he or she asks the patient to settle the prior balance at check-in. On a daily basis, the collections department can prepare a collection reminder tool for the front office staff (see Exhibit 7.3). If the patient is unable to settle the prior balance, the issue should be handed off by the front desk to the collections department, who should talk with the patient in a private place.

EXHIBIT 7.3 ■ **Front Desk Collection Tool**

"Before you see the physician today we need to settle your prior balance..."

Patient Name	Reference Account #	Appt. Time	Provider to Be Seen	Prior Amt. Due for Collection	See Collector

Note: This form is prepared by the collector.

New patients

New patients are particularly important to the practice and should be oriented to the practice in a way that makes them feel comfortable enough to come to the practice again. In addition to completing the face sheet and new patient paperwork, the organization must present to the patient a notification of the patient's right to privacy, and the patient must sign that he or she has received, read, and understood the information. If a patient does not understand the information, someone in the practice other than the front desk staff should read and explain it to him or her. In keeping with the patient's right to privacy, this is an opportunity to have the patient put in writing the individuals to whom he or she will allow you to release medical information. A patient should complete, sign, and date a standardized form that indicates his or her name and relationship to the insured. The practice should retain this form. Additional new patient paperwork consists of:

- **Present to patient** — notice of privacy rights and organization's privacy policy
- **Have patient sign** — form acknowledging receipt of Health Insurance Portability and Accountability Act (HIPAA) information
- **Record** — create standardized recording mechanism in PMS that patient has been informed of rights under HIPAA — notice of privacy rights and organization's privacy policy
- **Record** — patient's consent of individuals to whom information can be released

Special circumstances

Special circumstances sometimes occur during the visit portion of the meeting for which medical office insurance staff members may be asked to give guidance. One situation is when a patient is considered a new patient to the practice. Obviously, if the patient has never been seen in the practice before or by the physician before, the patient is a new patient. A patient may also be considered a new patient when billing the evaluation and management (E/M) code for an office visit under certain defined circumstances. Medicare defines a new patient as a patient who has not received any face-to-face professional services from the physician or the physician group in the same specialty in the three years prior to the visit. A patient is a new patient and billed as a new patient using the new patient set of E/M codes — 99201 through 99205 — based on the extent of the service provided. Otherwise, the face-to-face visit will be coded as an established patient using E/M codes 99211 through 99215. E/M codes are discussed at length in the Current Procedural Terminology lesson of this book (Chapter 11).

Another situation has to do with the Medicare provision relating to midlevel providers or physician extenders called nonphysician practitioners (NPPs) such as nurse practitioners (NPs), physician assistants (PAs), clinical nurse specialists (CNSs), certified nurse-midwives (CNMs) seeing patients under the definition of *incident-to services*. This is a confusing issue even for some midlevel providers/physician extenders, so insurance staff need to be clear on the billing rules.

For incident-to services, it is important to understand that the services must be an integral part of the professional service although incidental to the physician's service. The charge will be included in the physician's bill and sent under the physician's name and using the physician's National Provider Identifier (NPI). Incident-to services may occur in the office or a home setting only. When incident-to services are furnished, they must be services appropriate to those settings. Most importantly, incident-to services must be provided under the direct supervision of the physician. That is to say, the physician must be in the office suite immediately available to the NPP to provide direction or assistance. Incident-to services dictates that NPPs provide services for established patients whose treatment plan for a diagnosis was already established by a physician. The NPP provides services during the course of treatment but is not permitted to provide the initial service. An NPP may enter into a collaborative practice agreement with more than one physician in the practice, and Medicare considers physicians within a group interchangeable. So an NPP can be seeing a patient, carrying out the treatment of one physician who is not in the office suite, but another physician in the group is in the office suite while services are provided. In that instance, the incident-to service is reported using the name and NPI of the physician who was supervising in the office suite as the rendering physician on the claim.

All midlevel providers/physician extenders must meet the qualifications for state licensure, be licensed by the state, and work within the scope legally authorized by the state in which they are furnishing services. Qualifications for each group of physician extenders vary as follows.

Physician assistant

- Graduated from a program accredited by the Accreditation Review Commission on Education for the Physician Assistant; or
- Successfully passed the national certification exam of the National Commission on Certification of Physician Assistants (NCCPA); and
- Be licensed by the state where practicing.

  Note: PAs may not bill Medicare directly.

Nurse practitioner

- Be an RN licensed in the state of practice and provide services in keeping with state law,
- Earned a master's degree in nursing (required for NPIs issued after January 1, 2003), and
- Be certified as an NP by one of the recognized national certifying bodies.

  Note: NPs may bill Medicare directly.

Clinical nurse specialist

- Be an RN licensed in the state of practice and provide services in keeping with state law,
- Earned a master's degree in nursing in a defined clinical area from an accredited educational institution, and
- Be certified as a CNS by one of the recognized national certifying bodies.

  Note: CNSs may bill Medicare directly.

Certified nurse-midwife

- Be an RN licensed in the state of practice and provide services in keeping with state law and
- Meet one of the requirements either (1) as outlined by state regulations or (2) completion of formal education.

  Note: CNMs may bill Medicare directly.

Midlevel providers/physician extenders work under a collaborative agreement with a physician who is primarily responsible for the medical care they provide. Of the NPPs, only

PAs are unable to bill Medicare directly. Payment for PA services is made to the qualified employer of the PA who is enrolled in the Medicare program. The PA's employer's NPI number will be in box 33a on the CMS 1500 electronic equivalent, and the PA's NPI number will be in box 24j. All NPPs may enroll in the Medicare program. NPs, CNSs, and CNMs have the option to bill Medicare directly or reassign payment to their employer.

If the NPP is to receive payment directly, he or she should have the NPP's NPI number entered in box 33a on the CMS 1500 electronic equivalent. If the employer is to receive payment, the employer NPI number will be entered in box 33s on the CMS 1500 electronic equivalent and the NPI of the physician extender will be entered in box 24j on the CMS 1500 electronic equivalent. When an NPP uses his or her own NPI for billing purposes rather than billing under the collaborating physician's NPI number, payment is reduced. For example, if the NPP's NPI number is used for billing purposes, reimbursement will be paid at 85 percent of the fee that a physician would have been paid for providing the same service. If the physician's number is used for billing in the incident-to arrangement, the practice will be paid at the physician's rate, 100 percent, of reimbursement for the service. To recap, there are certain rules that must be adhered to when using incident-to billing.

- NPPs may not see new patients unless it is in conjunction with a physician. The physician must provide the "initial service."
- Physicians must furnish "subsequent services of a frequency which reflect his or her active participation in the management of the course of treatment." The medical record should always reflect physician involvement.
- NPPs may see established patients with established problems using incident-to billing *only* when the physician is in the same office suite *and* the physician has direct personal supervision of the service provided.
- Established patients seen by an NPP with a new problem must be seen by the physician or billed under the physician extender's NPI.
- The services provided by an NPP must be "integral, although incidental" to the professional service provided by a physician.
- All incident-to services provided must be within the midlevel provider's scope of state licensure and performed in the appropriate setting, typically a physician's practice, and services provided will be included in the physician's charge.

(*Note:* Quoted material in bulleted list comes from Medicare Benefit Policy Manual, Chapter 13, 70–80.3 www.cms.gov/manuals/Downloads/bp102c13.pdf.)

CLINICAL PORTION OF THE VISIT

Each organization has its own processes to facilitate support staff and the medical provider taking care of the patient's medical needs. From the insurance staff perspective, the important pieces of the clinical portion of the visit include making sure that the treatment meets the requirements for medical necessity and that the proper documentation is completed to support the charges of the visit.

Charge capture refers to the process of assigning the appropriate charges for every billable procedure or service delivered to the patient by the provider so that money can be collected for them. Charge capture is often a joint effort in the practice. Clearly, providers who provide service have the primary responsibility to initiate and capture charges.

Medical practices vary in their sophistication relating to the ability to integrate electronic medical records with electronic charge capture capabilities. A great many organizations still wait for the physicians to dictate charges, which must then be transcribed, coded, and finally posted as a charge to the patient's account. Organizations that intend to sufficiently capture charges for a date of service in a short time frame should create an organizational standard about the amount of time that is permitted to lapse between a service provided and the charge entered into the PMS to be billed. Unless the issue of timely and accurate charge capture is addressed and agreed on at the physician level, the process will likely come up short of ideal.

Medical office insurance staff members lack the authority to put charge capture policies in place, but they can make their supervisors and administrators aware when timeliness is an issue. Administrators can then point out to physicians what a detriment poor charge capture habits are to the entire practice. Sometimes fellow physicians are the best at pointing out to another physician the problems with poor charge capture. Medical office insurance staff members should empower themselves to advocate for effective charge capture processes and policies and to notify their practice managers if those processes are not followed.

CHECK-OUT

Check-out is another important patient touch point at which the actions of the front desk staff impact insurance staff. Front desk personnel must be diligent in following the organizational processes at check-out time.

- Check-out process:
  - Set the tone for another positive impression at parting
  - Schedule the next appointment
  - Schedule any follow-up procedures or testing from the appointment based on circumstances within the organization
  - Inform patients about follow-up intentions — future actions of provider and organization, and needed actions from patient
  - Collect all time-of-service payment due by the patient
  - Have processes in place to establish all legitimate payments that are due or past due
  - Use this face-to-face time to reiterate financial expectations of the patient
  - Settle any unresolved payments due by the patient in a private setting by the organization's collections department

Either after the patient has seen the medical provider, before check-out, or at check-out, he or she may be scheduled for further services such as diagnostic testing or surgical procedures that may require special attention by staff. Tests may need to be pre-authorized or surgeries may need to be precertified. Before these are scheduled, it is a good time to discuss how testing or surgery will be paid. It is essential for staff to know at this time if the patient's insurance deductible has been met. If not, then at least a portion of the deductible must be collected. In most organizations, staff efforts at this time should occur away from the front desk in the collections department. This is a time when patients will have questions, and staff in the collections department will want to provide patients with financial estimates of the charges for the upcoming tests or procedures. A private place is required. Patients should sign a financial agreement with the medical practice. The agreement should outline financial expectations and disclose to the patient the ramifications if the patient fails to comply with the agreement.

Immediately following check-out, charge entry should occur. Accuracy and timeliness are of utmost importance in charge entry. Once the charge is captured, logically, charge entry follows. This straightforward step can often be less efficient than it should be. A process for accurate charge entry must be established and followed. Charges posted in the computer system should balance to the charge tickets of each batch that is posted every day. Charge entry affects the practice both from a financial standpoint and a patient satisfaction standpoint. It is not enough to get the charge posted; it must be posted to the correct account and posted accurately.

Charges must also be posted promptly. Patients know when services are provided, and they expect members of the medical practice to know as well. When they have an interaction with the practice whose representative is not aware of services that have been provided, the patient may lose confidence in the practice. Patients are more apt to accept the responsibility to pay charges when they feel assured that the practice is on top of both providing the services and charging for the services. An organization that is financially sound inspires confidence in patients.

Regardless of the charge entry process, it is imperative for the medical practice to ensure that charge entry and charge capture processes have been given adequate planning attention. Likewise, monitoring must take place to ensure that the processes are being carried out.

In general, many important tasks must be done well at the front desk to support the functions that the insurance staff follow up on. These include:

- Accurately and completely recording information in PMS
- Having the financial policy written, developed in advance, and communicated to all staff and patients
- Having signage in the practice that supports financial policy expectations
- Performing essential tasks — do not try to do everything at the front desk — inform patients about additional fees and have them sign other forms at the appropriate time (Advance Benificiary Notice, record-copying fee, and so on)
- Creating organizational processes following good business principles to support time-of-service collections, daily posting of charges and receipts, computer balancing, daily depositing receipts, and so on

KEY TERMS AND DEFINITIONS

Administrative Simplification — A provision of HIPAA that defines standards for (1) electronic transaction requirements including the adoption of code sets; (2) national identifier requirements; (3) privacy requirement; and (4) security requirement.

Assignment of Benefits — The medical practice obtains the patient's signature, which allows the carrier to send payment for services directly to the medical practice.

Benefits Eligibility — Refers to individuals qualified to receive benefits as defined by a specific health plan.

Charge Capture — The process of assigning the appropriate charges for every billable procedure or service delivered to the patient by a provider so that money can be collected for it.

Charge Entry — The process of entering into the practice management system the procedure codes and the corresponding diagnosis codes that document the services provided.

Face Sheet — A form filled out by patients to provide medical practices with personal and demographic information.

The Health Insurance Portability and Accountability Act (HIPAA) of 1996 — Passed by Congress to (1) establish healthcare standards in several areas, (2) provide health insurance portability to individuals changing jobs — individuals who can prove continuous health insurance coverage cannot be denied benefits for pre-existing conditions when moving to another health plan for coverage — and (3) reduce fraud and abuse.

Insurance Coverage — An individual has a contract with an insurance carrier that has agreed to pay for certain healthcare services under defined terms.

Insurance Coverage Waiver — The medical practice obtains the patient's signature saying that the patient agrees to be responsible for payment for services if the insurance carrier determines that the patient is not eligible for coverage.

Referral — The process of one healthcare provider sending a patient to another provider, usually one who specializes in the area of treatment the patient needs. Some health plans require that they approve the referral process.

Signature on File — The medical practice obtains the patient's authorization for release of information for insurance purposes on the insurance claim seeking payment from the carrier for services.

Time-of-Service Collections — The policy of a healthcare organization to collect reimbursement for services due from patients when the service is delivered.

REVIEW OF OBJECTIVES

- **Identify the elements of the visit phase of the revenue cycle.**
  - Check-in
  - Clinical encounter
  - Check-out

- **Describe the information collected during the check-in process.**
  - Personal and demographic information
  - Insurance coverage
  - Benefits eligibility
  - Obtain referral or authorization
  - Sign paperwork
    - Signature on file
    - Assignment of benefits
    - Insurance coverage waiver

- **Describe the importance of charge capture and charge entry during the visit.**
  - Charge capture is the opportunity to identify every billable procedure or service provided to the patient.
  - Charge entry is the process of entering in the PMS the corresponding procedure and diagnosis codes of the services provided so that money can be collected for services.

- **Identify the essential aspects of the check-out process.**
  - Schedule follow-up appointments, tests, or procedures
  - Conduct pre-authorization or precertification if necessary
  - Sign financial agreement for tests or procedures
  - Resolve any outstanding financial issues

REVIEW EXERCISES: LESSON 7

MULTIPLE CHOICE

Please circle the best answer.

1. **The following are elements of the visit phase of the revenue cycle:**
   a. Check-in
   b. Check-out
   c. Both a and b

2. **Whenever possible it is preferable for medical practices to ensure use of:**
   a. Payment plans
   b. Time-of-service collections
   c. Collection agencies

3. **Efforts at the front desk support the work of the insurance department by:**
   a. Appointing self-pay patients
   b. Limiting the number of Medicaid patients
   c. Gathering and recording accurate and complete patient information

4. **For every patient, front desk personnel should scan the insurance card front and back as well as the patient's:**
   a. Birth certificate
   b. Immigration papers
   c. Driver's license

5. **If pre-visit functions were not carried out, the front desk staff should verify:**
   a. Benefits eligibility
   b. Immigration papers
   c. Birth certificate

6. **A new patient signs paperwork in the medical practice that authorizes the release of information for insurance purposes called:**
   a. Signature on file
   b. Assignment of benefits
   c. Insurance coverage waiver

7. **A new patient signs paperwork in the medical practice that allows the insurance carrier to send payment directly to the medical practice called:**
   a. Signature on file
   b. Assignment of benefits
   c. Insurance coverage waiver

8. **A new patient signs paperwork in the medical practice agreeing to be responsible for payment for services if the insurance carrier determines that the patient is not eligible for coverage called:**
   - **a.** Signature on file
   - **b.** Assignment of benefits
   - **c.** Insurance coverage waiver

9. **The clinical encounter portion of the visit produces:**
   - **a.** Insurance verification
   - **b.** Signature on a HIPAA form
   - **c.** Charge capture

10. **Medical practices are required by law to present new patients to a medical practice with notifications of privacy rights. That legislations is called:**
    - **a.** PNPR
    - **b.** PQRI
    - **c.** HIPAA

11. **Charge entry should be:**
    - **a.** Accurate and timely
    - **b.** Dictated and typed
    - **c.** Essential and delayed

12. **The check-out process provides a time to:**
    - **a.** Schedule the next appointment
    - **b.** Reiterate financial expectations
    - **c.** Both a and b

13. **The check-out process provides a time to:**
    - **a.** Verify eligibility for the prior visit
    - **b.** Sign a financial agreement for upcoming procedures
    - **c.** Both a and b

14. **A medical practice should set a process to:**
    - **a.** Collect prior balances for services
    - **b.** Ensure accurate charge entry
    - **c.** Both a and b

15. **Visit charges posted in the computer system should:**
    - **a.** Balance to the charge tickets of each batch that is posted every day
    - **b.** Affect the practice in a positive way
    - **c.** Be posted within the week of the visit

(Answers on page 150)

CASE STUDIES

Please select the best answer.

Case study 1: Robyn works in Dr. Layton's office at the front desk. The medical practice tries to have insurance eligibility conducted by schedulers when the appointment is made. Today Ms. Clark, a former patient of Dr. Layton who is a Medicaid patient, has come into the practice for the first time in months. Robyn notices that Ms. Clark's Medicaid eligibility hasn't been verified. Robyn is noticing that more and more patients are coming in who haven't had their insurance eligibility verified. What should Robyn do?

- **a.** Check in Ms. Clark as "arrived" in the computer system.
- **b.** Verify Ms. Clark's Medicaid eligibility online.
- **c.** Tell the schedulers if they miss insurance verification on one more patient she is going to the supervisor.

Case study 2: Robyn is working at the front desk for Dr. Layton. Mr. James has just arrived to see Dr. Layton. The collections department has put Mr. James's name on a list for Robyn to collect a prior balance for services. When Robyn asks Mr. James to settle his prior balance, he gets loud and says that he isn't going to pay a dime because the physician doesn't know what he is doing. What should Robyn do?

- **a.** Get Mr. James away from the front desk by asking someone in the collections department to see him.
- **b.** Tell Mr. James that, no matter how loud he gets, he won't see Dr. Layton without paying.
- **c.** Tell Mr. James he has to get out of the office because he said Dr. Layton was a bad doctor.

Case study 3: Dr. Shaw is disgusted with the amount that Medicare is paying her. She has decided that she will hire a nurse practitioner to see her patients in the office while she is doing surgery at the hospital. Dr. Shaw has told the insurance department that she wants them to bill as if she is seeing the patients in the office because they are her patients and not the nurse practitioner's patients. She has told the staff this is the only way that she will continue to see Medicare patients. She has explained the need to increase her volume in order to make enough money to continue to see Medicare patients. Is Dr. Shaw handling this situation correctly?

- **a.** Yes, the nurse practitioner can see new patients and bill under the physician's Medicare number if Dr. Shaw is in the suite when the patient is being seen.
- **b.** No, nurse practitioners must always bill under their own Medicare number.
- **c.** No, Dr. Shaw cannot be in two different locations at one time. It is an inappropriate billing practice to bill under Dr. Shaw's Medicare number for patients seen in the office when she is not there.

(Answers on page 150)

COMPLETION QUESTIONS

Please fill in the blank.

1. What identifying information should be collected at check-in?

____

2. Several items must be signed by the patient at the first visit to the practice. Name five items that need the patient's signature.

____

____

3. Why do patients need to sign an authorization for release of information form?

____

4. The CMS 1500 electronic equivalent makes reference to the authorization for release of information having been signed in box 12. What appears there?

____

5. Why does a patient sign a form called assignment of benefits?

____

6. The CMS 1500 electronic equivalent makes reference to the assignment of benefits having been signed in box 13. What appears there?

____

7. Why do patients need to sign a financial agreement/insurance coverage waiver?

____

____

8. What is the legislation called that mandates that a notice of privacy rights be given to patients?

____

9. What are the conditions for a patient considered a new patient in a practice even though he or she has received services from the practice in the past?

____

____

10. What are midlevel providers or physician extenders called?

____

11. Name four types of NPPs.

____

12. Medicare has certain rules relating to NPPs, but primarily the practice of NPPs is regulated by:

____

13. Which category of NPP cannot bill Medicare directly for payment?

____

14. Who receives Medicare reimbursement for the services a PA provides?

____

15. NPPs may bill under a Medicare provision called incident-to. When providing incident-to services, where is the physician?

____

16. Can an NPP provide initial treatment and establish a treatment plan?

____

17. If an NPP works in a group practice, which physician does Medicare consider the collaborating physician?

____

18. An NPP is seeing an established patient and carrying out the treatment plan of a physician in the practice but not in the office suite. However, another physician is in the office suite. Which NPI does the NPP use if billing incident-to?

____

19. What is the reimbursement for incident-to services provided by an NPP?

____

20. What is the reimbursement for services provided by an NPP when using the NPP's NPI?

____

(Answers on page 150)

MATCHING

Please match the letter of the definition to the term.
Write the letter of the definition next to the term.

Referral ____	**a.** Refers to individuals qualified to receive benefits as defined by a specific health plan.
Benefits eligibility ____	**b.** The medical practice obtains the patient's signature, which allows the carrier to send payment for services directly to the medical practice.
Face sheet ____	**c.** The policy of a healthcare organization to collect reimbursement for services due from patients when the service is delivered.
Insurance coverage waiver ____	**d.** The process of assigning the appropriate charges for every billable procedure or service delivered to the patient by a provider so that money can be collected for it.
Time-of-service collections ____	**e.** The medical practice obtains the patient's authorization for release of information for insurance purposes on the insurance claim seeking payment from the carrier for services.
HIPAA ____	**f.** A provision of HIPAA that defines standards for (1) electronic transaction requirements including the adoption of code sets; (2) national identifier requirements; (3) privacy requirement; and (4) security requirement.
Signature on file ____	**g.** The process of one healthcare provider sending a patient to another provider, usually one who specializes in the area of treatment the patient needs. Some health plans require that they approve the referral process.
Administrative Simplification ____	**h.** The process of entering into the practice management system the procedure codes and the corresponding diagnosis codes that document the services provided.
Assignment of benefits ____	**i.** The medical practice obtains the patient's signature saying that the patient agrees to be responsible for payment for services if the insurance carrier determines that the patient is not eligible for coverage.
Charge capture ____	**j.** An individual has a contract with an insurance carrier that has agreed to pay for certain healthcare services under defined terms.
Charge entry ____	**k.** The Health Insurance Portability and Accountability Act of 1996 passed by Congress to (1) establish healthcare standards in several areas, (2) provide health insurance portability to individuals changing jobs, and (3) reduce fraud and abuse.
Insurance coverage ____	**l.** A form filled out by patients to provide medical practices with personal and demographic information.

(Answers on page 151)

ANSWERS: LESSON 7

MULTIPLE CHOICE

1-c; 2-b; 3-c; 4-c; 5-a; 6-a; 7-b; 8-c; 9-c; 10-c; 11-a; 12-c; 13-b; 14-c; 15-a

CASE STUDIES

Case study 1-b; Case study 2-a; Case study 3-c

COMPLETION QUESTIONS

1. Take photo of patient, scan front and back of insurance card, and scan driver's license.
2. Authorization for release of information, assignment of benefits, insurance coverage waiver, acknowledgment of notice of privacy rights, and patient's consent of individuals to whom information can be released
3. This form gives the patient's permission to release information for insurances purposes.
4. Signature on file
5. This form allows the carrier to send payment for services directly to the provider.
6. Signature on file
7. The signature on this form shows that the patient has agreed to be responsible for payment for services if the insurance carrier determines that the patient is not eligible for coverage.
8. HIPAA
9. A patient who has not received any face-to-face professional services from the physician or the physician group in the same specialty in the three years prior to the visit is a new patient
10. Nonphysician practitioners (NPPs)
11. Nurse practitioners (NPs), physician assistants (PAs), clinical nurse specialists (CNSs), and certified nurse-midwives (CNMs)
12. The state laws in which they practice
13. PAs
14. The PA's qualified employer that is enrolled in the Medicare program
15. In the office suite
16. No, initial treatment and the treatment plan for a diagnosis must be established by a physician.
17. Medicare considers the physicians within a group interchangeable.
18. The number of the physician in the office suite
19. 100 percent of the rate that the physician would be paid for the service
20. 85 percent of the rate that the physician would be paid for the service

MATCHING

__ Referral: **g**

__ Benefits eligibility: **a**

__ Face sheet: **l**

__ Insurance coverage waiver: **i**

__ Time-of-service collections: **c**

__ HIPAA: **k**

__ Signature on file: **e**

__ Administrative simplification: **f**

__ Assignment of benefits: **b**

__ Charge capture: **d**

__ Charge entry: **h**

__ Insurance coverage: **j**

LESSON 8

Understanding the Revenue Cycle — Post-visit: Bulk Claims Management

OBJECTIVES

- Identify the elements of the post-visit phase of the revenue cycle dealing with bulk claims management.
- Describe the claims submission process.
- Clarify the role of the clearinghouse.
- Examine between electronic and paper claims filing.
- Understand the major elements of information included on the CMS 1500.
- Describe the importance of timely and accurate payment processing.

POST-VISIT

After the patient visit, the insurance staff's main work starts. The post-visit phase occurs after documentation, coding, charge capture, and charge entry have taken place. The post-visit phase is considered in terms of bulk claims management and individual claims management. It is important to note that each medical practice must assess processes based on the volume of generated claims and specialty type. It is critical that the claims management process be timely; the claim should be filed as quickly after the service is provided as possible. Filing or generating and submitting claims daily, is key to quick turn-around from insurance carriers. Exhibit 8.1 provides a general overview of the claims management process.

CLAIM SUBMISSION

After the patient has been seen, documentation of the visit has been completed, and charges have been entered, the claim should be generated and submitted to the insurance carrier as soon as possible, preferably the next day. Most medical practices submit claims electronically. The submission of electronic claims should be utilized whenever possible because it is more efficient and cost effective. It is important to have a computer vendor that can ensure correct formatting for the various claim types. Once the formatting is set, the issue of human error is less problematic. Claims filed electronically can be processed by internal computer functions.

EXHIBIT 8.1 ■ Overview of Claims Management Process

Daily Processes: Bulk Claims Management	➢ Claims generated ➢ Claims scrubbed ➢ Claims corrected before submission ➢ Claims submitted ➢ Confirm electronic claims submission ➢ Generate/mail paper claims ➢ Electronic payment posting ➢ Manual payment posting — insurance ➢ Manual payment posting — personal ➢ Verify payment amounts for accuracy
Manage Secondary Claims	➢ Batch ➢ Send ➢ Follow up on Medicare crossover claims ➢ Send letter – If two carriers paid as primary – Ask for carrier resolution
Payment: Daily Bulk Management	➢ Balance individual batches ➢ Balance collective batches ➢ Create daily deposit ➢ Deposit daily income

A 2005 Medicare rule requires that claims for beneficiaries be sent to comply with the electronic claims format outlined by HIPAA. Therefore, more than 90 percent of claims are sent electronically. However, based on the individual carrier's requirement, some claims are to be sent manually. Paper claims are likely to go through a more lengthy review or edit process at the carrier that delays payment. Insurance staff must know the elements of the paper claim, because those elements are mapped to the electronic claim. The flowchart in Exhibit 8.2 provides a general overview of how to process bulk claims.

The computer system should have some capability to scrub the claim before it is filed to identify whether it is a clean claim. If the claim needs to be corrected, it must be done before the claim is filed. If the claim-scrubbing process is not electronic, then the process must occur manually in order to guarantee that claims that leave the practice are clean claims. Only clean claims will have a good chance of being paid.

EXHIBIT 8.2 ■ **Post-visit Claims: Daily Bulk Management Flowchart**

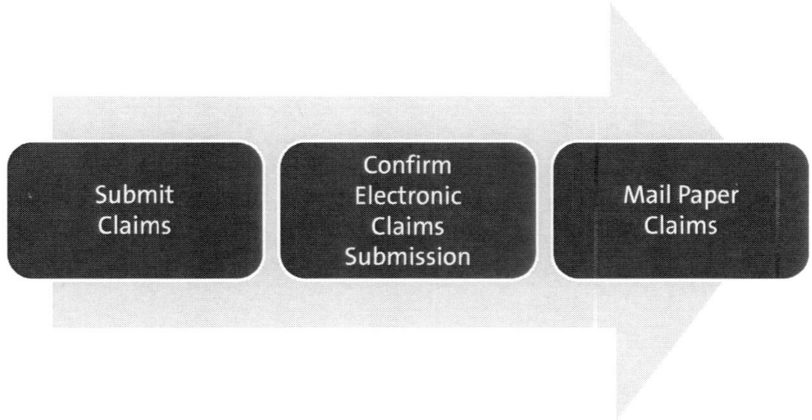

CLEARINGHOUSES

Claims sent from a medical practice typically do not go directly to the insurance carrier. Rather, when a claim leaves the medical practice, it goes through a clearinghouse before it reaches the carrier. The clearinghouse, selected by the practice, facilitates claims processing and delivery. The role of the clearinghouse is to provide an interface for claims management. Clearinghouses receive claims from a practice management system (PMS) through an interface and move that information to the appropriate payers, both government and commercial. In the role of facilitating claims processing, clearinghouses may receive information containing nonstandard elements in a non-standard format and move that information into a format acceptable to the payer intended to pay the claim. The reverse may also be true; standard transactions received by the clearinghouse may be put into a non-standard format or the receiving organization. Clearinghouses, like healthcare providers and health plans, are governed under the Privacy Rule. Clearinghouses operate with providers and health plans on a business-to-business level and do not deal directly with individual patients. You can find the official definition of a healthcare clearinghouse in the Department of Health and Human Services final HIPAA Privacy Rule in Section 160.103 (www.hhs.gov/ocr/privacy/hipaa/understanding/summary/privacysummary.pdf).

Clearinghouses typically use decision-support tools to validate that claims are clean in regard to completeness and accuracy to ensure they are correct when submitted to the payer. Not all clearinghouses are alike, varying in their commitment to the provider and in their ability to deliver high-quality services to providers.

Some clearinghouses have high claims acceptance rates and good editing processes with short time frames for reviewing claims for billing conflicts. Clearinghouses are good business associates if they are able to provide the medical practice with ease in viewing, editing, correcting, and submitting claims. However, some clearinghouses may prove to be costly business associates if they do not have good editing processes and do not report information to the medical practice in a timely manner. Months after a set of claims has left the medical practice, clearinghouses have been known to report back to the medical practice that the claims sent were not received by the carrier. Practices should enter into agreements with clearinghouses only after conducting complete due diligence.

Once a claim is filed and arrives at the carrier, it goes through the carrier's adjudication process to determine if the claim will be paid as filed or if there are conditions that will cause the claim not to be paid. Even if the claim is a clean claim, the carrier may determine that the claim will not be paid for a number of possible reasons, including that all the charges are applied to the patient's deductible, the carrier determines that services provided do not meet medical necessity requirements, or the carrier determines that the patient was ineligible for services covered by them on the date of service. Processes in the medical practice should have identified these issues before or at the time of service so that the issues could have been addressed with the patient. Finding out these payment problems after the fact delays payment and may result in not receiving payment for the services the patient received even though the services provided were legitimate.

Filing claims every day ensures a short time between the date of providing services and submitting the claim for payment. The quicker a claim is filed after the date of service, the sooner that claim will be paid. In addition, timely filing increases the likelihood that the claim will be paid as billed. Most organizations that file claims quickly know this anecdotally. Their aging analysis provides evidence that quick turnaround pays off.

ELECTRONIC FORMATTING

Correct formatting of electronic claims is crucial to receiving payment. Electronic claims formatting is particularly at risk when organizations move to a new PMS. It is the organization's contracted computer vendor/information technology (IT) partner that does electronic claims formatting in compliance with HIPAA regulations. Yet it is essential that the person working in the medical practice communicating with the IT company on claims formatting understand the organization's billing needs. The medical practice's liaison must be able to communicate those needs to the IT representative and stand firm in his or her requests. Likewise, it is necessary for the IT representatives to listen to the organization's personnel and accurately program for the organization's needs.

The financial ramifications of incorrect electronic claims formatting cannot be overstated. If the right combinations of billing group number, procedure, place of service, physician, and modifiers are not set correctly, payment will not be made correctly. These mistakes have a compounding effect on the insurance department. In addition to the volume of claims that medical office insurance staff must keep up with, they will also receive an influx of incorrect claims due to mistakes made in submitting the claims.

Good records relating to the setup of electronic claims formatting are indispensable to medical organizations. Without question there will be staffing changes in the practice. Just as certain, there will be need for changes to the electronic claims format. Without good documentation of the initial setup of electronic claims formatting, the organization is at risk for making changes that are broader than necessary for the issue at hand. Unintended consequences can occur even with a small change, if the change is not well thought through. Mistakes of this kind can take weeks to identify and put the organization at financial risk. It is incumbent on organizational management to take electronic claims formatting seriously and assign the proper level of supervision to the process.

PAPER CLAIMS

It may be necessary to submit some paper claims. While the majority of claims will be filed electronically, paper claims should be managed consistently and efficiently. Paper claims may be required when additional information is necessary to receive payment. Paper claims may be printed as programmed by formats that are set up in the PMS, but the medical office insurance staff person should be familiar with each element of the CMS 1500 paper claim form (see Exhibit 8.3)

Each box on the claim form provides distinct information that is standardized so that each carrier can pick up the required information if the form is filled out completely and accurately based on the carriers' requirements. Claims formatting is set in the PMS, in conjunction with the computer vendor partner, to ensure that fields are populated automatically and appropriately. The computer vendor partner should know the requirements of the medical practice's various payers. Not all payers require the same information to be completed in all boxes. Some fields must be completed; some are only required if applicable. In addition, some carriers do not use some fields. Medicare has particular filing requirements for certain fields, while Medicaid or commercial carriers may have other requirements.

Medical office insurance staff can use the sample claim form to review each box on it to get a general idea of the required information. First, notice that the form to be used has the following printed in the lower right hand of the form: APPROVED OMB-0938-0999 FORM CMS-1500 (08-05). If the form does not contain the information cited, it is incorrect. Second, notice that the form has two sections: PATIENT AND INSURED INFORMATION (boxes 1–13) and PHYSICIAN OR SUPPLIER INFORMATION (boxes 14–33).

Patient and Insured Information (Boxes 1–13)

Box 1 TYPE OF INSURANCE

The PMS will be programmed to check the appropriate box to distinguish the correct payer.

Box 1a INSURED'S ID NUMBER

This is the ID number of the individual whom the insurance recognizes as the subscriber. This number may be the patient's identification number. However, if the patient is insured as a dependent of the policyholder, then it may be the number of the policyholder. This is not a standardized field; various payers require particular sequences of numbers or letters or a combination of numbers and letters that they recognize for payment.

EXHIBIT 8.3 ■ CMS 1500 Form

1500

HEALTH INSURANCE CLAIM FORM

APPROVED BY NATIONAL UNIFORM CLAIM COMMITTEE 08/05

PICA | PICA

CARRIER

1. MEDICARE (Medicare #) | MEDICAID (Medicaid #) | TRICARE CHAMPUS (Sponsor's SSN) | CHAMPVA (Member ID#) | GROUP HEALTH PLAN (SSN or ID) | FECA BLK LUNG (SSN) | OTHER (ID)

1a. INSURED'S I.D. NUMBER (For Program in Item 1)

2. PATIENT'S NAME (Last Name, First Name, Middle Initial)

3. PATIENT'S BIRTH DATE MM DD YY SEX M F

4. INSURED'S NAME (Last Name, First Name, Middle Initial)

5. PATIENT'S ADDRESS (No., Street)

6. PATIENT RELATIONSHIP TO INSURED Self Spouse Child Other

7. INSURED'S ADDRESS (No., Street)

CITY STATE

8. PATIENT STATUS Single Married Other

CITY STATE

ZIP CODE TELEPHONE (Include Area Code) ( )

Employed Full-Time Student Part-Time Student

ZIP CODE TELEPHONE (Include Area Code) ( )

9. OTHER INSURED'S NAME (Last Name, First Name, Middle Initial)

10. IS PATIENT'S CONDITION RELATED TO:

11. INSURED'S POLICY GROUP OR FECA NUMBER

a. OTHER INSURED'S POLICY OR GROUP NUMBER

a. EMPLOYMENT? (Current or Previous) YES NO

a. INSURED'S DATE OF BIRTH MM DD YY SEX M F

b. OTHER INSURED'S DATE OF BIRTH MM DD YY SEX M F

b. AUTO ACCIDENT? PLACE (State) YES NO

b. EMPLOYER'S NAME OR SCHOOL NAME

c. EMPLOYER'S NAME OR SCHOOL NAME

c. OTHER ACCIDENT? YES NO

c. INSURANCE PLAN NAME OR PROGRAM NAME

d. INSURANCE PLAN NAME OR PROGRAM NAME

10d. RESERVED FOR LOCAL USE

d. IS THERE ANOTHER HEALTH BENEFIT PLAN? YES NO *If yes*, return to and complete item 9 a-d.

READ BACK OF FORM BEFORE COMPLETING & SIGNING THIS FORM.

12. PATIENT'S OR AUTHORIZED PERSON'S SIGNATURE I authorize the release of any medical or other information necessary to process this claim. I also request payment of government benefits either to myself or to the party who accepts assignment below.

SIGNED DATE

13. INSURED'S OR AUTHORIZED PERSON'S SIGNATURE I authorize payment of medical benefits to the undersigned physician or supplier for services described below.

SIGNED

PATIENT AND INSURED INFORMATION

14. DATE OF CURRENT: MM DD YY ILLNESS (First symptom) OR INJURY (Accident) OR PREGNANCY(LMP)

15. IF PATIENT HAS HAD SAME OR SIMILAR ILLNESS. GIVE FIRST DATE MM DD YY

16. DATES PATIENT UNABLE TO WORK IN CURRENT OCCUPATION MM DD YY FROM TO

17. NAME OF REFERRING PROVIDER OR OTHER SOURCE 17a. 17b. NPI

18. HOSPITALIZATION DATES RELATED TO CURRENT SERVICES MM DD YY FROM TO

19. RESERVED FOR LOCAL USE

20. OUTSIDE LAB? YES NO $ CHARGES

21. DIAGNOSIS OR NATURE OF ILLNESS OR INJURY (Relate Items 1, 2, 3 or 4 to Item 24E by Line)

1. ___ . ___ 3. ___ . ___

2. ___ . ___ 4. ___ . ___

22. MEDICAID RESUBMISSION CODE ORIGINAL REF. NO.

23. PRIOR AUTHORIZATION NUMBER

	24. A. DATE(S) OF SERVICE From MM DD YY To MM DD YY	B. PLACE OF SERVICE	C. EMG	D. PROCEDURES, SERVICES, OR SUPPLIES (Explain Unusual Circumstances) CPT/HCPCS MODIFIER	E. DIAGNOSIS POINTER	F. $ CHARGES	G. DAYS OR UNITS	H. EPSDT Family Plan	I. ID. QUAL.	J. RENDERING PROVIDER ID. #
1									NPI	
2									NPI	
3									NPI	
4									NPI	
5									NPI	
6									NPI	

25. FEDERAL TAX I.D. NUMBER SSN EIN

26. PATIENT'S ACCOUNT NO.

27. ACCEPT ASSIGNMENT? (For govt. claims, see back) YES NO

28. TOTAL CHARGE $

29. AMOUNT PAID $

30. BALANCE DUE $

31. SIGNATURE OF PHYSICIAN OR SUPPLIER INCLUDING DEGREES OR CREDENTIALS (I certify that the statements on the reverse apply to this bill and are made a part thereof.)

SIGNED DATE

32. SERVICE FACILITY LOCATION INFORMATION

a. b.

33. BILLING PROVIDER INFO & PH # ( )

a. b.

PHYSICIAN OR SUPPLIER INFORMATION

NUCC Instruction Manual available at: www.nucc.org *PLEASE PRINT OR TYPE* APPROVED OMB-0938-0999 FORM CMS-1500 (08-05)

Box 2 PATIENT'S NAME

The patient's name on the claim should appear exactly as it is on the insurance card and must be recorded in the PMS in exactly that same way to print correctly. For example, if the patient's name on the card is Cynthia Jones but the name is recorded in the practice management system as Cindy Jones, the claim may not be paid.

Box 3 PATIENT'S BIRTH DATE AND SEX

The identifying information must be recorded as directed—mm/dd/ccyy—and the box for male or female checked. This information is used as a source, along with other data, to verify that the individual is insured by the carrier. The information must be accurate to assist in tracking for appropriateness of treatment and medical necessity.

Box 4 INSURED'S NAME

This information must be submitted by last name, first name, and middle initial. The name may be the same as the patient's name in box 2 or it may be different. This is where the name of the person to whom the insurance was issued appears. This person could be the parent or the spouse of the person whose name is in box 2.

Box 5 PATIENT'S ADDRESS

This box requires the street address as well as the city, state, and zip code where the patient is living at the time of the appointment. The fields should be recorded based on U.S. Postal Service requirements, including correct abbreviations for states. This box also requires the patient's 10-digit telephone number beginning with the area code.

Box 6 PATIENT RELATIONSHIP TO INSURED

This box supplies information as to whether the patient is the insured or is a dependent of the insured. For example, the patient may be insured under the health insurance policy of a spouse or parent. There is also an option to check "other." This is relevant for situations such as domestic partner relationships.

Box 7 INSURED'S ADDRESS

This is the area to record the policyholder's address. The same rules as in Box 5 apply. Ensure that street address, city, state, zip, and 10-digit phone number are recorded accurately.

Box 8 PATIENT STATUS

This box records the patient's marital and employment status. The options relating to marital status are single, married, or other. The employment options are employed, full-time student, or part-time student. This information should be recorded in the PMS so that box 8 can be populated accurately.

Box 9 OTHER INSURED'S NAME

This is the area for information about secondary insurance coverage. Some patients have a primary insurance, which pays first, and a secondary insurance that will pay after the primary insurance. For example, a husband and wife both work, and each is covered by insurance offered by his or her respective employer. In addition, each spouse is named for coverage on the other's health insurance. In this case, each has secondary insurance. The husband's primary insurance is from his employer, and his secondary insurance is from his spouse's employer. The wife's primary insurance is from her employer, and her secondary insurance is from her spouse's employer. Some carriers allow SAME to be entered in this box if the entry is the same as box 2.

Box 9a OTHER INSURED'S POLICY OR GROUP NUMBER

This box relates to Box 9 to give the policy or group number of the secondary insurance. This is not a standardized field. Various payers require particular sequences of numbers or letters or a combination of numbers and letters that they recognize for payment.

Box 9b OTHER INSURED'S DATE OF BIRTH AND SEX

The identifying information must be recorded as directed—mm/dd/ccyy—and the box checked male or female. This information is used as a source, along with other data, to verify that the individual is insured by the carrier. The information must be accurate to assist in tracking for appropriateness of treatment and medical necessity.

Box 9c EMPLOYER'S NAME OR SCHOOL NAME

Enter the name of the employer or school of the insured for the secondary insurance payer ID or enter the claims processor's abbreviated address.

Box 9d INSURANCE PLAN NAME OR PROGRAM NAME

Record the name of the insurance plan that provides secondary coverage. This is the final box dealing with secondary insurance.

Box 10 IS PATIENT'S CONDITION RELATED TO

The information in this box provides important data for the insurance carrier to determine the appropriate payer for the services. This box establishes if workers' compensation insurance, auto insurance, or some other accident policy should pay for the services. This box allows three options:

a EMPLOYMENT? (CURRENT OR PREVIOUS)

YES NO

b AUTO ACCIDENT? PLACE (STATE)

YES NO

c OTHER ACCIDENT?

YES NO

Box 10d RESERVED FOR LOCAL USE

Individual payers may have particular requirements for this box.

Box 11 INSURED'S POLICY GROUP OR FECA NUMBER

Box 11 requires the insured's policy identification number. Medicare requires that box 11 be completed to ensure that the provider has made a good faith attempt to establish if Medicare is the primary payer or the secondary payer. Boxes 11 through 11d are dedicated to information about the primary insurance.

Box 11a INSURED'S DATE OF BIRTH AND SEX

Enter mm/dd/ccyy and sex if different from box 3.

Box 11b EMPLOYER'S NAME OR SCHOOL NAME

Enter employer's name or school name, if applicable.

Box 11c INSURANCE PLAN OR PROGRAM NAME

Enter the claims processor's abbreviated address.

Box 11d IS THERE ANOTHER HEALTH BENEFIT PLAN?

Completion of this box is not required by Medicare.

Box 12 PATIENT'S OR AUTHORIZED PERSON'S SIGNATURE

This box will contain SIGNATURE ON FILE. This signifies that the patient has signed paperwork, retained by the practice, authorizing the release of medical information that is necessary to process the claim.

Box 13 INSURED'S OR AUTHORIZED PERSON'S SIGNATURE

This box will contain SIGNATURE ON FILE. This signifies that the patient has signed paperwork, retained by the practice, authorizing payment of medical benefits sent directly to the provider. Box 13 is the last box in the section that is marked: PATIENT AND INSURED INFORMATION.

Physician or Supplier Information (Boxes 14–33)

Box 14 DATE OF CURRENT ILLNESS

This box requires date of the first symptom of the current illness. Box 14 is the first box in the section marked PHYSICIAN OR SUPPLIER INFORMATION.

Box 15 IF PATIENT HAS HAD SAME OR SIMILAR ILLNESS

Not required by Medicare. Complete as required. Leave blank if unknown.

Box 16 DATES PATIENT UNABLE TO WORK IN CURRENT OCCUPATION

Complete if patient is unable to work in current occupation.

Box 17 NAME OF REFERRING PROVIDER OR OTHER SOURCE

Complete with referring or ordering physician. Medicare defines a referring physician as one who requests services for a beneficiary who will have those services paid under the Medicare program. Medicare defines an ordering provider, physician or nonphysician practitioner, as one who orders services for such items as diagnostic or clinical laboratory tests, pharmaceutical services, or durable medical equipment.

Box 17a

Not required.

Box 17b NPI (National Provider Identifier)

Enter 10-digit NPI of referring or ordering physician.

Box 18 HOSPITALIZATION DATES RELATED TO CURRENT SERVICES

In the FROM space, enter inpatient hospital date. In the TO space, enter the discharge date, if appropriate. If the patient is still an inpatient, leave blank.

Box 19 RESERVED FOR LOCAL USE

May not be used by some carriers.

Box 20 OUTSIDE LAB? $ CHARGES

Complete if appropriate.

Box 21 DIAGNOSIS OR NATURE OF ILLNESS OR INJURY

Enter up to four diagnosis codes, using the highest level of specificity.

Box 22 MEDICAID RESUBMISSION

Complete if appropriate, for Medicaid only.

Box 23 PRIOR AUTHORIZATION NUMBER

Enter prior authorization number assigned by payer.

Box 24A–J

Box 24A–J provides billing information for up to six services. Shaded areas allow for reporting supplemental information such as description of an unlisted code.

Box 24A is used for dates of service. For continuous service complete dates in both the FROM and TO section. For only one service date use the FROM section.

Box 24B is used to identify the place of service. Place of service codes are found in the CPT book.

Box 24C is used to indicate emergency services. This box can be completed with Yes or No. Box 24C is not required by Medicare.

Box 24D is used to enter CPT and Healthcare Common Procedure Coding System (HCPCS) codes for procedures, services, or supplies. If necessary use up to four modifiers to add information about the codes submitted.

Box 24E is used to enter the diagnosis code reference number that indicates which of the diagnosis codes from box 21 relate to the CPT or HCPCS code on that line. Only one reference number is allowed per line. Refer back to box 21 to enter either 1, 2, 3, or 4 as appropriate.

Box 24F is used to enter charge for each listed service using the dollar and cents format.

Box 24G is used to identify units or days. The field can express how many of the same service was provided and can be used for identifying units of supplies, anesthesia minutes, or multiple visits. Otherwise, this field should be programmed to default to 1.

Box 24H is used to identify Medicaid Early & Periodic Screening & Diagnostic Treatment (EPSDT) benefits or family planning. Enter Yes or No.

Box 24I is used to enter ID qualifier.

Box 24J is used to enter the 10-digit NPI of the rendering provider.

Box 25 FEDERAL TAX ID NUMBER

This box is used to submit the federal tax ID. The number should be identified with an X in the appropriate box to indicate whether the number submitted is a Social Security Number (SSN) or an employer identification number (EIN).

Box 26 PATIENT'S ACCOUNT NUMBER

This box is meant to aid the provider in tracking payment back to the correct patient in the medical practice. This is an optional field.

Box 27 ACCEPT ASSIGNMENT?

This box is used for Medicare beneficiaries and should be checked as appropriate to indicate if the provider is accepting assignment or not.

Box 28 TOTAL CHARGE

This box is used to represent the total charge.

Box 29 AMOUNT PAID

This box is used to enter the payment amount as received from any other carrier. Use as appropriate.

Box 30 BALANCE DUE

Leave this box blank.

Box 31 SIGNATURE OF PHYSICIAN OR SUPPLIER INCLUDING DEGREES OR CREDENTIALS

This box is used as indicated. The signature, degree or credentials, and date are entered in this box.

Box 32 SERVICE FACILITY LOCATION INFORMATION

This box is used to enter the address of the facility where services were provided. The first line provides the name of the physician or clinic; the second, the address; and the third, the city, state, and zip code of the facility.

Box 32a is to provide the 10-digit NPI.

Box 32b is for other ID.

Box 33 BILLING PROVIDER INFO & PH#

By the title of the box, to the right, enter the phone number. The phone number is not required.

In the body of the box enter the name of the physician or clinic on the first line. On the second line, enter the address. On the third line, enter the city, state, and zip code.

Box 33a is to provide the 10-digit NPI.

Box 33b is for other ID.

Remember that claims should always be filed electronically when possible. If paper claims must be submitted, they should be printed from the practice management system with appropriate claims formatting. The insurance personnel should make sure that printer alignment is set so that the paper claim can be easily read by the insurance carrier's scanner. As a last resort, claims may be prepared manually. If claims are prepared manually, make sure that they are legibly printed with black or blue ink without the use of whiteout. CMS 1500 should be submitted in the most efficient, professional way possible. CMS 1500 forms are not supplied by CMS or by the Department of Health and Human Services (HHS), rather, they may be purchased from local business forms suppliers or from the U.S. Government Printing Office.

SECONDARY CLAIMS

For situations in which patients are covered by two or more insurance plans, it is essential for the medical practice to have a process to manage those claims. Secondary insurance can be managed by the same process as primary claims — they are batched and sent. It is particularly important to follow up on Medicare claims that cross over to Medigap or supplemental insurance automatically.

A problem often arises with patients' accounts when more than one insurance carrier is providing coverage: both carriers may pay as if they are the primary payer. This results in an overpayment on the patient's account, creating a credit balance. The overpayment should not be sent back to the patient, but to one of the carriers. The question is: Which one?

A letter must be sent to the carriers advising them of the situation, and the carriers should be asked to resolve the issue. Medical office insurance staff members should not spend their valuable time trying to help insurance carriers determine which one is the primary payer and which the secondary. Until the payers make a decision, it is not wise to refund the overpayment, because the payment may be recouped by one of the carriers without knowledge that the overpayment was refunded. Even if the practice initiated the refund and sent it to the correct carrier, the carrier may recoup the overpayment by withholding payment on another insured's account who is a patient of the physician organization.

These confusing issues are difficult to straighten out. However, medical office staff members should keep the following in mind:

- The medical practice is best served to notify the payers of the overpayment and wait for the payer to act or instruct the medical practice about the action to take.
- If a patient has insurance through his or her own employer and through his or her spouse's employer, the insurance provided by the patient's employer will be billed as primary and the insurance provided by the spouse's employer will be secondary.

The flowchart in Exhibit 8.4 provides a general overview of how to manage secondary claims.

EXHIBIT 8.4 ■ Flowchart for Managing Secondary Claims

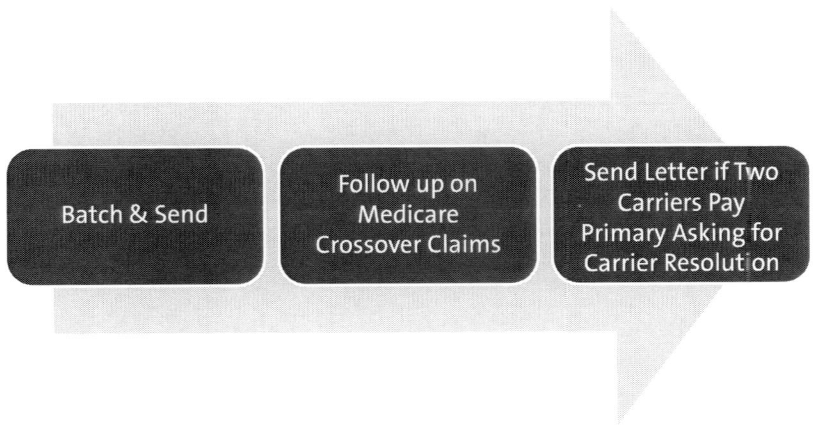

PAYMENT POSTING

There are two critical pieces to payment posting: it must be timely, and it must be accurate. Filing electronic claims is essential to the medical practice; so is payment posting. Optimally, all payments received by the medical practice should be posted the day they are received.

Although not all organizations follow this model, it is the prudent model to implement for many reasons. First, the time value of money is significant to all medical practices. Any revenue should be accessible to the practice as soon as it is available. Second, from a good business practice standard, money or checks should not be retained in the medical practice, as holding them can invite problems. Medical practice organizations should have a policy defining their own threshold of reasonableness that lays out expectations relating to payment posting for current and future employees. Once the criteria relating to payment posting is established, employees must be held to executing the expected process. In many organizations, this important aspect of the revenue cycle is delayed by staff members who postpone payment posting due to the pressure of attending to other work responsibilities.

There are two ways a payment may be posted to the medical practice's account: manually or electronically with electronic funds transfer. Manual payment posting is labor intensive and expensive to the medical practice. It is fraught with human error and should be avoided. Payment posting, like all other aspects of the medical office insurance department, should rely on technology as much as possible. Moving from manual posting to electronic posting with electronic funds transfer from the carrier is a good option whenever possible. Electronic posting and electronic funds transfer can help organizations manage the volume of paperwork inherent in the system. Also, using Medicare's electronic posting can give billing departments an opportunity to improve productivity.

As mentioned earlier, payment posting is an important aspect of the revenue cycle. It is also the point in time when payments should be audited for correctness. As each check is posted, payment should be critically reviewed to ensure the correct amount was paid by the insurance carrier. Generally, mistakes are noticed if a payment is lower than it should be. The insurance carriers have little motivation to make correcting these problems their priority. Ensuring that insurance carriers are paying the contracted amount per CPT code is easier if each carrier's contracted fee schedule is loaded into the practice management system. Efficient ways of loading carriers' fee schedules should be explored with practice management system vendors. Tracking and appealing payment discrepancies is essential to guarantee that the carrier is paying correctly; if it isn't, the loss of income for the medical practice can be significant over time. It is the insurance staff members' responsibility to manage denials aggressively so that revenue is not lost.

Payment comes from insurance carriers and individuals paying copayments, coinsurance, payment plan installments, or self-pay patient fees. These individual payments must be posted manually and should be posted daily so that anytime a patient receives a statement, it shows an accurate balance. Any time a patient knows he or she has made a payment but it is not reflected on the most recent statement, doubt is raised in the patient's mind about the trustworthiness of the medical practice.

DAILY PAYMENT MANAGEMENT

Each person involved in charge or payment posting must balance each individual posting based on charges, receipts, and adjustments. The computer input amounts must be in sync with each individual's total charges posted from encounter forms or charge tickets, the total receipts posted from cash, checks, and all receipt sources. Adjustments must be verified. Once each individual has "balanced" to the computer system, all the collective batches must be balanced to the computer practice management system. A daily deposit is then created and daily income deposited and accounted for in the medical practice's bank account. The practice should only retain enough money to reasonably support the practice for the next day's business. This supports good business principles and, along with electronic payment posting, gives the medical practice quicker access to funds. See the flowchart in Exhibit 8.5 for an overview of daily bulk management of payments.

EXHIBIT 8.5 ■ **Payment: Daily Bulk Management Flowchart**

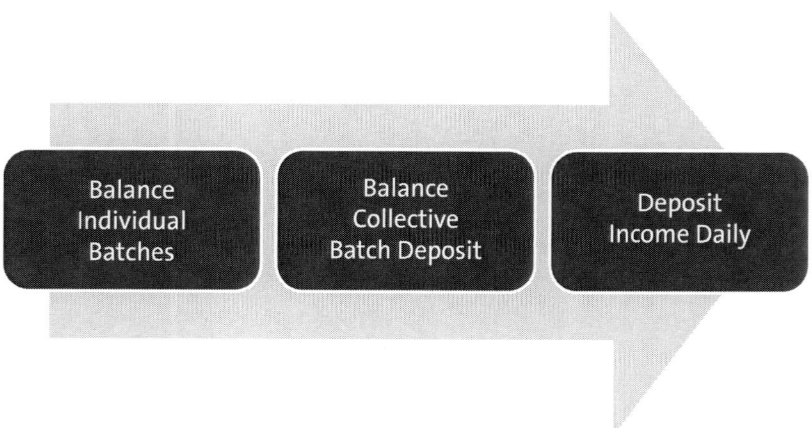

In addition to providing staff quicker access to funds and improved processing accuracy, the electronic approach assists the medical office insurance department in retrieving information for accounts follow-up. For example, because patient information is already in electronic format, it is not necessary for insurance staff employees to scan explanation of benefits for future retrieval when following up on the account. Anything that can be done in the organization to guarantee that payment posting is occurring accurately and quickly improves the opportunity to have successful account follow-up. Individual account follow-up is discussed in the next lesson.

KEY TERMS AND DEFINITIONS

Claim Scrubbing — A process conducted before the claim is sent to the carrier to identify if the claim is a clean claim that will be paid by the carrier.

Clearinghouse — An organization that receives data, in standard or non-standard format, on behalf of one entity and, after processing the data, sends it to another entity. Clearinghouses include organizations that provide billing, repricing, value-added networks, and community health information systems.

CMS 1500 — The official paper form will have printed in the lower right hand of the form: APPROVED OMB-0938-0999 FORM CMS-1500 (08-05).

Electronic Formatting — Refers to ensuring that the claim submitted electronically is in a standard format that will be accepted by the payer. Health Insurance Portability and Accountability Act (HIPAA) of 1996 requirements will standardize all communication formats for transactions with movement to 5010 formats.

Medigap Insurance — Medicare supplemental insurance claims are automatically sent when Medicare has the appropriate information.

Secondary Claims — Claims generated in those situations where patients have health insurance coverage by two or more insurances; the process of sending a claim to the next responsible carrier after the primary carrier has paid on services provided.

REVIEW OF OBJECTIVES

➢ **Identify the elements of the post-visit phase of the revenue cycle dealing with bulk claims management.**

Daily processes: bulk claims management

- Claims generated
- Claims scrubbed
- Claims corrected before submission
- Claims submitted
- Confirm electronic claims submission
- Generate/mail paper claims
- Electronic payment posting
- Manual payment posting — insurance

- Manual payment posting — personal
- Verify payment amounts for accuracy

Manage secondary claims
- Batch
- Send
- Follow up on Medicare crossover claims
- Send Letter
  - If two carriers paid as primary
  - Ask for carrier resolution

Payment: daily bulk management
- Balance individual batches
- Balance collective batches
- Create daily deposit
- Deposit daily income

➢ **Describe the claims submission process.**
- Claims should be generated and submitted daily.
- Claims should be edited for correctness before they leave the medical practice.
- Most medical practices submit claims electronically as a result of a 2005 Medicare requirement.
- Some claims requiring attachments will be sent manually.
- Manual claims are likely to be paid more slowly.
- Only clean claims have a good chance of being paid.

➢ **Clarify the role of the clearinghouse.**
- Clearinghouses facilitate claims processing.
- Sending claims from the medical practice to a clearinghouse is done for the clearinghouse to move the information into the format required by payers.
- Clearinghouses may receive claims in standard format and, after converting, send out in non-standard format or vice versa.
- Clearinghouses use decision-support tools to validate that claims are clean.
- A clearinghouse should provide medical practices the ability to view, edit, correct, and submit claims.
- Once a claim arrives at a carrier, it goes through an adjudication process to determine if and how the claim will be paid.

➢ **Examine between electronic and paper claims filing.**
- Electronic claims are formatted in compliance with HIPAA regulations.
- Medical office insurance staff should not make any changes in claims formatting without authorization .
- Unintended consequences of changing claims formatting can negatively impact the revenue cycle.

- Paper claims may be required when a carrier needs additional information.
- Paper claims can be formatted in the practice management system to print according to carriers' stipulations.
- Paper claims should be managed consistently and efficiently.

Understand the major elements of information included on the CMS 1500.

- CMS 1500 is a standardized form.
- The version to use is: APPROVED OMB-0938-0999 FORM CMS-1500 (08-05).
- Not all carriers require all fields of CMS 1500 to be completed.
- CMS 1500 is divided in two sections:
    - Boxes 1–13 Patient and Insured Information
    - Boxes 14–33 Physician and supplier information

Describe the importance of timely and accurate payment processing.

- Payment can be posted electronically or manually.
- Payments should be posted the day they are received.
- It is not a good business practice to hold checks or cash in the practice without posting to the appropriate account.
- When patients receive a statement that does not reflect money they paid to the medical practice, doubt is raised about the medical practice.
- Electronic payment posting is faster and more accurate than manual payment posting.
- After receipts are posted, individual and collective batches should be balanced to the practice management system and a bank deposit should be made daily.

REVIEW EXERCISES: LESSON 8

MULTIPLE CHOICE

Please circle the best answer.

1. **The main work of insurance staff starts:**
   - **a.** Before the patient visit
   - **b.** During the patient visit
   - **c.** After the patient visit
2. **The key to quick turnaround from insurance carriers is:**
   - **a.** Generating and submitting claims daily
   - **b.** Generating and submitting claims weekly
   - **c.** Generating and submitting claims monthly
3. **Most claims from medical practices are submitted:**
   - **a.** Manually
   - **b.** Computer printed
   - **c.** Electronically
4. **A clearinghouse:**
   - **a.** Should provide medical practices the ability to view, edit, correct, and submit claims
   - **b.** Should provide medical practices payment within 14 days
   - **c.** Should provide medical practices remittance advice within 60 days
5. **Adjudication is the process of:**
   - **a.** Scrubbing the claim so that it is clean
   - **b.** Determining if the claim will be paid as filed
   - **c.** Making a determination at the clearinghouse
6. **Incorrect electronic claims formatting can:**
   - **a.** Be detrimental to quality in the medical practice
   - **b.** Be detrimental financially to the medical practice
   - **c.** Be detrimental to patient satisfaction
7. **The following can be said about the CMS 1500 form:**
   - **a.** It is a standardized form
   - **b.** Not all payers require the same information on the form
   - **c.** Both a and b

8. **The following can be said about the CMS 1500 form:**
   a. It is divided into two distinct parts
   b. It is supplied to medical groups by HHS
   c. Both a and b

9. **The following can be said about the CMS 1500 form:**
   a. A box on the form makes inquiry about whether the claim should be paid by workers' compensation insurance, auto insurance, or another accident policy
   b. A box on the form makes inquiry about whether the claim should be paid by workers' compensation insurance, auto insurance, or life insurance
   c. Neither a nor b

10. **The term SIGNATURE ON FILE on the CMS 1500 form refers to:**
    a. Assignment of benefits
    b. HIPAA
    c. Notice of privacy

11. **A secondary claim is filed:**
    a. When the patient is out-of-network
    b. When a patient has more than one healthcare insurance
    c. Neither a nor b

12. **Payments may be posted:**
    a. Electronically
    b. Manually
    c. Both a and b

13. **It is critical for payments:**
    a. To equal the standard charge
    b. To be posted timely and accurately
    c. Neither a nor b

14. **The practice management system should:**
    a. Be populated with all physician credentialing information
    b. Be populated with each carrier's fee schedule
    c. Be populated with clinical data about each patient

15. **Electronic payment posting:**
    a. Gives the medical practice quicker access to funds
    b. Makes EOB retrieval easier because it is already in electronic format
    c. Both a and b

(Answers on page 175)

CASE STUDIES

Please select the best answer.

Case study 1: Rhonda works in the insurance department at the Southwest Medical Clinic. The medical practice has a policy that all payments are to be posted on the day that they are received. Rhonda's coworker, Jan, is assigned to post all personal payments. Rhonda noticed by accident that Jan has a stack of checks in her drawer and that the check on the top of the stack was three weeks old. Concerned, Rhonda pulled up the account number written on the check. The check had not been posted to the account. How should Rhonda handle this situation?

- **a.** Tell her coworker that she is going to get her fired.
- **b.** Get the checks out of Jan's drawer and post them.
- **c.** Find an opportunity to make the supervisor aware of the situation and volunteer to help Jan if needed.

Case study 2: Rhonda received a primary payment from two insurance carriers on the same service provided to Jane Green. How should Rhonda handle the situation?

- **a.** Call Jane to see which insurance is primary and offer to send one of the checks to Jane.
- **b.** Write a letter to both carriers to see which insurance is primary and send one of the checks to Jane.
- **c.** Write a letter to both carriers, explain the situation, and ask them to notify you as to which carrier is primary.

(Answers on page 175)

COMPLETION QUESTIONS

Please fill in the blanks.

1. Why is claim scrubbing important?

2. Most claims are sent electronically. Sending claims electronically reduces:

3. Why is it important to file claims daily?

4. Why are good records relating to claims formatting important?

5. What are the two ways that payments can be posted?

6. What are the two critical pieces of payment posting?

7. Why is electronic payment posting recommended?

8. What payment posting will require manual payment posting?

9. It is necessary for medical offices to make a determination about when Medicare is primary or when it is secondary. How should medical offices handle situations when two commercial carriers pay as if each is the primary payer?

10. What is the rule of thumb to determine the primary payer relating to a group health plan?

(Answers on page 175)

MATCHING

Please match the letter of the definition to the term.
Write the letter of the definition next to the term.

CMS 1500_____	**a.** Medicare supplemental insurance claims are automatically sent when Medicare has the appropriate information.
Secondary claims_____	**b.** An organization that receives data, in standard or non-standard format, on behalf of one entity and, after processing the data, sends it to another entity. Includes organizations that provide billing, repricing, value-added networks, and community health information systems.
Clearinghouse_____	**c.** The official paper form will have printed in the lower right hand of the form APPROVED OMB-0938-0999 FORM CMS-1500 (08-05).
Electronic formatting_____	**d.** A process conducted before the claim is sent to the carrier to identify if the claim is a clean claim that will be paid by the carrier.
Medigap insurance_____	**e.** Claims generated in those situations where patients have health insurance coverage by two or more insurances; the process of sending a claim to the next responsible carrier after the primary carrier has paid on services provided.
Claim scrubbing_____	**f.** Refers to ensuring that the claim submitted electronically is in a standard format that will be accepted by the payer. HIPAA requirements will standardize all communication formats for transactions with movement to 5010 formats.

(Answers on page 176)

ANSWERS: LESSON 8

MULTIPLE CHOICE

1-c; 2-a; 3-c; 4-a; 5-b; 6-b; 7-c; 8-a; 9-a; 10-a; 11-b; 12-c; 13-b; 14-b; 15-c

CASE STUDIES

Case study 1-c; Case study 2-c

COMPLETION QUESTIONS

1. To ensure that a clean claim is sent to the carrier so that payment can be made.
2. Human error
3. Filing claims daily ensures a short time between the date of service provided and payment on the claim.
4. Staff changes in the practice and needs of the practice change so good records avoid unintended consequences that could impact finances negatively when changes are made.
5. Manually or electronically with electronic funds transfer
6. Posting must be timely and accurate.
7. Manual payment posting is labor intensive and expensive and creates opportunity for human error.
8. Copayments, coinsurance, payment plan payments, and payments from self-pay patients
9. The medical practice should send a letter to each carrier asking both to sort out the issue.
10. When a patient has healthcare insurance provided by an employer's group health plan and insurance provided by a spouse's group health plan, the patient's group health plan is primary.

MATCHING

__ CMS 1500: **c**

__ Secondary claims: **e**

__ Clearinghouse: **b**

__ Electronic formatting: **f**

__ Medigap insurance: **a**

__ Claim scrubbing: **d**

LESSON 9

Understanding the Revenue Cycle — Post-visit Individual Account Follow-up

OBJECTIVES

- Describe an efficient process for individual account follow-up.
- Identify the process for incorrect payment amounts paid by the carrier.
- Explain the importance of early claims follow-up.
- Explain the importance of consistent follow-up on aging buckets.
- Identify important denial management processes.
- Describe the process for individual account resolution after insurance pays.

INDIVIDUAL ACCOUNT FOLLOW-UP

So far we have reviewed the revenue cycle as divided into three distinct phases: pre-visit — before the patient arrives in the medical practice; visit — the time that the patient is in the medical practice; and post-visit — after the patient has left the medical practice. In Lesson 8 we discussed the bulk claims management of the post-visit phase. In this lesson we review the individual account follow-up aspect of the post-visit phase. It is in account follow-up that medical office insurance staff members become critical to the medical practice. Based on the average number of claims denied — one in five — the medical practice must have good individual account follow-up to ensure that it is paid for the services provided to patients. A general discussion provides background for a step-by-step road map to follow in working claims.

It is essential that an organization establish a system for account follow-up. The system should be communicated in such a way that all members of the insurance department, both current employees and new hires, are aware of organizational expectations. Written processes or decision trees for account follow-up are helpful reminders to staff. Staff members should understand the processes within the system and internalize the reasoning behind each process. Understanding and internalizing processes will ensure that the organization's goals are passed on to new insurance department employees. Developing a system takes some investment of time and input from management but is well worth the effort in terms of the positive results produced.

PRIORITIZING WORK

Prioritizing work should be an organizational decision; it should not be left up to the discretion of staff members. An organized approach to working accounts receivable aging should be designated to staff, and staff members should be held accountable for results. Possible approaches are to prioritize work based on carriers, physicians, or aging buckets. Limitations or capabilities of practice management systems (PMSs) may play a role in dictating the best approach in an organization.

Some organizations favor having staff members specialize in working claims from a particular carrier. This approach assumes that learning the processes of various carriers streamlines operations and creates an advantage toward increasing efficiency. Other organizations create the impression of a small organization within a large organization, or a multispecialty organization, by assigning account follow-up to staff members per physician. While this can give staff members an opportunity to specialize in the follow-up for particular specialties, it may be a disadvantage to specific physicians if the insurance staff members assigned to their accounts are not as efficient and effective as other staff members. On the other hand, some organizations assign follow-up work to insurance staff members by aging buckets using the traditional 30+, 60+, 90+, 120+, 150+, and 180+ days categories. Organizations intent on achieving best practice status may conduct follow-up on accounts even before they rotate into the 30+ day bucket. These organizations have learned that attacking accounts follow-up sooner rather than later gives a better opportunity to deal with the rejections, denials, and appeals processes within the time limits set by carriers so that getting paid for services is more likely.

REJECTIONS AND DENIALS

Many rejection/denial determinations from carriers are based on the insurance policy's benefit structure. Denials from carriers due to services or procedures considered not medically necessary or conditions not covered are almost impossible for the insurance department to preempt. Only the prior authorization process makes information known that will likely result in a denial from the insurance carrier to cover services. The difficulty of insurance follow-up is compounded because most patients do not understand what is covered by their policy. Once again, these situations point to the necessity of gathering and retaining accurate patient information. If insurance staff members have accurate contact information, they can contact patients so that they become involved early in the insurance payment process when there is a problem. The insured may be able to assist in clarifying with his or her human resources department or insurance carrier the terms and conditions of his or her policy. Early contact with patients provides better understanding about the limitations of their insurance policy and sets the stage for them to accept financial responsibility for the service.

Many denials are corrected by minor adjustments to the insurance claim. Most of these issues are a result of human error on the part of medical practice employees, ranging from physicians to data entry staff. The organization is well served to discover these claims errors before the claims are filed. Large organizations try to correct minor issues by using claims scrubbers. This approach may not be financially viable for small organizations, which may need staff to use a manual process of verifying that information is accurately entered into the PMS before claims are filed. Some small, tightly staffed organizations may ignore the process of auditing information prior to the claim leaving the practice. This decision may prove to be more costly in the long run than making accommodations to verify accurate information before the claim leaves the practice. To reiterate from the discussion of clearinghouses in Lesson 8, this is a role that differentiates a mediocre clearinghouse from a valuable one. Regardless of the process, medical office insurance staff members must work rejections/denials to resolve the account. It is well known that many payment denials are not resolved favorably for the medical practice. Resolution of the account often means filing an appeal.

APPEALS

Insurance staff members must familiarize themselves with the appeals process of the various carriers, so the practice has a better chance of winning an appeal for itself and its patient. Medical insurance staff should be aware that there are national organizations as well as state regulations and federal mandates relating to the appeals process when health insurance claims are denied. For example, the National Committee for Quality Assurance (NCQA) dictates that both physicians and health plans review appeals based on previous denials for payment of services. NCQA requires health plans to provide an opportunity for appeals review. After the internal appeals process has been exhausted, health plans must allow for an external review process.

State departments of insurance appeals process

State departments of insurance are important to the appeals process. Although states may vary, typically state regulations provide that physicians have the right to advocate for appropriate medical care for patients and, therefore, allow physicians to have a role in determining medical necessity. States may also provide assistants to help patients with insurance appeals.

Medicare appeals process

Federal mandates require all federal insurance programs as well as health plans that contract with Medicare to follow the processes for appeals recommended in the Consumer Bill of Rights and Responsibilities that was compiled by the Advisory Commission on Consumer Protection and Quality in the Healthcare Industry (www.hcqualitycommission.gov). The Medicare appeals process for original, fee-for-service Medicare considers appeals at five different progressive levels: (1) redetermination, (2) reconsideration, (3) hearing by an administrative law judge (ALJ) in the Office of Medicare Hearings and Appeals, (4) Review by the Medicare Appeals Council, and (5) judicial review in federal district court. After an initial determination is made on a Medicare claim, appeals on both coverage and payment decisions can be made by beneficiaries, providers, or suppliers.

Redetermination

The first level of appeal is a redetermination that is filed in writing to the Medicare contractor using Form CMS-20027. Medicare contractors may also provide online forms for filing appeals. In such cases it is best to follow the appeal method preferred by the carrier in order to facilitate a quick response. The appeal must be filed within 120 days from the receipt of the initial determination, and any supporting documentation should be provided. The Medicare Administrative Contractors (MACs) will typically issue a decision within 60 days. The appeal for redetermination may be filed without regard to meeting a monetary threshold.

Reconsideration

The second level of appeal may be filed if you disagree with the redetermination. The level of appeal is reconsideration by a qualified independent contractor (QIC). The appeal must be filed with the QIC within 180 days of receiving the redetermination. The reconsideration request can be filed following the instructions on the Medicare Redetermination Notice (MRN) and can be filed on Form CMS-20033 that accompanies the MRN. The reconsideration request must explain evidence that supports disagreeing with the first level of appeal. At this level of appeal it is not necessary to resubmit information that has already been submitted to the contractor. The QIC will typically respond within 60 days from the request for consideration.

Hearing by an ALJ in the Office of Medicare Hearings and Appeals

The right to a third level of appeal exists if the QIC cannot provide a decision that is fully favorable and within the applicable time frame. A monetary threshold of $120 must remain in controversy in order to request an administrative law judge hearing. This request must be made within 60 days from the QIC reconsideration decision. Using Form CMS-20034 A/B, practices can make a request for a hearing with an ALJ. At this level and subsequent levels of appeal, it is important to submit all information that should be considered in decision-making. The ALJ will typically issue a determination within 90 days, but the decision may take longer based on the availability of all necessary information.

Review by the Medicare Appeals Council

The fourth level of appeal applies if there is dissatisfaction with the ALJ's decision. A request for review by the Medicare Appeals Council must be submitted in writing within 60 days of the ALJ's decision. The ALJ's response will contain information about how to move to the fourth level of appeal. There is no monetary threshold at this level, but the appeal must be specific about the issues and prior findings being contested. Typically the Medicare Appeals Council will make a decision within a 90-day time frame.

Judicial review in federal district court

Filing a request for a judicial review before a federal district court judge is the fifth and final level of appeal. This level requires that a substantial amount of money be in controversy — $1,180 for 2008. The amount is increased annually based on a percentage of the consumer price index component for medical care and can be found on the Centers for Medicare & Medicaid Services (CMS) Web site. This hearing must be requested within 60 days of the Medicare Appeals Council's determination.

A *reopening* is similar to an appeal. A reopening can occur because of an over- or underpayment. The primary difference between a reopening and an appeal is the initiating party. Medicare contractors take action to reopen a determination. Although a provider can initiate reopening, the decision to reopen is at the discretion of the Medicare contractor. On the other hand, the right to appeal is mandatory. Typically a provider can request a reopening if there is a minor clerical error. However, if the provider disagrees with the decision relating to a claim, an appeal should be filed.

INSURANCE CORRESPONDENCE

Insurance correspondence can be both verbal and written.

Verbal correspondence

Medical office insurance staff members do much of their work talking on the telephone to resolve issues. That type of verbal communication is inevitable in the course of resolving accounts. The skill of asking the right question at the right time can be essential to moving the claims process toward resolution. Therefore, developing verbal skills is critical for insurance staff.

Written correspondence

Written communication to insurance carriers is no less important. All types of written communication to carriers should be well thought through by staff and management. By doing so, templates can be developed and established for use by all staff members. Standardized templates within the organization can save time for busy staff and be more apt to convey the appropriate message to resolve the issue at hand. Sample letters, indexed by problem type, saved in a computer file accessible to all staff members is optimal.

It is also necessary for insurance staff to have ready access to the terms of the contract with various insurance carriers. Contracts can be scanned for easy access. Management or lead insurance staff members can create summary documents for the entire staff to use. These summary documents should outline the major points of insurance contracts and list the carriers' contact information. An investment of time and energy at the time of contracting can have major payoffs when communicating with insurance carriers.

PATIENT CORRESPONDENCE

Like correspondence with insurance carriers, correspondence with patients will be both verbal and written. Patients are often confused about communication relating to their healthcare. They might wonder whether the communication really relates to them if it has a name listed as the provider other than the name of their physician. Particularly when patients have diagnostic testing, they are surprised to receive a bill for services from someone other than their physician. Patients in our society have heard many horrendous stories in the popular media about negative aspects of healthcare. This climate has made them suspicious and distrustful of the healthcare industry. It is extremely important to the medical practice that insurance staff members present the practice as a competent, helpful, and empathetic organization even when they are serious about collecting for services provided.

The Medical Group Management Association, in conjunction with the Healthcare Financial Management Association and the American Hospital Association, has developed a patient-friendly billing philosophy. *Patient Friendly Billing* outlines voluntary standards designed to communicate better with patients when conveying financial information. Patient Friendly Billing states that the communication should be "clear, concise, and correct." This philosophy asserts that following that simple principle would help produce many benefits such as better patient satisfaction, fewer financial questions from patients, and patients paying their portion of the service faster. Medical practices should always make an effort to keep the patient informed about what is transpiring in relationship to the patient's account. For example, when an appeal is made to a payer relating to a patient's account, it is a good idea to send a letter to the patient informing him or her of the medical provider's action on behalf of payment on the account. This correspondence establishes goodwill between the patient and the practice.

Insurance staff members should be familiar with every piece of financial communication that goes out to patients, so that they can identify the communication piece that patients are speaking about when they call insurance staff. Insurance staff members should be acquainted with the format of statements. Often medical practices send out statements that are so difficult to read that individuals working in the organization are not able to understand the information. Insurance staff should be able to read a statement sent out by the organization and readily help the patient interpret what the information on the statement means. Insurance staff should be able to look at their practice management screen and track with the patients the information that is on the patient's statement. The explanation that staff members give regarding charges and balances due will incline patients to pay sooner or delay payment. In general, when giving explanation to patients, individuals working in healthcare should be careful to use language that patients can understand rather than jargon that is common only to those working in the healthcare industry. Staff members should make certain that their communications with patients give the patient the impression that the staff member is friendly, fair, and informed.

INDIVIDUAL ACCOUNT FOLLOW-UP ON CLAIMS

Every medical practice should have clear assignments within the insurance department about following up on each account after insurance has paid. A hazard in working individual claims is that accounts are not worked consistently.

It is understandable that individual employees do not work at the same pace. Problems arise, however, when one staff member cannot or does not work the accounts he or she is supposed to. There are several reasons this may occur, and they are not all the fault of the insurance employee. For example, perhaps the schedulers or front desk personnel are not performing their tasks competently, and management is not holding these individuals accountable for their work. Another possibility is that there is simply too much volume for the number of employees assigned to complete the tasks. High-volume medical practices that are short-staffed are probably costing themselves revenue. High-performing medical practices tend to have more employees to ensure that they have enough staff to efficiently handle processes they have deemed important to the revenue cycle.

Sometimes it is the fault of the individual staff member. Perhaps he or she does not manage time well, does not understand how to do the job, or is not well suited for it. Individual staff members must have the characteristics that support being successful in the insurance department. These characteristics include the ability to be persistent and self-reliant, as well as the willingness to take on responsibility to the medical practice on behalf of patients. Medical practices should track accounts receivable (A/R) based on aging buckets and by carrier type. Each bucket should be assigned to a particular staff member who will break the bucket down into individual accounts to see why the account balance is still outstanding. A/R buckets should be worked weekly, and insurance staff members should meet with management weekly to ensure that accounts are being managed well.

IMMEDIATE FOLLOW-UP ON INCORRECT PAYMENT AMOUNT

Certain processes should be in place to ensure that most follow-up occurs as soon as the insurance carrier responds initially to the claim filed by the medical practice. The payment-posting process is a decisive opportunity to signal the practice that action must be taken on the claim when payment is not correctly made. That action should occur immediately based on the processes in place in the medical practice.

When it is unclear why the carrier did not pay correctly, a call to the carrier can resolve the issue. When it is clear why the carrier did not pay correctly, the claim should be fixed and resubmitted immediately. This is often the juncture where the medical practice falls short in capturing revenue, because the staff members posting payments are intent on finishing the electronic or paper check and do not consider it their responsibility to respond to the small claim issue. However, the person posting the payment should take the very short time required to correct the claim so that it can be resubmitted in the next batch of claims that is filed. By doing so, payment can be expected in a short period of time. When organizations allow minor issues to sit unresolved, it may take weeks to finally work the claim with a minor problem and resend it, delaying payment to the practice and putting the claim at risk of never being paid correctly by the carrier. The best policy for ensuring revenue recovery is to appeal the claim immediately.

BEGIN ACCOUNT FOLLOW-UP WITH 15-DAY BUCKET

Organizations dedicated to maximizing revenue start working the claims process early. Contact is made to the carrier before the claim pays to ensure that the claim is being considered for payment. Medicare pays clean claims filed electronically within 14 days of the date that the claim was filed. It is an effective process for medical practices to print a list of claims filed 15 days prior to work each day. This time invested early in the claims process can decrease the amount of time required later in the claims process.

To reiterate, sending a claim does not guarantee that it got to the payer or, if it did, the payer is processing it for payment. A simple call to payers can ensure that a claim is being processed and payment will be made. This 15-day list can be divided among staff to lessen the burden of making 15-day outstanding claims calls. When making this call, the insurance staff member asks a series of questions:

- Was the claim received?
- Was it a clean claim?
- When will it be paid?

Insurance staff should fix the claim if needed. That effort may reduce the revenue cycle by up to eight weeks; it could easily take that amount of time to hear from the carrier. A carrier has little inclination to respond quickly when the claim is incorrect. The insurance staff person should be required to make a note in the PMS that other staff members can refer to if following up on the claim. The note will give the date the carrier was called, the response to the questions, actions taken, and follow-up instructions. Some PMSs may allow accounts to be put in a tickler queue by account number to make follow-up easier. The note in the PMS should contain the expected payment date, so that insurance staff can follow-up if payment is not received in the expected time period.

The ages of accounts with outstanding balances are expressed on a report called an *aging analysis*. The aging analysis may be the most important financial document in the organization. You can learn to read one by using the aging analysis in Exhibit 9.1; its various sections are discussed following the exhibit.

EXHIBIT 9.1 ■ Aging Analysis Report

	Current 0–30 days	31–60 days	61–90 days	91–120 days	121–150 days	151–179 days	180 days plus	Aging
Coinsurance	$53,541.35	$41,730.63	$23,447.32	$18,940.05	$19,422.15	$21,689.88	$126,213.82	$304,985.20
Self Pay	$35,743.00	$26,777.00	$17,844.00	$42,950.00	$32,807.00	$36,663.00	$82,875.90	$275,659.90
Blue Cross	$1,890.67	$174.49	$0.00	$1,311.13	$0.00	$0.00	$3,411.47	$6,787.76
Medicaid	$45,388.89	$7,185.61	$6,026.08	$4,317.78	$18,503.26	$9,958.26	$50,509.49	$141,889.37
Non Contractual	$22,029.62	$15,793.95	$8,650.40	$6,826.64	$2,251.67	$3,568.04	$37,611.81	$96,732.13
Medicare	$113,162.37	$3,862.53	$3,598.71	$1,137.11	$4,760.56	$5,319.43	$39,656.01	$171,496.72
Discounted Fee	$87,983.80	$23,686.10	$6,633.20	$3,977.31	$15,973.12	$6,470.25	$54,032.58	$198,756.36
HealthLink	$74,563.81	$12,787.79	$1,628.88	$584.78	$2,600.68	$2,516.91	$31,463.30	$126,146.15
Insurance Class Total	**$434,303.51**	**$131,998.10**	**$67,828.59**	**$80,044.80**	**$96,318.44**	**$86,185.77**	**$425,774.38**	

Aging analysis format

Coinsurance
Self Pay
Blue Cross
Medicaid
Non Contractual
Medicare
Discounted Fee
HealthLink
Insurance Class Total

First, look at the column on the far left. That column lists all the major payers in the practice.

Self Pay	$35,743.00	$26,777.00	$17,844.00	$42,950.00	$32,807.00	$36,663.00	$82,875.90	$275,659.90

It may include a row that breaks out money that is out in coinsurance, a row noting patients who have no insurance and are self-pay, a row for money that is in Medicare responsibility, and a row that is in Medicaid responsibility. Then, you may have rows that lump all discounted fee-for-service contracts together. The other rows will consist of the two or three biggest contracts — those contracts whose insured comprise the largest portion of the organization's patient population. The last row of the report is reserved to show the total of each column.

	Current 0–30 days
Coinsurance	$53,541.35
Self Pay	$35,743.00
Blue Cross	$1,890.67
Medicaid	$45,388.89
Non Contractual	$22,029.62
Medicare	$113,162.37
Discounted Fee	$87,983.80
HealthLink	$74,563.81
Insurance Class Total	**$434,303.51**

Moving from the far left column to the next column to the right, you will see the heading "0–30 days." That column represents the money that is out for services that are considered current.

The heading on the next column is 31–60 days. The numbers in this column represent money that has been outstanding for more than 30 days but has not yet reached 60 days outstanding. It is not current but not significantly past due. When you look at the last row, which shows the total of this column, you will see that the total is significantly less than the total of the 0–30 day column. This is the way an aging analysis should look, demonstrating that the practice is collecting a large part of receivables in a timely manner.

Moving on to the next column, 61–90 days, you see that the total of this column is even less. Again, this is the way an aging analysis should look and is good news for the medical practice.

	Current 0–30 days	31–60 days	61–90 days
Coinsurance	$53,541.35	$41,730.63	$23,447.32
Self Pay	$35,743.00	$26,777.00	$17,844.00
Blue Cross	$1,890.67	$174.49	$0.00
Medicaid	$45,388.89	$7,185.61	$6,026.08
Non Contractual	$22,029.62	$15,793.95	$8,650.40
Medicare	$113,162.37	$3,862.53	$3,598.71
Discounted Fee	$87,983.80	$23,686.10	$6,633.20
HealthLink	$74,563.81	$12,787.79	$1,628.88
Insurance Class Total	**$434,303.51**	**$131,998.10**	**$67,828.59**

The remaining columns don't look so good for the practice. Reviewing both the rows and the columns helps get a clear understanding of where the outstanding revenue rests. This report, however, cannot tell you what is going on in the organization. Following are several possibilities:

- The insurance staff is not working claims appropriately when account balances lie in insurance responsibility.
- The coinsurance row is too high, meaning that the process has broken down for collecting coinsurance after insurance has paid.
- The self-pay row is too high because the practice is providing services to self-pay patients before establishing how those services will be paid.
- There are issues with one or more payers that are outside of the control of the insurance department — for example, a payer may have started paying as if the medical practice is out-of-network by mistake.

Regardless, insurance staff members must be aware of information on the aging analysis to know if they are working effectively to resolve claims.

On this aging analysis, the remaining columns are out of control likely for one of the reasons just described. When reading an aging analysis, remember each row is totaled in the far right column, and the total of the far right column is the total A/R amount for the medical practice. You will note that adding the total of the columns, represented by the last row, will also equal the A/R amount of the medical practice.

Working the aging buckets

For the insurance staff, working insurance consists of working each column and row account by account until the balance on the account is resolved. The columns are sometimes referred to as *aging buckets*. Assignments within the organization may be made according to the aging buckets. Responsibility for working aging accounts may also be assigned by insurance type. Insurance staff members often prefer this arrangement of assignments, because each insurance type has a different requirement for follow-up to get the claims paid. Once staff members become familiar with a carrier's requirements, they are able to resolve more accounts more quickly because less research is required to learn each carrier's particular expectations. Staff members should work their aging bucket assignments starting with the largest claims in order for the practice to realize that revenue first. This does not mean, however, that the entire list should not be worked. Even the small dollar items must be resolved to keep the A/R up to date.

Working a particular carrier or category

It is not a good practice for one insurance staff member to work a particular carrier or category on the aging report from the current column, 0-30 days, through the 180-day column without any other department members assuming responsibility for those accounts at some point in time. This division of responsibility provides checks and balances for the organization. If one person is not living up to the responsibility he or she has been given, that inadequacy will be exposed when another person assumes responsibility for working on that carrier or payer category.

When the division of work is being considered, the medical practice's percentages with various payer communities should be reviewed. For example, if one staff member primarily works Medicare (49 percent of the practice's patient population) and another works non-contracted insurance (30 percent of the practice's patient population), it might appear to be an unfair division of work. However, the majority of Medicare claims are filed electronically, and clean claims are paid within 14 days filing. In addition, the number of clean claims initially sent should be considered and then weighted beside the number of non-contracted insurances and the variety of requirements of each. It may be that working 49 percent of the practice's Medicare claims takes less time than working 30 percent of the practice's non-contracted claims, because the requirements between the non-contracted claims vary so widely.

Working claims for one provider only

Another opportunity for process mistakes in the medical practice when working insurance is when one staff member is assigned to work all the insurance for a particular physician or provider. This is especially problematic if the organization pays physicians or providers primarily based on receipts. Although compensation based on receipts is probably not a good measure for compensating providers and is a decision that rests outside of the control of insurance staff, it sometimes enters into the provider compensation equation. Making insurance follow-up assignments by provider allows receipts to rest largely on the competency and work integrity of the insurance staff person.

Processes for assigning each aspect of the analysis report

The medical practice is responsible for setting up processes that assign each aspect of the aging analysis report by column and row, so that no gaps exist in working insurance. Once assignments have been made, a process must be developed for how the accounts will be worked and when. An effective way is to divide assignment responsibility by payer type by aging bucket column, supporting the assignment completion by printing a report that shows each account that comprises the aging bucket. The report should be worked one account at a time, and notes should be made in the PMS based on what was done to resolve the account for payment and when the account should be worked again.

The largest amounts can be worked first to ensure that the practice is able to collect the greatest outstanding balances quickest. This process is repeated regularly until the account is resolved. Accounts may be resolved while still in the current aging column. Regardless, they must be worked in each column, 30-day, 60-day, 90-day, 120-day, 150-day, or 180-day plus, until the account is resolved.

To reiterate, it is *not* a good idea to make assignments so that one insurance staff member works the same payer throughout the entire revenue cycle. For the same reason, one individual should not have the sole assignment for a particular physician. These situations cause the receipts in that category to rest on the shoulders of a single staff member. Even if that person is extremely competent and trustworthy, it is good for more than one staff person to have experience with various payers. This way, the knowledge and skills acquired by experience do not rest with only one person. Even when insurance staff members typically work with a particular payer, they should be comfortable to move from payer to payer.

DENIAL MANAGEMENT

Insurance staff members are always too busy. They are on the phone answering questions and/or getting additional information from patients, calling carriers to sort out information, and the list goes on and on. It is unlikely that the most conscientious insurance staff member is ever satisfied with his or her production. Because there is so much demand for their time, insurance staff members are sometimes unable to get to an essential part of their work — working denials. Each year a large percentage of insurance claims is denied. Of those denied claims, only a small percentage is ever refiled. This means that organizations are being denied the receipt of money that rightfully belongs to them.

This can happen because insurance staff members are so busy attending to the tasks at hand that they ignore the tasks waiting to be addressed. Working denials is not considered fun, but it is necessary for the organization's financial health. The importance of working denials must be stressed to all staff members, and the organization must help facilitate that effort by creating formats from which denials will be worked.

CONTRACTS

Medical office insurance staff should have access to the payer contracts with the practice, because they contain much information that impacts the work of insurance staff. A reference sheet can be developed for insurance staff to use in understanding the payer requirements and practice expectations. Exhibit 9.2 is an example of a reference sheet by payer.

EXHIBIT 9.2 ■ Sample Reference Sheet by Payer

Carrier Name	XYZ Insurance Group
Carrier Contact Information	Phone: 1.877.555.5555 Fax: 1.877.555.5552 Address: Street City, State, Zip Preferred Contact Name: Mary Preferred Contact Phone: 1.877.555.5555
Contract Effective Date	mm/dd/ccyy Termination: method (in writing, 180-days notice)
Claims Submission Details	
Timely Filing Requirements	12 months from date of service
Claim Appeals Process	Standard form (saved in Microsoft® Word) Folder: File name: Levels of appeal: 3
Medical Necessity Definition	
Global Period	
Multiple or Bilateral Procedure Payment	First: 100% Second: 50% Third: 50%
Medical Review Policy	
Fee Schedule	Attached

DENIALS DRIVEN BY PRACTICE OR PAYER

Each practice must understand the characteristics of denials within the organization. There are many reasons for denials. Understanding what are the largest categorizes of denials within the practice can be instructive in teaching staff how to correct regularly occurring mistakes. For example, the practice discovers the top reason payments are being denied is because some patients were not covered on the date of service. If that is the case, then the organization knows that data collection about insurance coverage and insurance verification during the pre-visit or visit phase of the revenue cycle did not occur as required by organizational processes. In this case the denials are due to errors made in the practice.

As another example, say the practice realizes that the top reason for denials is due to payer errors. Accurate claims should be paid by the payer. If evidence substantiates that denials are occurring because of actions by payers, different actions are required. Organizations should track denials by payers. This information too should be analyzed and is very informative to the practice.

A practice could be experiencing a large volume of denials by a payer due to a problem in the practice. Perhaps staff members are omitting a step that the payer requires. For example, staff may be ignoring the referral process. This is an opportunity to inform staff members about the required actions needed to avoid these denials.

In other situations, denials may be driven by payers when the practice is processing and supplying accurate claims to the payer. These may occur categorically because of changes that have occurred in the payer's organization. For example, perhaps the carrier has migrated to a new computer system and the system is set incorrectly in relationship to the medical practice's information. It is always important to categorize denials, so that the practice can recognize patterns that can be corrected. The denial trends should be recognized and corrected quickly to minimize the volume of claims that must be reprocessed. The volume of current insurance work is enough to keep insurance staff busy without enlarging the volume of work with old claims.

Much of the work in dealing with denials requires calling the payer. Some payers have online access to help track and decipher the situation with claims; other payers or situations can only be resolved by calling the carrier. Just as in the medical office, much of the work done in a carrier's organization is done manually. Individuals working for carriers can make innocent mistakes, just as medical practice staff members can. When calling the carrier is required, medical insurance staff should always document the name of the carrier's representative. Often, organizations can find a person working for the carrier who is particularly knowledgeable and helpful. When insurance staff can find a credible contact with a carrier, they can save valuable time asking their contact person to help them resolve a difficult issue. The medical insurance staff should be very respectful of the carrier relationship and make sure that they have researched the issue thoroughly before enlisting help from the carrier contact. Medical practices should have a list, shared with all in the insurance department, of carrier contact information, telephone, fax, addresses, and unique processes.

DENIAL MANAGEMENT — NO-PAYS

No-pays must be posted. More than one medical practice has had staff members assume that because the claim did not have any money attached, they did not have to make posting claims without payment a priority. This attitude points to a lack of understanding of the entire process. Once staff members understand that posting no-pay claims is important to the financial process, they give posting no-pay claims a higher priority. An initial investigation of why the carrier did not pay is required.

For example, a claim may have $0.00 payment because the entire amount was applied to the patient's deductible. In today's environment deductibles can be quite large; many deductibles are $5,000 per year. Patients insured with high deductibles may have many services, even a surgery, without meeting the deductible requirement. If the no-pay is not posted and transferred to patient responsibility, the organization will not get paid. Some organizations that have overlooked these situations for years have cost themselves thousands of dollars.

Research of the claim may disclose that the claim did not pay because of an exclusion of the policy's benefits. In those situations, the amount of the claim should be transferred to patient responsibility. The patient signed an insurance coverage waiver form as a new patient stating that he or she would be responsible for payment for services if the insurance carrier determined that the patient was ineligible for coverage.

In another instance, research may show that the claim did not pay because of some minor error on the claim. In that event, the claim can be corrected and re-sent to the carrier immediately. Under no circumstances should a claim be re-sent to a carrier without correcting the claim. Resubmitting a claim containing the same information that was already sent is considered a duplicate and will not be paid.

Researching the reason a claim did not pay may reveal that the carrier made an error. That will require a call to the carrier, and an appeal will result.

DENIALS MANAGEMENT: APPEAL CLAIMS INDIVIDUALLY

Claims may require appeal because the insurance carrier did not pay the claim, or it paid the claim incorrectly. Every claim that is paid incorrectly should be appealed. Appealing every claim is necessary to retain the practice's financial viability. Suppose an insurance carrier has a contracted amount to pay $48.98 on a service, and, for no apparent reason, the carrier starts paying $45.98 on that service. If an insurance staff member adjusts off the $3.00 on the service and no appeal is filed, there is no reason for the carrier to ever pay more than the new fee of $45.98. Let us assume that the service is a visit that will be repeated in the practice thousands of times in the next five years — imagine how much money the organization has lost on one code where the price cut seemed insignificant. This is an example using a small dollar amount, but the same situation can occur on large amounts where the practice may lose hundreds of dollars per code. The important point is that every claim that is paid incorrectly must be appealed to keep the carrier on notice. Medical practices can suffer financially because of sloppy practices in the organization.

The best way to ensure that payment is made correctly is to have the fee schedule of each contracted insurance carrier loaded in the practice management system fee schedule. This creates an obvious difference in the amount that was to be paid and the amount that was paid. The probable underpayment leaves a balance on the service. In the unlikely event that an overpayment occurs, the overpayment creates a credit balance on the service. In either case, the service balance is not resolved and requires attention for insurance staff members.

Appealing claims requires intensive effort on the part of medical office insurance staff. Appealing the claim should be made as easy as possible. Insurance staff should be aware that most carriers have standardized forms to use when appealing claims. There is not one standard format common to all carriers. Many forms exist, and insurance staff must know the carriers that have a form and those that do not.

Carriers that have a standard form are showing a good faith effort to assist medical practices in appealing claims. A payer's standard form allows the payer to respond more easily to the request because the payer's staff does not have to dig the needed information out of the body of a letter. The standard form creates a better chance of a timely response.

Insurance staff members are familiar with the standard forms, even though they may be titled in various ways. For example, a common Medicare MAC, Wisconsin Physician Services (WPS), uses a form titled WPS Medicare Redetermination Request Form. Medicare's form, Medicare Reconsideration Request Form, is widely used. Commercial carriers also have standard forms; for example, UnitedHealthcare's form is titled UnitedHealthcare Claim Reconsideration Request Form.

When an insurance carrier has no standard form, the medical practice can assist in the appeals process by creating its own standardized letters. The practice should create letter formats by carrier or formats in which information from the carrier file can be copied and pasted into the standard appeals letter. A standard letter format can be created in the practice with a file for various reasons why the claim is being appealed. Insurance staff can quickly create an appeal letter by using the standard letter format and inserting the language that is particular to the reason for the appeal.

Claims may need to be appealed for various reasons, including:

- Corrected claim — coding error (procedure code or diagnosis code)
- Claim underpayment
- Claim overpayment
- Justify medical necessity
- Disagree with carrier in claim adjudication: clarify modifier use, bundling issue, supporting documentation
- Network issues: participating versus non-participating provider discounts

See Exhibit 9.3 for a sample appeal letter and Exhibit 9.4 for a list of reasons to plug into the [REASON] paragraph in the appeal letter.

EXHIBIT 9.3 ■ **Sample Appeal Letter**

[Use Organization Letterhead]

Date ________________

Insurance Provider Company Name
Address
City, State, Zip Code

RE: Identification Number

Insured Member Name: ________________________________

Insured Patient Name: ________________________________

Group Number: ________________________________

Claim Number: ________________________________

Date(s) of Service: *(mm/dd/yyyy — mm/dd/yyyy)* ________________________________

Total Charges: *($xxx.xx)* ________________________________

Dear [Health Insurer]:

This letter is written on behalf of *(physician providing service, MD)*, *(NPI)*, who provided services, *(CPT codes)* on the service date listed above. We are asking reconsideration of your initial payment determination dated, *(mm/dd/yyyy)*.

Please review this claim considering the following information. [REASON]*

Thank you for reviewing and revising the claim determination. We will expect payment promptly. If you require additional information from us please contact: *(staff person's name)* at *(telephone number xxx.xxx.xxxx)*.

Supporting documentation is attached. [Use preceding sentence ONLY IF Appropriate]

Sincerely,

[Insurance Department Staff Member]

**See Exhibit 9.4 for list of reasons for claim appeal.*

EXHIBIT 9.4 ■ Reasons for Claim Appeal

[REASON]*

1) These charges should be allowed, [give reason].

2) These charges should be allowed because the timely filing requirement was satisfied. The original submission date was *(mm/dd/yyyy)* and the corrected claim was submitted on *(mm/dd/yyyy)*.

3) The claim is not a duplicate, [give reason].

4) Modifier *(xx)* was inadvertently submitted when the correct modifier was *(xx)*. The claim was corrected and resubmitted but remains unpaid.

5) Modifier *(xx)* was billed correctly. [Give definition of modifier from CPT book.]

6) ICD-9 code *(xxx.xx)* was inadvertently submitted when the correct [ICD-9] was *(xxx.xx)*. The claim was corrected and resubmitted but remains unpaid.

7) ICD-9 code *(xxx.xx)* was billed correctly. [Give definition of modifier from ICD-9 book].

8) CPT code *(xxxxx)* was inadvertently submitted when the correct CPT code was *(xxxxx)*. The claim was corrected and resubmitted but remains unpaid.

9) CPT code *(xxxxx)* was billed correctly. [Give definition of code from CPT book].

10) The procedure, CPT code *(xxxxx)* is a distinct procedure, not a bundled procedure. [Give definition of code from CPT book].

11) The service was authorized. The claim was resubmitted with the authorization number, *(xxxxxxx)*, on *(mm/dd/yyyy)* but the remains unpaid.

12) The claim was denied because of medical necessity. In fact, the services were medically necessary. The service meets your definition for medical necessity and is supported by professional standard of care criteria. Attached is the supporting documentation.

13) The service, CPT code *(xxxxx)* was performed more than once on the date of service and the correct modifier was applied. Attached is the supporting documentation to justify the reason for performing the second service.

**See paragraph in Exhibit 9.3.*

INSURANCE RESOLUTION: INDIVIDUAL ACCOUNTS

Immediately following insurance resolution, the balance should be transferred to the patient's responsibility so that the patient will pay coinsurance. Statements should be sent to the patient immediately. Each organization must decide the time frame it is willing to give patients to pay their coinsurance. Certainly, medical practices should establish a short time frame that should not come as a surprise to patients. The expectation of financial responsibility should have been established with the patient when he or she received services. The patient should also have a copy of the organization's financial policy. It is important that an organization establish a policy and communicate that policy to patients. Often, organizations that create policies do not put the principles of that policy into action. Financial policies should be implemented and applied fairly throughout the practice.

Patients will present in the medical practice with different financial situations, just as they present with different medical situations. Organizations should think through the various possibilities to ensure that some patients are not favored over others. For example, will the organization offer charity care, and, if so, what will be the criteria? This kind of decision is outside of the authority of medical office insurance staff. However, if charity care is to be extended to a patient, medical office insurance staff should be aware of this before care is provided.

Insurance staff members should also be aware that filing insurance without making every effort to collect the coinsurance portion of the insurance agreement from the patient is considered insurance fraud. To reiterate, physicians can provide care charity or professional courtesy care, but it is inappropriate to omit collecting coinsurance.

COLLECTIONS

Collections is a sensitive topic in many medical practices. Turning patients' account balances over to a collections agency may be even more sensitive. Each organization must develop a philosophy relating to how it deals with account balances it is unable to collect. If a medical practice makes a conscious effort to increase standards in every aspect of the practice, including better performance with greater accuracy in billing, one can only hope that patients who can pay will be more apt to do so. Most medical practices today find that it is necessary to use an outside collection agency for those accounts that they are unable to collect. Clearly, it serves the practice well to keep that number to a minimum. Increasing efficiencies inside the organization is a better investment in the long run than paying an outside agency.

CREDIT BALANCES/OFFSETS/RECOUP

Medical practices should be as diligent about refunding money to patients as they are about collecting money from them. Many different situations can credit balances on accounts. Money may be owed to carriers or to patients. A quick turnaround in sending out patient refunds builds goodwill with patients and reinforces the impression that the medical practice is efficient and effective. If patients can trust the medical practice both to provide good care and be reliable in financial matters, they will choose that practice when they need care in the future for themselves and their family.

When carriers have overpaid, they often compensate by making an adjustment in future payments. These offsets or recoups are legitimate and give the carriers an opportunity to compensate themselves for money due from the practice. Medical practices should exercise care when dealing with amounts that the carrier reports as an overpayment. Sometimes the communication coming from the carrier indicates that the medical practice is to refund the overpayment, but the practice of the carrier may be to recoup the overpayment by deducting the amount overpaid from the next check sent to the practice. These situations are difficult to resolve and can become lengthy. While it is right for the carrier that overpaid to recover the overpayment, it is not a good use of the practice's resources to try to recover the income for services a second time. Staff members who know the working habits of carriers can help formulate policy within the organization about which carriers they refund and under what circumstances, as opposed to those carriers they know will recoup money.

KEY TERMS AND DEFINITIONS

Accounts Receivable — The total money due to the practice for services provided.

Accounts Receivable Aging — The total money due to a medical practice categorized by the period of time the money has been due. Typically the categories are current, >30 days, >60 days, >90 days, >120 days, >150 days, and >180 days.

Aging Analysis — A report expressing the unpaid balance on patient accounts by responsibility for payment and in the number of days the account has been outstanding. The report is the total of accounts receivable due to the practice from services provided.

Appeal — A written request asking the insurance carrier to review or critically examine the initial determination of payment for services provided. Claims that were paid incorrectly are appealed by the medical practice to ask the payer for reconsideration on payment. Every claim that pays incorrectly should be appealed.

Carrier — An insurance organization that adjudicates and processes claims. Medicare Part B claims are processed by carriers called MACs.

Charity Care — Care that is given to patients who do not have the ability to pay for services. The determination for charity care is made before any collection attempt is made.

Claim — A request for payment from an insurance carrier after medical services have been provided.

Coinsurance — The percentage of the covered charge that the insured individual is required to pay to satisfy payment for services provided. Coinsurance is paid after insurance pays its portion. The coinsurance percentage amount is established in the benefit plan purchased from the insurance carrier. The insurance deductible must be met before coinsurance is applicable.

Collection Agency — A third-party entity that collects unpaid bills for an organization. Medical practices that are unable to collect payment on accounts from patients may hire a collection agency to collect the debt for medical services. The collection agency receives a contracted percentage of the amount it collects as payment for its services.

Deductible — The amount an insured individual must pay before insurance begins to pay for covered services. Deductibles are met at the beginning of each plan year and are defined by the insurance contract.

Duplicate Claims — The act of billing for the same service more than one time. Medicare condemns this practice when repeated regularly.

Financial policy — An organizational policy outlining the financial expectations of the organization toward patients relating to collecting for services provided. Each practice should develop how it intends to handle those practices.

Medical Necessity — Services and supplies that align with the accepted standard of care for a particular medical diagnosis meet the criteria for medical necessity.

Modifiers — Numeric codes that increase or decrease the relative value unit (RVU) of a Current Procedural Terminology (CPT) code. A complete list of modifiers with definitions is found in the CPT codebook.

No-pays — Claims for which the medical practice has received $0.00 payment. No-pays may result from several reasons. Some may be from errors made by the practice or the payer, or they may result from all charges being applied to the patient's deductible or because the payer determines that the requirement of medical necessity was not met.

Payer — One who pays for health services.

Payer Contract — The document that represents the agreement between the medical practice and the payer outlining the requirements for filing claims and being paid on those claims.

REVIEW OF OBJECTIVES

- **Describe an efficient process for individual account follow-up.**
  - Have clear assignments of responsibility.
  - Work A/R buckets weekly.
  - Management meets weekly with staff for accountability.
- **Identify the process for incorrect payment amounts paid by the carrier.**
  - Immediately followup on incorrect payment amount.
    - Call carrier for direction if unclear,
    - Fix claim and resubmit claim, or
    - Appeal claim immediately.
- **Explain the importance of early claims follow-up.**
  - Begin account follow-up with 15-day bucket.
    - Was the claim received?
    - Was it a clean claim?
    - When will it be paid?
    - Create note in PMS (account and tickler).
    - Follow up if not received.

- **Explain the importance of consistent follow-up on aging buckets.**
  - Continue individual account follow-up.
    - 60-day
    - 90-day
    - 120-day
    - 150-day
    - 180-day+
- **Identify important denial management processes.**
  - By practice and by payer
    - Categorize reasons.
    - Is it practice driven?
    - Is it payer driven?
  - No-pays
    - Post all no-pays, without delay.
    - Transfer balance to patient responsibility as appropriate.
    - Research reason for no-pay and take action.
    - Correct.
    - Resend corrected claim.
  - Denials management: appeal claims individually.
    - Follow payer's process for appeal.
    - Create standardized letters used by everyone in insurance department.
    - Use appropriate standardized letter.
    - Create tickler file to follow-up on appeals.
- **Describe the process for individual account resolution after insurance pays.**
  - Transfer balance to patient after insurance pays.
  - Send statement to patient immediately.
  - Follow up in short time frame based on expectation already established with patient.
  - Collect based on organizational time frame as established in financial policy — already communicated to patient.
  - Follow established policy, turn accounts over to collection as necessary.
  - Process credit balance refunds promptly.

REVIEW EXERCISES: LESSON 9

MULTIPLE CHOICE

Please circle the best answer.

1. **The most effective way for a medical practice to follow up on insurance claims is to:**
   - **a.** Allow staff to choose work assignments each day
   - **b.** Have clear assignment responsibility
   - **c.** Work the checks with the largest payments
2. **A/R buckets should be worked:**
   - **a.** Weekly
   - **b.** Monthly
   - **c.** Semi-annually
3. **Insurance staff members are persistent, responsible, and self-reliant. Management should:**
   - **a.** Allow them to do their work without interference
   - **b.** Give them new assignments daily
   - **c.** Meet with them often and hold them accountable for their work
4. **It is important for medical practices to ensure that aging buckets are worked:**
   - **a.** Consistently
   - **b.** After all money is posted
   - **c.** When all work is caught up
5. **It is important for the medical practice to categorize denials by:**
   - **a.** Practice and by payer
   - **b.** Payer
   - **c.** Practice
6. **Medical practices are better served to make A/R account assignments by:**
   - **a.** Physician
   - **b.** A/R bucket by payer
   - **c.** Payer only
7. **It is correct to say about no-pay claims that:**
   - **a.** No-pays must be posted immediately
   - **b.** No-pays are unimportant to post because no money is attached
   - **c.** No-pays can be posted monthly

8. A claim can be classified as a no-pay claim because:

- **a.** The medical practice does not participate with the payer
- **b.** The entire claim was applied to the deductible
- **c.** The patient has met 100 percent of his or her out-of-pocket amount

9. When a claim does not pay because the service was excluded as a covered benefit:

- **a.** The service should be transferred from insurance responsibility to the patient's responsibility
- **b.** The service should be automatically refiled for the payer to reconsider
- **c.** The service should be appealed on medical necessity grounds

10. A contract reference file can inform medical office insurance staff about:

- **a.** Payer contact information
- **b.** Claims appeal process
- **c.** Both a and b

11. It is appropriate to say about appealing a claim that has paid incorrectly that:

- **a.** Every claim should be appealed
- **b.** The claim should be resubmitted for the correct payment
- **c.** The remaining balance should be written off

12. After an insurance carrier pays correctly:

- **a.** The account is resolved
- **b.** Any balance on the account should be transferred to the patient's responsibility immediately
- **c.** Any balance on the account should be transferred to a collection agency

13. Credit balances due to patients:

- **a.** Should be refunded immediately
- **b.** Should be retained on the account to apply on the next service
- **c.** Should be retained on the account

14. Credit balances due to payers:

- **a.** Should be refunded immediately
- **b.** Should result in generating a letter to the carrier to inform of the overpayment
- **c.** Should be ignored

15. When considering standard appeals forms provided by carriers, it can be said that:

- **a.** They are all standardized
- **b.** They may be unique to the payer
- **c.** They are ignored by carriers

(Answers on page 204)

CASE STUDIES

Please select the best answer.

Case study 1: Janice works in the insurance department of the Always Best Care medical practice. One of her responsibilities is to post the no-pay claims from two of the largest carriers. Another of her responsibilities is to post checks that are received from patients who are making personal payments. Janice has been pulled from the insurance department to fill in at the front while Sue is out sick. Janice has had time to complete some of her insurance work while covering the front desk. She has been able to post the person-pay checks, but she has not had an opportunity to post the no-pay claims for the past three days. How should Janice handle this situation?

- **a.** Realize that she is doing the most important thing by getting the money posted.
- **b.** Discuss the situation with her supervisor because she knows that the no-pay claims must be posted.
- **c.** Look through the no-pay claims and post the ones she can.

Case study 2: Mary is assigned to work the 90-day Medicaid A/R bucket. As soon as she starts working it, she realizes that the Medicaid accounts have not been worked at all for the last three months. Beth is assigned to work Medicaid accounts in all A/R buckets prior to 90 days. Mary has noticed that Beth is spending a great deal of time on Facebook, even though there is an organizational policy that staff members are only to use the Internet for work purposes. Mary spoke to Beth about the Medicaid account not being worked. Beth replied that Medicaid is not a good payer anyway and that it doesn't matter if the accounts are worked or not. How should Mary handle this situation?

- **a.** Mary knows that Medicaid is not a good payer and that the money really doesn't matter.
- **b.** Mary is furious with Beth because of her attitude and vows to get her fired.
- **c.** Mary should inform her supervisor because the entire insurance department's results are negatively impacted by Beth's actions.

(Answers on page 204)

COMPLETION QUESTIONS

Please fill in the blank.

1. What process in the medical practice is required to preempt services denied for not meeting medically necessary requirements or non-covered service denials?

   ____

2. Most denials on non-clean claims are due to:

   ____

3. What should occur before claims leave the practice?

   ____

4. What are the levels of Medicare appeals for original, fee-for-service Medicare?

   ____

   ____

5. The first level of Medicare appeal must be filed in a certain time frame. What is the time frame?

   ____

6. What form is used to file the first level of Medicare appeal?

   ____

7. The second level of Medicare appeal must be filed in a certain time frame. What is the time frame?

   ____

8. What form is used to file the second level of Medicare appeal?

   ____

9. What is the monetary threshold for filing the third level of Medicare appeal?

   ____

10. Insurance denials may be driven by different parties, and insurance staff should be aware of which party is responsible for the denial. What are the two parties?

    ____

(Answers on page 204)

MATCHING

Please match the letter of the definition to the term.
Write the letter of the definition next to the term.

Charity care _____	**a.** The total money due to a medical practice categorized by the period of time the money has been due. Typically the categories are current, >30 days, >60 days, >90 days, >120 days, >150 days, and >180 days.
Accounts receivable _____	**b.** The document that represents the agreement between the medical practice and the payer outlining the requirements for filing claims and being paid on those claims.
Carrier _____	**c.** The percentage of the covered charge that the insured individual is required to pay to satisfy payment for services provided and Is paid after insurance pays its portion. The percentage amount is established in the benefit plan purchased from the insurance carrier. The insurance deductible must be met before it is applicable.
Accounts receivable aging _____	**d.** A third-party entity that collects unpaid bills for an organization. Medical practices that are unable to collect payment on accounts from patients may hire this entity to collect the debt for medical services. The entity receives a contracted percentage of the amount it collects as payment for its services.
Payer _____	**e.** The amount an insured individual must pay before insurance begins to pay for covered services. Are met at the beginning of each plan year and are defined by the insurance contract.
Aging analysis _____	**f.** An insurance organization that adjudicates and processes claims. Medicare Part B claims are processed by carriers called MACs.
Payer contract _____	**g.** Services and supplies that align with the accepted standard of care for a particular medical diagnosis meet the criteria for medical necessity.
Financial policy _____	**h.** The act of billing for the same service more than one time. Medicare condemns this practice when repeated regularly.
Appeal _____	**i.** Numeric codes that increase or decrease the relative value unit (RVU) of a Current Procedural Terminology (CPT) code. A complete list with definitions is found in the CPT codebook.

Modifiers _____	**j.** A request for payment from an insurance carrier after medical services have been provided.
Claim _____	**k.** Care that is given to patients who do not have the ability to pay for services. The determination for this type of care is made before any collection attempt is made.
Coinsurance _____	**l.** One who pays for health services.
Duplicate claims _____	**m.** A written request asking the insurance carrier to review or critically examine the initial determination of payment for services provided. Claims that were paid incorrectly are appealed by the medical practice to ask the payer for reconsideration on payment. Every claim that pays incorrectly should be appealed.
Collection agency _____	**n.** Claims for which the medical practice has received $0.00 payment. May result for several reasons. Some may be from errors made by the practice or the payer, or they may result from all charges being applied to the patient's deductible or because the payer determines that the requirement of medical necessity was not met.
Deductible _____	**o.** A report expressing the unpaid balance on patient accounts by responsibility for payment and in the number of days the account has been outstanding. The report is the total of accounts receivable due to the practice from services provided.
Medical necessity _____	**p.** An organizational policy outlining the financial expectations of the organization toward patients relating to collecting for services provided. Each practice should develop how it intends to handle those practices.
No-pays_____	**q.** The total money due to the practice for services provided.

(Answers on page 205)

ANSWERS: LESSON 9

MULTIPLE CHOICE

1-b; 2-a; 3-c; 4-a; 5-a; 6-b; 7-a; 8-b; 9-a; 10-c; 11-a; 12-b; 13-a; 14-b; 15-b

CASE STUDIES

Case study 1-b; Case study 2-c

COMPLETION QUESTIONS

1. Prior authorization
2. Human error
3. Claim auditing or claim scrubbing to ensure clean claims
4. Redetermination, reconsideration, hearing by an administrative law judge, review by Medicare Appeals Council, and judicial review in federal district court
5. Within 120 of the initial determination
6. Form CMS-20027
7. Within 180 days of receiving the redetermination
8. Form CMS-20033
9. $120.00 remaining in controversy
10. Payer and practice

MATCHING

__ Charity care: **k**

__ Accounts receivable: **q**

__ Carrier: **f**

__ Accounts receivable aging: **a**

__ Payer: **l**

__ Aging analysis: **o**

__ Payer contract: **b**

__ Financial policy: **p**

__ Appeal: **m**

__ Modifiers: **i**

__ Claim: **j**

__ Coinsurance: **c**

__ Duplicate claims: **h**

__ Collection agency: **d**

__ Deductible: **e**

__ Medical necessity: **g**

__ No-pays: **n**

LESSON 10

Reading an Explanation of Benefits

OBJECTIVES

- Review the role of claim adjustment reason codes.
- Characterize the role of remittance advice remark codes.
- Analyze an EOB.

OVERVIEW

An Explanation of Benefits (EOB) is sent to providers in response to claims filed to explain what was paid by the carrier and why the claim was paid the way it was. An important part of working insurance in a medical office is to understand how to read an EOB and react appropriately to what it communicates. Reading an EOB can be a daunting task, but knowing what to pay attention to on the EOB allows medical office insurance staff a better opportunity to be good detectives. When reading the EOB, it is important to become familiar with two important aspects — claim adjustment reason codes and remark codes.

Claim adjustment reason codes

Claim adjustment reason codes convey to insurance staff that an adjustment has been taken on a submitted claim or service on the claim. In other words, a claim adjustment reason code signals that the claim or service line was paid in a different way than the claim was billed. If no claim adjustment reason code is used, the claim was paid as billed, as was expected by the organization that submitted the claim. There are certain claim adjustment group codes. They are:

- **CO** — Contractual obligation (used based on contracted or legislated agreement)
- **CR** — Corrections and reversals (used to correct a prior claim)
- **OA** — Other adjustments (used when no other group code is appropriate)
- **PI** — Payer-initiated reductions (used when no contract exists between provider and payer but payer thinks patient should not be responsible)
- **PR** — Patient responsibility (used when adjustment amount should be billed to patient)

The group codes are used with claim adjustment reason codes, which are both numeric and alphanumeric. For example, on an EOB you might see **CO-45.** The group code **CO** means that the terms of the contractual agreement are being met. Often these adjustment amounts are written off by the provider organization because of the contractual agreement between the provider and payer. These amounts are not typically billed to the patient. In addition, the CO is used with the numeric code 45. The 45 means that the charge exceeds fee schedule/maximum allowable or contracted/legislated fee arrangement. The numeric code 45 could also be paired with the PR group code, if the adjustment amount were the patient's responsibility.

Reason Code 1 signifies deductible, and **Reason Code 2** indicates coinsurance. Each of these codes is used with a group code such as CO (contractual obligation) or PR (patient responsibility). When the medical office insurance staff person working an EOB sees PR-1, the message is conveyed that the service line on the claim has been adjusted because what might have been paid by the carrier was applied to the patient's deductible.

The numeric codes may be accessed through Washington Publishing Company at www.wpc-edi.com/cintent/view/69511. All claim adjustment reason codes have instructive information attached. They have a **Start:** date, which is the date the code became available for use. Because the code list is dynamic, the code may have been updated. If that is the case, the code has a **Last Modified:** date. Last modified indicates when the maintenance committee last modified the definition of the code. Also, a code may not be in use anymore. In that case it has a **Stop:** date. Often a code with a stop date also directs the user to a different code that should be used by a **Notes:** comment. For example code 71 — Primary Payer amount. Start: 01/01/1995 with Stop: 06/30/2000 and Notes: Use code 23.

The codes are maintained by the Claim Adjustment Status Code Committee and are updated three times a year — end of January or beginning of February, first of June, and end of September or beginning of October. Code modifications or additions may be initiated broadly. They may be requested by Medicare or by individuals. Individuals may find a code request form on the Washington Publishing Company Web site (as noted previously) with instructions about how to submit a request for a new code or to change a code message. Code change requests are at the discretion of the committee.

Medical office insurance staff should keep the online version of claim adjustment reason codes handy to use when working with EOBs. Because the lists changes, relying on a paper copy is not recommended.

Remittance advice remark codes

Remark codes are used for two purposes: (1) to provide general information about processing a remit or (2) to provide supplemental information to clarify the claim adjustment status code, a reason code. The remark code as a supplemental explanation clarifies the information of the reason code.

The reason code signals that an adjustment was taken on a claim or a service line, and the remark code provides further explanation. The Health Insurance Portability and Accountability Act (HIPAA) requires that reasons use the ASC X12N format (835) transaction, so that all claim payment advice is standardized. This standardization is discussed at length in Lesson 13, "Regulations."

Remarks may be identified at the claim or be line specific at the service level. Remark codes are rarely used unless an adjustment has been taken; **REMARK** alone does not explain an adjustment. Remark codes are generic enough to be useful across the payer spectrum. Remark codes that are very specific are extremely limited because they need to be used by the maximum number of payers within the industry for creation. At one time, remark codes were proprietary, created and maintained to support Medicare requirements.

Now, by HIPAA mandate, all covered entities use remark codes. As noted in the discussion of reason codes, reasons are maintained by a committee separate and apart from remark codes. Remark codes are maintained by the Remittance Advice Remark Code Committee, which is made up of representatives from the Centers for Medicare & Medicaid Services (CMS). Remark codes may change if a justification for change is submitted to the committee, but changes to remark codes are made in light of the remark code being paired with a reason code. Remark codes should be accessed online and may be found at the Washington Publishing Company Web site www.cmsremarkcodes.info/RemarkCodesMenu.aspx. Remark codes, like reason codes, have instructive information attached. They have a **Start:** date, which is the date the code became available for use. If the code definition has been modified, the code has a **Last Modified:** date. The code may also include an informative note. The updated list of remittance advice remark codes is published each year at the end of March, July, and November.

HOW TO READ AN EOB

Learning to read an EOB is essential to working in the business of medical insurance. It is a skill that many individuals working in medical practices don't have — it is fair to say that many of you may have an administrator who doesn't know how to read an EOB.

The EOB gives you the insurance carrier's rationale for payment. Being able to read the EOB tells you *what* the insurer made the determination to pay and *why* it made that determination. This information lets you know if the charge submitted was approved to pay or if the claim was denied. With this understanding, you then know what to do in response. For example, you may post money, make an adjustment to the account, need to appeal the determination, or move the balance on the service to personal patient responsibility. You can be sure that when an individual working in the insurance department does not understand how to read an EOB, he or she is costing the practice lost revenue. By the same token understanding how to read an EOB and responding correctly helps a medical practice capture more revenue. An accurate response to an EOB cannot be overvalued.

The complicating factor with EOBs is that before the 835 transaction requirements, there was no standard format. That means that every carrier has used a different format to display the information that insurance departments need to understand what the carrier determined about payment.

MEDICARE EOB

Let's start with a Medicare EOB, because if you understand the elements on Medicare's EOB you can transfer that knowledge to interpret other carriers' EOBs. It is important for you to know that you are looking at a mockup of information from an actual EOB

EXHIBIT 10.1 ■ Full Medicare EOB

MEDICARE EOB

WISCONSIN PHYSICIANS SERVICE INS.
PROVIDER 1357777782 **ALWAYS EXCELLENT CLINIC**
CHECK/EFT 880888171 **8/25/2009**

MEDICARE REMITTANCE NOTICE

PERF PROV	SERV DATE	POS	NOS	PROC	MODS	BILLED	ALLOWED	DEDU	COINS	GPR/RC-AMT		PROV PD
					HIC 499999999	**ACNT 00140265S**	**ICN 180916224996**			**ASG Y MOA MA01 MA18**		
0000099999	1213 121307	21	1	49568	5979	936.00	235.44	0.00	47.09	CO-45	700.56	188.35
										PR-2	47.09	
LATE FILING REDUCTION		18.84										
PT RESP	47.09			CLAIM TOTALS:		936.00	235.44	0.00	47.09		747.65	188.35
***NOTE: CLAIM FORWARDED TO COMPLIMENTARY INSURER: WAKELY AND ASSOCIATES, INC.												
CLAIM LATE FILING REDUCTION: 18.84										188.35 net		
					HIC 488888888	**ACNT 00149784S**	**ICN: 180917308756**			**ASG Y MOA MA01 MA19**		
1111188888	0618 061809	11	1	99203		155.00	84.73	84.73	0.00	CO-45	70.27	0.00
										PR-1	84.73	
PT RESP	84.73			CLAIM TOTALS:		155.00	84.73	84.73	0.00		155.00	0.00
***NOTE: CLAIM FORWARDED TO COMPLIMENTARY INSURER: ANTHEM CENTRAL - FACETS												
											0.00	
					HIC 477777777	**ACNT 00149222S**	**ICN: 180916224962**			**ASG Y MOA MA01**		
2222277777	609 60909	11	1	11401		506.00	112.34	0.00	22.47	CO-45	339.66	89.87
										PR-2	22.47	
2222277777	609 60909	11	0	A4550		62.00	0.00	0.00	0.00	CO-B15	62.00	
PT RESP	22.47			CLAIM TOTALS:		568.00	112.34	0.00	22.47		478.13	89.87
											89.87	

ADJUSTMENT REASON......: LATE CHARGE
AJUSTEMENT AMOUNT.....: 18.84
TOTAL LATE FILING REDUCTIONS: 18.84

TOTALS	TOTAL CLAIMS	TOTAL BILLED	TOTAL ALLOWED	TOTAL DEDUCT	TOTAL COINS		TOTAL RC AMT	TOTAL PROV PD
	75	29199.00	7553.52	84.73		1493.63	23223.84	5975.16
ADJS:	**TOTAL PREV PD**	**TOTAL PD TO BEN**	**TOTAL INT**	**TOTAL PRIMARY**	**TOTAL OFFSET**		**TOTAL OTHER A**	**TOTAL OF CHECK**
	0.00	0.00	0.00	0.00		18.84	0.00	5956.32

(see Exhibit 10.1). The only thing that has been changed is the identifying information about patients.

Note the area that we are focusing on. In the far left corner you will see the name of the carrier — in this case it is Wisconsin Physicians Service Insurance Corporation (WPS). This organization has contracted with Medicare to process Part B claims. WPS started processing claims for Wisconsin; it now processes both Parts A and B Medicare and provides services in Illinois, Iowa, Kansas, Michigan, Minnesota, Missouri, and Nebraska.

Under the name of the carrier is the provider's NPI — the National Provider Identifier. In this case the provider is the Always Excellent Clinic, and you can see that name of the group to the right of the NPI number. Under the provider number you see "Check/EFT # 880888171." That is the electronic funds transfer number. All providers enrolling with Medicare now must participate in electronic funds transfer. You would normally see the date of the funds transfer to the right of the number.

To the right you see that this is a Medicare Remittance Notice, called an RA, for remittance advice. That is another name for EOBs.

The heading below gives you a list of the items that you will see regarding each patient. Look from left to right.

PERF PROV	SERV DATE	POS	NOS	PROC	MODS	BILLED	ALLOWED	DEDU	COINS	GPR/RC-AMT	PROV PD

- **PERF PROV** — This is the *number of the provider* who delivered the service, the performing provider. Remember that the check went to the group, but this is the number of the billing provider.
- **SERV DATE** — This is the *date of service.* Each service date will have a start date and an end date. The end date includes the year. We will point this out for each patient.
- **POS** — This is the *place of service,* that is, where the service was provided. The place of service can make a difference in payment. For example, some services can only be provided in an office or what is called a *non-facility* setting, while others are only appropriate to be provided in a *facility* setting.
- **NOS** — This means the *number of services.*
- **PROC** — This is the *procedure or service* that was provided to the insured and is represented by a Current Procedural Terminology (CPT) code. Every service has a five-digit code that differentiates one service from another.
- **MODS** — This means *modifiers.* Modifiers are attached to CPT codes to give some particular information about the service that was provided. We will talk more about modifiers later.
- **BILLED** — The *billed* amount is the standard fee that the organization charges; however, it has little relationship to what will be paid to the provider of the service — particularly on a Medicare EOB.
- **ALLOWED** — This is the *maximum* amount that a participating provider can expect to collect from a Medicare patient, typically called a beneficiary. The allowed amount is dictated by the current Medicare fee schedule. In fee-for-service Medicare, 80 percent of the allowed amount will be paid and the other 20 percent is the patient's responsibility.
- **DEDU** — Every Medicare patient has a *deductible.* If the deductible has not been met, the portion of the charge will be applied to the deductible until the deductible is satisfied.
- **COINS** — Coinsurance is the 20 percent that is the patient's responsibility. That 20 percent will typically be paid by the patient's Medigap or supplemental insurance. And you should note that the claim will be "crossed over" or forwarded to that carrier.
- **GRP/RC-AMT** — This is the *group reason code amount.* Under that heading you see the dollar amount in excess of the limiting charge.
- **PROV PD** — This is how much the *provider is paid.*

Patient 1

Let's look specifically at the first patient.

PERF PROV	SERV DATE	POS	NOS	PROC	MODS	BILLED	ALLOWED	DEDU	COINS	GPR/RC-AMT		PROV PD
					HIC 499999999	ACNT 00140265S		ICN 180916224996		ASG Y	MOA MA01 MA18	
0000099999	1213 121307	21	1	49568	5979	936.00	235.44	0.00	47.09	CO-45	700.56	188.35
										PR-2	47.09	
LATE FILING REDUCTION		18.84										
PT RESP	47.09			CLAIM TOTALS:		936.00	235.44	0.00	47.09		747.65	188.35
***NOTE: CLAIM FORWARDED TO COMPLIMENTARY INSURER: WAKELY AND ASSOCIATES, INC.												
CLAIM LATE FILING REDUCTION: 18.84										188.35 net		

In addition to the information just covered, each patient has another line of information that will be consistent across patients. Consider the half line that is highlighted.

- **HIC 499999999A** — The HIC is the *Medicare health insurance claim number.*
- **ACNT** — This is the *patient account number* as assigned by the provider of the service.
- **ICN** — This is the *internal control number.*
- **ASG** — This lets you know *whether assignment is accepted or not.* The "Y" indicates that assignment is accepted. An "N" would mean that assignment was not accepted.
- **Remark codes** — You see MOA with the codes MA01 and MA18 following.
  - **MOA (Medicare Outpatient Adjudication):** This refers to the *remark codes that are approved by CMS.* A maximum of five codes per ICN are printed in the MOA fields.
  - **Code MA01:** This means if you do not agree with what the carrier approved for these services, you may appeal our decision.
  - **Code MA18:** This means the claim information is also being forwarded to the patient's supplemental insurer.

Based on the information that was considered initially, go back and see what is known from reading this EOB. Starting from the left, see that the performing provider's NPI number is 0000099999.

The date of service was 12/13. Note that the beginning date and end date are the same.

The place of service is 21. Place-of-service codes are found in the front of the CPT codebook. POS 21 tells us that the service was provided as inpatient in a hospital.

There was one service provided, and the procedure was CPT 49568, with modifiers 59 and 79 attached. CPT 49568 is the code to describe implantation of mesh.

Modifiers are listed on the inside cover of the CPT codebook. Modifier 59 is used to denote distinct procedural service. In "Appendix A — Modifiers" of the CPT 2011 codebook you will see:

> **59 Distinct Procedural Service:** Under certain circumstances it may be necessary to indicate that a procedure or service was distinct or independent from other non-E/M services performed on the same day. Modifier 59 is used to identify procedures/

> services, other than E/M services, that are not normally reported together, but are appropriate under the circumstances. Documentation must support a different session, different procedure or surgery, different site or organ system, separate incision/excision, separate lesion, or separate injury (or area of injury in extensive injuries) not ordinarily encountered or performed on the same day by the same individual. However, when another already established modifier is appropriate it should be used rather than modifier 59. Only if no more descriptive modifier is available, and the use of modifier 59 best explains the circumstances, should modifier 59 be used. **Note:** Modifier 59 should not be appended to an E/M service with anon-E/M service performed on the same date, see modifier 25.[1]

And the 79 modifier denotes an "unrelated procedure or service by the same physician during the postoperative period."[2] An example could be if the patient was in a postoperative period from having hernia surgery and had to be taken to the operating room for gallbladder surgery. The gallbladder surgery would be billed with a 79 modifier. In "Appendix A — Modifiers" of the CPT 2011codebook you will see:

> **79 Unrelated Procedure or Service by the Same Physician During the Postoperative Period:** The physician may need to indicate that the performance of a procedure or service during the postoperative period was unrelated to the original procedure. This circumstance may be reported by using modifier 79. (For repeat procedures on the same day, see modifier 76.)[3]

The charge submitted was $936.00 and the allowed amount was $235.44.

No dollars were applied toward the patient's deductible so we know that this patient has already met his or her deductible. The coinsurance amount is $47.09 cents. Look at CO-45. CO stands for the contractual obligation and is used to identify amounts that law prohibits Medicare from paying and absolves the beneficiary of any financial liability. Examples are limiting charge violations, late filing penalties, or amounts for services not reasonable and necessary. Here CO-45 is referring to the $700.56 and is indicating that the patient may not be billed for that amount.

Under the CO-45 you see PR-2. PR indicates patient or supplemental insurance responsibility and the reason code 2 indicates coinsurance.

The other information that you can glean about this service is that there has been a late filing reduction of $18.84. As we move to look at the other patients on this EOB you will note that the service dates on those were in 2009 whereas this service date was in 2007 — that explains the late filing reduction.

You can also see that the claim was forwarded to the supplemental or complementary insurer, in this case Wakely and Associates.

---

1. American Medical Association. 2010. "Appendix A – Modifiers" in *CPT® 2011 Standard Edition.* Chicago: American Medical Association, p. 390.
2. Ibid.
3. Ibid, p. 391.

Patient 2

Let's move on to the second patient. What do you notice about this patient that was different from the first patient?

```
                                                HIC 488888888   ACNT 00149784S  ICN: 180917308756ASG Y  MOA  MA01  MA19
 1111188888 0618  061809     11     1   99203            155.00    84.73  84.73     0.00 CO-45     70.27              0.00
                                                                                         PR-1      84.73
PT RESP          84.73               CLAIM TOTALS:       155.00    84.73  84.73     0.00                    155.00    0.00
***NOTE: CLAIM FORWARDED TO COMPLIMENTARY INSURER: ANTHEM CENTRAL - FACETS
                                                                                                            0.00
```

Note that there is a different performing provider number. That means a different physician from the first provided these services.

This POS code is 11: this service was provided in the office. The procedure code is 99203. That is the CPT code for a new patient who was provided services that met the level 3 criteria for an Evaluation and Management code.

The charges for this code were $155.00, and $84.73 was allowed by Medicare. You will also note that the entire amount was applied toward the deductible amount.

Going all the way over to the right you can see that the provider was paid $0.00 dollars.

We also have an MA19 code, which means:

> Information was not sent to the Medigap insurer due to incorrect/invalid information you submitted concerning that insurer. Please verify your information and submit your secondary claim directly to that insurer. (www.wpc-edi.com/content/view/739/1)

Information was not sent to the Medigap insurer due to incorrect/invalid information that was submitted by the practice concerning that insurer. In this case, you would need to verify your information and submit the secondary claim directly to that insurer.

You might get the impression from the claim-forwarded message that the claim was sent, even if you ignored the reason code. This is a perfect example of conflicting information on the EOB and why no piece of information can be ignored. Unfortunately, this is not the only time that you will see conflicting or incorrect information on the EOB.

In this case a call must be made to Medicare to see if the claim was forwarded. A call must be made to find out the correct information, and then it is the responsibility of the practice to file the secondary claim if it did not cross over to the secondary carrier.

Patient 3

As we move on to the third patient, there are several things to note.

```
                                                HIC 477777777   ACNT 00149222S  ICN: 180916224962ASG Y  MOA  MA01
 2222277777  609  60909      11     1   11401            506.00   112.34   0.00    22.47 CO-45    339.66              89.87
                                                                                         PR-2      22.47
 2222277777  609  60909      11     0 A4550               62.00     0.00   0.00     0.00 CO-B15    62.00
PT RESP          22.47               CLAIM TOTALS:       568.00   112.34   0.00    22.47                    478.13    89.87
                                                                                                            89.87
```

First, look at **PERF PROV.** We have yet another performing provider number. That means that this remittance notice deals with services provided by three different physicians.

There is a procedure code of A45550, indicating use of a surgical tray. Surgical trays are not allowed for payment by Medicare, so you will see the use of CO-B15.

This reason code means that this service/procedure requires that a qualifying service/procedure be received and covered. The qualifying other service/procedure has not been received/adjudicated.

The patient is not responsible to pay because Medicare disallows surgical trays.

Also note here that the claim was not forwarded by Medicare to the supplemental insurance. Because because the claim was not crossed over (which means "forwarded" in office billing jargon) to the supplemental insurance, a claim must be sent by the medical practice to supplemental insurance carrier along with a copy of the Medicare EOB.

Summary box

Finally at the bottom of the page, there is a summary of the EOB.

ADJUSTMENT REASON......: LATE CHARGE
AJUSTEMENT AMOUNT.....: 18.84
TOTAL LATE FILING REDUCTIONS: 18.84

TOTALS	TOTAL CLAIMS	TOTAL BILLED	TOTAL ALLOWED	TOTAL DEDUCT	TOTAL COINS	TOTAL RC AMT	TOTAL PROV PD
	75	29199.00	7553.52	84.73	1493.63	23223.84	5975.16

This box shows:

- The late filing reduction for patient 1: $18.84.
- This remittance addressed 75 claims in all.
- The total billed amount was $29,199.00, but the allowed amount was only $7,553.52.
- The $84.73 from patient 2 was applied to her deductible.
- The practice needs to collect $1,493.63 in coinsurance either from the patients or from the patients' supplemental insurance.

ADJS:	TOTAL PREV PD	TOTAL PD TO BEN	TOTAL INT	TOTAL PRIMARY	TOTAL OFFSET	TOTAL OTHER A	TOTAL OF CHECK
	0.00	0.00	0.00	0.00	18.84	0.00	5956.32

Remember that *supplemental insurance* is also called *Medigap* insurance and is on the NOTE: section of the EOB or remittance by the wording claim forwarded to the complementary insurer. The total RC AMT is the total amount of non-covered services. This is the difference between the total billed amount and the total allowed amount.

Finally you see the total paid to the provider. But as you look beneath the $5,975.16 and note the Total of Check, you see that the amount is $5,956.32. Why two different amounts? The answer is because the $18.84 late filing amount was deducted.

PAYMENT NOT APPLIED EOB

ALWAYS EXCELLENT CLINIC **USER: RMH** **8/25/2009 9:11A**

Acct#: 00132953 Name: HIC#: 46666666 ICN: 1809170260690 Msg Codes: MA01

Prov.	Date	Pro/MO	Chg-Am	C-Allow	P-Allow	Deduct	Co-Ins	Paymen	Remark Cod	Claim Status	GPMS chg#
###	4/1/2008	49659	2343	0.00	0.00	0.00	0.00	0.00	CO226	Payment Denied	309192

PAYMENT NOT APPLIED --REASON: 888 PAYMENT AND DEDUCT
ADDITIONAL REMARK CODES: NIMA127

Acct#: 00149786 Name: HIC#: 45555555 ICN: 1809166044050 Msg Codes: MA103

Prov.	Date	Pro/MO	Chg-Am	C-Allow	P-Allow	Deduct	Co-Ins	Paymen	Remark Cod	Claim Status	GPMS chg#
###	6/10/2009	99243	267	0.00	0.00	0.00	0.00	0.00	CO140	Payment Denied	312423

PAYMENT NOT APPLIED --REASON: 888 PAYMENT AND DEDUCT
ADDITIONAL REMARK CODES: MA130

Acct#: 00149848 Name: HIC#: 44444444 ICN: 1809173087480 Msg Codes: MA27

Prov.	Date	Pro/MO	Chg-Am	C-Allow	P-Allow	Deduct	Co-Ins	Paymen	Remark Cod	Claim Status	GPMS chg#
###	6/10/2009	99223/57	286	0.00	0.00	0.00	0.00	0.00	CO18	Payment Denied	313582

PAYMENT NOT APPLIED --REASON: 888 PAYMENT AND DEDUCT

Acct#: 00149848 Name: HIC#: 43333333 ICN: 1809173087500 Msg Codes: MA27

Prov.	Date	Pro/MO	Chg-Am	C-Allow	P-Allow	Deduct	Co-Ins	Paymen	Remark Cod	Claim Status	GPMS chg#
###	6/10/2009	44143	5364.00	0.00	0.00	0.00	0.00	0.00	CO18	Payment Denied	313582

PAYMENT NOT APPLIED --REASON: 888 PAYMENT AND DEDUCT

Acct#: 00149222 Name: HIC#: 42222222 ICN: 1809162249620 Msg Codes: MA01

Prov.	Date	Pro/MO	Chg-Am	C-Allow	P-Allow	Deduct	Co-Ins	Paymen	Remark Cod	Claim Status	GPMS chg#
###	6/9/2009	A4550	62.00	0.00	0.00	0.00	0.00	0.00	COB15	Primary Payment	311639

PAYMENT NOT APPLIED --REASON: 888 PAYMENT AND DEDUCT
ADDITIONAL REMARK CODES: M15

********************************PROVIDER ADJUSTMENT DATA ENCOUNTERED*********************************

NO ACCOUNT NUMBER RETURNED SEQUENCE NUMBER: 0001
NO HIC NUMBER RETURNED NO CTRL NUMBER RETURNED
REASON: LATE CHARGE
ADJUSTMENT AMT: 18.84

TOTALS				
	INTEREST..............................		**TOTAL:**	0.00
	INPUT PAYMENTS..................:	77	**TOTAL:**	5975.16
	PAYMENT APPLIED...........	72	**TOTAL:**	5975.16
	PAYMENTS NOT APPLIED......:	5	**TOTAL:**	0.00

PAYMENT NOT APPLIED EOB

Now let's review rejected claims on the EOB and figure out why payment was not made.

Because we have gone through the previous exercise, you will already be familiar with much of this information. During this exercise, pay special attention to the Msg codes and the remark codes.

Patient 1

Acct#: 00132953 Name: HIC#: 46666666 ICN: 1809170260690 Msg Codes: MA01

Prov.	Date	Pro/MO	Chg-Am	C-Allow	P-Allow	Deduct	Co-Ins	Paymen	Remark Cod	Claim Status	GPMS chg#
###	4/1/2008	49659	2343	0.00	0.00	0.00	0.00	0.00	CO226	Payment Denied	309192

PAYMENT NOT APPLIED --REASON: 888 PAYMENT AND DEDUCT
ADDITIONAL REMARK CODES: NIMA127

Look at the first patient, **Acct# 00132953.** On the same line but on the right-hand side is Msg code **MA01,** which you have seen before. The complete definition attached to this code means that, if you do not agree with what was approved for these services, you may appeal the decision. To ensure that the carrier is fair to you, the carrier is required to have another individual who did not process your initial claim to conduct the appeal. However, in order to be eligible for an appeal, you must write to us within 120 days of the date you received this notice, unless you have a good reason for being late. Note that you have 120 days to appeal; any appeal filed beyond that point will be rejected because of timely response factors.

Under **Remark Codes** you have **CO226.** Remember that **CO** is the contractual obligation and indicates the beneficiary is not financially responsible. The **226** is taken from the reason code list and means that the information requested from the billing/rendering provider was not provided or was insufficient or incomplete.

At least one remark code must be provided (may be composed of the remittance advice remark code or NCPDP reject reason code.) This example reinforces the need for working knowledge of what is on the remark code and reason code lists. As you can see, reading a Medicare EOB is neither simple nor easy.

You will note there is an additional remark code: **NI** and **MA127. NI** means you may appeal this decision in writing within the required time limits following receipt of this notice by following the instructions included in your contract or plan benefit documents. **MA127** means reserved for future use and is neither a code that is no longer used.

Patient 2

Acct#: 00149786 Name: HIC#: 45555555 ICN: 1809166044050 Msg Codes: MA103

Prov.	Date	Pro/MO	Chg-Am	C-Allow	P-Allow	Deduct	Co-Ins	Paymen	Remark Cod	Claim Status	GPMS chg#
###	6/10/2009	99243	267	0.00	0.00	0.00	0.00	0.00	CO140	Payment Denied	312423

PAYMENT NOT APPLIED --REASON: 888 PAYMENT AND DEDUCT
ADDITIONAL REMARK CODES: MA130

For patient 2, you see Msg code **MA103.** It means Hemophilia Add On.

Note that MA130 is an additional remark code that means your claim contains incomplete and/or invalid information, and no appeal rights are afforded because the claim is unprocessable. You should submit a new claim with the complete/correct information.

Under remark codes you have **CO140.** You know what the CO indicates. Go back to the reason code list to find 140, and you will see that means: patient/insured health identification number and name do not match.

Patient 3

Acct#: 00149848 Name: HIC#: 44444444 ICN: 1809173087480 Msg Codes: MA27

Prov.	Date	Pro/MO	Chg-Am	C-Allow	P-Allow	Deduct	Co-Ins	Paymen	Remark Cod	Claim Status	GPMS chg#
###	6/10/2009	99223/57	286	0.00	0.00	0.00	0.00	0.00	CO18	Payment Denied	313582

PAYMENT NOT APPLIED --REASON: 888 PAYMENT AND DEDUCT

Look at the third patient's account. Here you see Msg code: **MA27.** This means missing/incomplete/invalid entitlement number or name shown on the claim.

CO18 indicates duplicate claim/service.

Acct#: 00149848 Name: HIC#: 43333333 ICN: 1809173087500 Msg Codes: MA27

Prov.	Date	Pro/MO	Chg-Am	C-Allow	P-Allow	Deduct	Co-Ins	Paymen	Remark Cod	Claim Status	GPMS chg#
###	6/10/2009	44143	5364.00	0.00	0.00	0.00	0.00	0.00	CO18	Payment Denied	313582

PAYMENT NOT APPLIED --REASON: 888 PAYMENT AND DEDUCT

When you look at the fourth line, you can see that this is the same patient, but this $0 payment is for a different procedure. On the prior service the CPT code was 99223 with a 57 modifier. This CPT code is a 44143 with, again, MA27 and CO18.

Acct#: 00149222 Name: HIC#: 422222222 ICN: 1809162249620 Msg Codes: MA01

Prov.	Date	Pro/MO	Chg-Am	C-Allow	P-Allow	Deduct	Co-Ins	Paymen	Remark Cod	Claim Status	GPMS chg#
###	6/9/2009	A4550	62.00	0.00	0.00	0.00	0.00	0.00	COB15	Primary Payment	311639

PAYMENT NOT APPLIED --REASON: 888 PAYMENT AND DEDUCT
ADDITIONAL REMARK CODES: M15

As we have already noted, the last patient's Msg code is **MA01.** An additional remark code **M15** is given. That means separately billed services/tests have been bundled as they are considered components of the same procedure. Separate payment is not allowed.

Earlier we discussed code A4550 and noted that Medicare never allows payment for a surgical tray.

Remark code **COB15** represents this message: "This service/procedure requires that a qualifying service/procedure be received and covered. The qualifying other service/procedure has not been received/adjudicated."

Note that this service differs from the others. Under **Claim Status** all the others said *Payment Denied* while this one says *Primary Payment.*

This **Payment Not Applied box** ties back to the payment of the primary procedure and indicates that it has already been paid.

DISCUSSION

As we have already pointed out, EOBs are complex at best, and the lack of standardization makes understanding them and knowing what to look for even more difficult. Reading an EOB is like being a detective. You are looking for pieces of information, and together those pieces tell a story.

Part of your detective work is to identify conflicting information, such as what we saw in one of our examples. And sometimes an EOB contains incorrect information. You have to look for those situations. For example, commercial carriers often apply the discount incorrectly and give incorrect information about the allowed amount on the contract; therefore, the non-covered amount will be incorrect. As a medical practice insurance staff member, it is up to you to catch these errors.

If you have contracted prices with carriers that are not loaded into your practice management system (PMS), you should encourage your supervisor or administrator to do so. By loading the prices into the PMS, it automatically takes the correct discounts. Errors are easier to spot, and you know at a glance when to act.

It takes time to load fee schedules in the PMS. However, this investment of staff time will produce a good financial payoff and make the work of the insurance department easier and more accurate.

It is important to remember that the information we have covered is contained on *every* EOB regardless of carrier, but each carrier has a different format based on its preference.

KEY TERMS AND DEFINITIONS

Claim Adjustment Reason Codes — Used on an EOB to convey to insurance staff that an adjustment has been taken on a submitted claim or service on the claim.

Claim Adjustment Group Code CO — Contractual obligation (used based on contracted or legislated agreement).

Claim Adjustment Group Code CR — Corrections and reversals (used to correct a prior claim).

Claim Adjustment Group Code OA — Other adjustments (used when no other group code is appropriate).

Claim Adjustment Group Code PI — Payer-initiated reductions (used when no contract exists between provider and payer but payer thinks patient should not be responsible).

Claim Adjustment Group Code PR — Patient responsibility (used when adjustment amount should be billed to patient).

Explanation of Benefits (EOB) — A written description of payment made by a health plan that is sent to both provider and patient.

Remark codes — Used for two purposes: (1) to provide general information about processing a remit or (2) to provide supplemental information to clarify the claim adjustment status code.

REVIEW OF OBJECTIVES

- **Review the role of claim adjustment reason codes.**
  - Signal that a claim was paid in a different way than it was billed
  - Claim adjustment group codes:
    - CO – contractual obligation (used based on contracted or legislated agreement)
    - CR – corrections and reversals (used to correct a prior claim)
    - OA – other adjustments (used when no other group code is appropriate)
    - PI – payer initiated reductions (used when no contract exists between provider and payer but payer thinks patient should not be responsible)
    - PR – patient responsibility (used when adjustment amount should be billed to patient)
  - Codes are maintained by the Claim Adjustment Status Code Committee
  - Codes are updated three times per year
- **Characterize the role of remittance advice remark codes.**
  - Serve two purposes
    - to provide general information about processing a remit
    - to provide supplemental information to clarify the claim adjustment status code
  - Adjustment may be taken on a claim or on line-specific items on a service
  - Codes are maintained by the Remittance Advice Remark Code Committee, which is a representative body of CMS
  - Codes are updated three times per year
- **Analyze an EOB.**
  - EOB headings indicate where information from claim billed is located — PERF PROV, SERV DATE, POS, NOS, PROC, MODS, BILLED, ALLOWED, DEDUCT, COINS, GPR/RC-AMT, PROV PD.
  - EOB subheading indicate specific information about the individual claim — HIC, ACNT, ICN ASG, CODES.
  - EOBs may contain claims from more than one provider and services for more than one patient.
  - A summary section at the bottom of the EOB recaps the information found on the EOB.

REVIEW EXERCISES: LESSON 10

MULTIPLE CHOICE

Please circle the best answer.

1. **An EOB provides information about:**
   - **a.** What was paid on a claim and why it was paid
   - **b.** What one carrier pays as compared to another carrier
   - **c.** What one physician charges compared to another physician

2. **The following may be found on an EOB:**
   - **a.** HIPAA Privacy Notice
   - **b.** Claim adjustment reason codes
   - **c.** Neither a nor b

3. **Contractual obligation (CO) found on an EOB is classified as:**
   - **a.** Remittance advice remark code
   - **b.** Payment contractual remark code
   - **c.** Claim adjustment group code

4. **Claim adjustment reason code 1 signifies:**
   - **a.** Deductible
   - **b.** Coinsurance
   - **c.** Neither a nor b

5. **PR-1 on an EOB means that:**
   - **a.** The patient is responsible for the amount that is coinsurance
   - **b.** The patient is responsible for the amount applied to deductible
   - **c.** The physician regulations says that the patient is not responsible for charges

6. **Claim adjustment reason codes are maintained by:**
   - **a.** CMS
   - **b.** HIPAA
   - **c.** The Claim Adjustment Status Code Committee

7. **The words "Last Modified:" attached to a code means:**
   - **a.** The last time the payment amount was modified
   - **b.** The last time the definition was modified
   - **c.** The last time the code was put back on the list

8. Remittance advice remark codes serve the purpose to:

- **a.** Provide general information about processing a remittance
- **b.** Provide supplemental information to clarify the claim adjustment status code
- **c.** Both a and b

9. Remarks may be identified:

- **a.** At the claim level
- **b.** Line specific at the service level
- **c.** Both A and B

10. The standardized HIPAA format used for reasons and remarks transactions is:

- **a.** ASC X12N format 834
- **b.** ASC X12N format 835
- **c.** ASC X12N format 836

11. It is true to say that remark codes alone:

- **a.** Explain an adjustment
- **b.** Do not explain an adjustment
- **c.** Do not explain a payment

12. It is true to say that remark codes are maintained by:

- **a.** A committee made up of representatives from CMS
- **b.** The Remittance Advice Remark Code Committee
- **c.** Both a and b

13. Which of the following is not a heading commonly included on an EOB?

- **a.** PERF PROV
- **b.** SERV DATE
- **c.** HIPAA

14. EOBs include such information as a patient's:

- **a.** Race
- **b.** Ethnicity
- **c.** Neither a nor b

15. EOBs include such information as a patient's:

- **a.** Performing provider
- **b.** Date of birth
- **c.** Both a and b

(Answers on page 226)

CASE STUDIES

Please select the best answer.

Case study 1: Joan works in the insurance department processing EOBs. She is processing a claim for services that Dr. Johnson provided to Mary Sampson last month. Joan sees that PR-1 is on the EOB. What should Joan do?

- **a.** Take the contractual obligation adjustment and don't bill the patient.
- **b.** Move the charge amount to patient responsibility because the charge was applied to her deductible.
- **c.** Correct the claim and resubmit.

Case study 2: Joan works in the insurance department processing EOBs. She is training a new employee, Julie, who has been hired to help her with her work. Joan shows Julie the printout of claim adjustment reason codes and the remittance advice remark codes. Julie notices that the printouts are from a year ago. Julie knows that both code sets are updated three times per year, so she asks Joan why she is using printed copies rather than using the online list of reason and remark codes. Joan explains that their supervisor won't allow insurance staff to use the Internet for fear that someone may get on Facebook during work hours. How should Julie handle this situation?

- **a.** Use the printed version.
- **b.** Refuse to use the printed version and get on the Internet when working EOBs.
- **c.** Talk to the supervisor to explain how important using the Internet is to the insurance department and let the supervisor know that insurance staff must stay up to date on the definition of reason and remark codes as defined on the Internet.

(Answers on page 226)

COMPLETION QUESTIONS

Please fill in the blank.

1. What is the purpose of claim adjustment reason codes?

   ____

2. What are the claim adjustment group codes?

   ____

3. What does claim adjustment group code CO indicate?

   ____

4. What does claim adjustment group code CR indicate?

   ____

5. What does claim adjustment group code OA indicate?

   ____

6. What does claim adjustment group code PI indicate?

   ____

7. What does claim adjustment group code PR indicate?

   ____

8. How many times per year are claim adjustment reason codes and remittance advice remark codes updated?

   ____

9. When are claim adjustment reason codes updated?

   ____

10. When are remittance advice remark codes updated?

    ____

(Answers on page 226)

MATCHING

Please match the letter of the definition to the term.
Write the letter of the definition next to the term.

Claim adjustment group code CO ______	**a.** Used on an EOB to convey to insurance staff that an adjustment has been taken on a submitted claim or service on the claim.
Claim adjustment reason codes ______	**b.** Contractual obligation (used based on contracted or legislated agreement)
Claim adjustment group code CR ______	**c.** Used for two purposes: (1) to provide general information about processing a remit or (2) to provide supplemental information to clarify the claim adjustment status code.
Claim adjustment group code PI ______	**d.** Patient responsibility (used when adjustment amount should be billed to patient)
Explanation of Benefits (EOB)______	**e.** Corrections and reversals (used to correct a prior claim)
Remark codes______	**f.** Payer-initiated reductions (used when no contract exists between provider and payer but payer thinks patient should not be responsible)
Claim adjustment group code PR ______	**g.** Other adjustments (used when no other group code is appropriate)
Claim adjustment group code OA ______	**h.** A written description of payment made by a health plan that is sent to both provider and patient.

(Answers on page 226)

ANSWERS: LESSON 10

MULTIPLE CHOICE

1-a; 2-b; 3-c; 4-a; 5-b; 6-c; 7-b; 8-c; 9-c; 10-b; 11-b; 12-c; 13-c; 14-c; 15-a

CASE STUDIES

Case study 1-b; Case study 2-c

COMPLETION QUESTIONS

1. To convey to insurance staff that the claim was paid differently than it was billed
2. CO, CR, OA, PI, and PR
3. That an adjustment was taken based on contracted or legislated agreement
4. That an adjustment was taken to correct a prior claim
5. Used when no other group code adjustment is appropriate
6. The group code used when no contract exists between provider and payer but payer thinks patient should not be responsible.
7. The adjustment code is used when adjustment amount should be billed to patient.
8. Three times per year
9. End of January/beginning of February, June, and end of September/beginning of October
10. End of March, July, and November

MATCHING

__ Claim adjustment group code CO: **b**
__ Claim adjustment reason codes: **a**
__ Claim adjustment group code CR: **e**
__ Claim adjustment group code PI: **f**
__ Explanation of Benefits (EOB): **h**
__ Remark codes: **c**
__ Claim adjustment group code PR: **d**
__ Claim adjustment group code OA: **g**

LESSON 11

CPT Coding

OBJECTIVES

- Summarize Current Procedural Terminology® (CPT) codes' impact on charges and payments.
- Examine relative value units (RVUs).
- Describe the correct Coding Initiative (CCI).
- Outline use of documentation and coding evaluation and management (E/M) codes.
- Analyze modifiers.
- Review Place-of-Service codes.

OVERVIEW

The ultimate goal of the billing process is reimbursement from insurance carriers. For the reimbursement process to work correctly, several conditions must be met at distinct junctures in the billing process. Each juncture presents situations of ambiguity for medical office insurance staff members. Much of the uncertainty exists because of complex and confusing sets of regulations that do not exist in isolation, but are compounded by a lengthy programmatic attempt on the part of the Centers for Medicaid & Medicare Services (CMS) to control the cost and rate of growth in healthcare. A review of the items that determine the charge value of services and procedures sets the stage for an understanding of this process.

CURRENT PROCEDURAL TERMINOLOGY® CODES*

Current Procedural Terminology (CPT) codes are designed to pay for physician services — both procedures and evaluation and management (E/M) services. The CPT codes assign a specific five-digit number that identifies each medical service and procedure that providers may deliver to patients. As long as physician collaboration exists and general supervising rules are followed, Medicare will pay for E/M services provided by a physician assistant (PA), nurse practitioner (NP), clinical nurse specialist (CNS), or certified nurse-midwife (CNM).

Payment is determined by medical necessity of the service combined with billing under the appropriate individual CPT code requirements. Descriptive terms help identify which CPT codes should be used for billing purposes. The purpose of CPT codes is to provide uniformity across the spectrum of care — medical, surgical, and diagnostic services. CPT codes are a nomenclature or classification language used broadly by all healthcare entities, so that there can be no misunderstanding of what services were provided. The directive is to use the CPT code that most closely describes the service or procedure that was provided to the patient. CPT codes are not intended to approximate the service but to describe the service *exactly.* When a new service or procedure is developed and no CPT code exists, the American Medical Association (AMA) invites medical professionals to request that a new descriptive code be developed. Request forms may be found at www.ama-assn.org/ama/pub/category/3866.html.

The AMA maintains CPT yearly. While CPT predated the Health Insurance Portability and Accountability Act (HIPAA) of 1996, HIPAA mandates the use of CPT when filing all electronic transactions for financial reimbursement. The CPT codebook begins with complete instructions for using the book. The book is divided into six sections — E&M, Anesthesia, Surgery, Radiology, Pathology and Laboratory, and Medicine — and contains a wealth of knowledge. Although managers may consider the CPT codebook to serve primarily as a resource for coders, it is also an indispensable resource for insurance staff members. Organizations should provide easy access to current CPT codebooks for insurance department staff members to use when working insurance claims. If insurance staff members have access to updated books and feel comfortable using and making notations in the book, they will work claims more efficiently with less guesswork and mystery.

RESOURCE-BASED RELATIVE VALUE SYSTEM

Relative value unit (RVU) is a term that comes from the Resource-Based Relative Value System (RBRVS). RBRVS is a national uniform system that went into effect in 1992. It is used for reimbursing all physician services. The intent of the RBRVS was to create consistent payment policies for physician reimbursement equitable to physicians all over the country.

Prior to RBRVS, physician reimbursement was based on actual, customary, and prevailing charges. There was little rhyme or reason to physicians' reimbursement schedules, and costs continued to rise significantly each year with no end in sight. CMS, with the clear understanding that reimbursement for healthcare services is a complex process, shaped the RBRVS system to establish, as accurately as possible, a cost base for the skill, time, and resources involved in every physician service provided to patients — both procedures and E/M codes. CMS's use of RBRVS ensures that the agency can prudently purchase healthcare services for its beneficiaries. Further, the establishment of RBRVS was to ensure that CMS could achieve the objective of statutory requirements to control costs in Medicare for physician reimbursement under the sustainable growth rate (SGR) mandates.

The case can be made that RBRVS is similar to the time and motion studies used in the industry sector since the Industrial Revolution's outgrowth of the assembly line. RBRVS has, without question, been revolutionary in changing physicians' reimbursement. There are three major factors used to calculate fees using RBRVS: RVUs, Geographical Practice Cost Indices (GPCIs), and Conversion Factor (CF). CMS, as required by law, uses these three factors to calculate physician fees or payment amounts annually under the RBRVS system.

Relative value unit

The RVU, the first major factor, is itself divided into three components — work, practice expense, and malpractice expense, which are defined in the CPT codebook. The first of these components, *work (RVUw),* reflects the physician's "resources of skill, time, and intensity of effort to furnish the service." Procedures and services with higher RVUs produce higher reimbursement for physicians. The second component, *practice expense (RVUpe),* represents "the overhead expenses incurred to provide the space, equipment, supplies, and support personnel cost for providing the services." The third component, *malpractice expense (RVUm),* represents the impact that each procedure or service has on the cost of professional liability insurance that the physician pays. (Definitions from Ingenix®. April 2011 "Introduction," in *Medical Correct Coding Guide* [CCI — Version 17.1], p. 5.)

Geographical Practice Cost Indices

The second factor of RBRVS is the GPCI. The GPCI varies by region and compares each region to a national average. There may be several regions per state. A GPCI for each region is established for each of the RVU elements — work, practice expense, and malpractice expense. Each of the established GPCIs is multiplied by its corresponding RVU element value to help determine physicians' fees.

Conversion Factor

The third major factor of RBRVS is the CF. The CF is a fixed-dollar amount that is multiplied by RVUs to establish the fee for a service provided. The CF is updated annually by CMS but is subject to change by legislation passed by Congress. The fully implemented resource-based formula for calculating fees is:

$$[(\text{RVUw} \times \text{GPCIw}) + (\text{RVUpe} \times \text{GPCIpe}) + \text{RVUm} \times \text{GPCIm})] \times \text{CF}$$

Another mandated consideration when calculating physicians' payment is budget neutrality (BN). In a growing program, BN accounts for program growth by reducing programmatic costs so total program cost does not grow. A budget neutrality adjustment (BNA) may be applied in a given year that may change the formula when calculating physicians' fees. In an attempt to properly represent the value of a procedure or service, CMS continually refines the Medicare Physicians Fee Schedule (MPFS) based on research and credible input from groups such as the AMA's Relative Value System Update Committee (RUC). Annually CMS provides an updated MPFS to carriers. The MPFS, published yearly, can be downloaded from the CMS Web site. Medical office insurance staff members are not regularly required to calculate fees but should be familiar with the process.

CORRECT CODING INITIATIVE (CCI)

In addition to the role of CPT, ICD-9-CM, RVU, GPCI, and CF in paying for physician services, the National Correct Coding Initiative (NCCI) was developed to help control cost to the Medicare system. For practical purposes, medical office insurance staff members should note that NCCI and CCI are used interchangeably. CMS recognized improper coding as a situation that was leading to improper payments to physicians. The greatest source of improper payments occurred when a combination of codes was reported. The NCCI's intent was to clarify how and when codes should be reported. Practically speaking, NCCI gives instruction about which codes can be reported together and which must be reported separately. That is not to say that the NCCI made physician billing easier for medical office insurance staff. Remember that the AMA is responsible for the CPT code manual. CMS relied on CPT to base its policies relating to the CCI and to define coding conventions to use as a payment guide for Medicare contractors. Edits under the NCCI were implemented in 1996.

CCI edits are used to prevent improper payment from incompatible combinations of codes by allowing certain modifiers that are found and defined in the CPT code manual. The global surgery modifiers are 25, 78, 58, and 79. Other modifiers are 59 and 91. Additionally, several anatomic modifiers are allowed. To further help ensure correct coding, CCI edits are organized by ranges of column 1 codes and specific chapters — 00000–99999, 10000–19999, 20000–29999, and so on. Specialty-specific sections may be downloaded as needed.

To help sort out information, CMS supports a coding policy manual titled *National Correct Coding Initiative Coding Policy Manual for Medicare Services*, which is updated annually. The manual may be acquired in two different ways. You can download it from the CMS Web site at www.cms.hhs.gov/NationalCorrectCodInitEd/, or you can purchase it in its entirety in printed and electronic form or in sections from the National Technical Information Service (NTIS). NTIS provides access for purchase from its Web site, including an electronic version, at www.ntis.gov/products/families/cci/. It may also be purchased by calling 1-800-363-2068 toll free or 1-703-605-6060.

NCCI breaks down edits into two sets of tables. Using these tables is not intuitive and, in fact, is complex to understand. Exhibit 11.1 shows the two tables in a side-by-side comparison. The first table is marked A, and the second table is marked B. The first table is defined as the **Column 1/Column 2 Correct Coding Edits**, formerly called Comprehensive/Component. The Column 1 portion, referred to in the title, represents what has been known as comprehensive code edits, and the Column 2 portion represents what has been known as component code edits. The second table contains **Mutually Exclusive Edits**. Each table contains two columns — Column 1 and Column 2. However, the Column 1 codes and the Column 2 codes are defined differently in each table. Because the Column codes are defined differently in the first table than in the second table, these two tables are difficult to understand and remember.

EXHIBIT 11.1 ■ CCI Edits Tables

	A	B
	Column 1/Column 2 Correct Coding Edits	**Mutually Exclusive Edits***
Column 1 means	Comprehensive code for a major procedure or service and represents a **higher** work RVU (RVUw) value	Procedure or service with a **lower** work RVU (RVUw) value
Column 2 means	Component code that is an integral part of the Column 1 code and represents a **lower** work RVU (RVUw) value than the Column 1 code	Procedure or service with a **higher** work RVU (RVUw) value (When the higher work RVU code of Column 2 is reported with the Column 1 code, the Column 2 code is the procedure or service that will not be paid.)

*Mutually Exclusive Edits outline procedures or services that cannot reasonably be performed at the same session by the same provider on the same beneficiary. Both codes are paid only when indicated by clinical circumstances and billed with the appropriate modifier. Without the correct modifiers, only the Column 1 code will be paid. Modifiers must justify for the Column 2 code to also be paid.

Source: Holt, Sarah J. 2009. *Get the Money in the Door.* Englewood, Colo.: Medical Group Management Association, p. 50. Reprinted with permission from Medical Group Management Association.

To break down the two tables for understanding, look first at the **Column 1/Column 2 Correct Coding Edits** table. This table includes two kinds of code pair edits; however, the two kinds are not obvious. The first kind of code pair is the combination of Column 1 comprehensive code and Column 2 component code that is an integral part of Column 1.

The second, less obvious, kind of code is not related to the comprehensive/component relationship. Rather, the second kind of code pair edits includes codes that simply should not be reported together, in other words, a misuse of the code. This second kind of edit is the reason that the name of the column was changed from Comprehensive/Component to **Column1/Column 2 Coding Edits**. Certain pairs of CPT and Health Care Common Procedure Coding System (HCPCS) Level II codes should not be paid separately unless certain circumstances exist. The CCI edits address these code pairs when the same beneficiary receives more than one service by the same provider on one date of service. Modifiers that should be used in these instances are also provided.

To reiterate, in this first table Column 1 represents a comprehensive code. Not only is the Column 1 code defined as the comprehensive code, but also the Column 1 code is generally the major procedure or service and represents a higher RVUw value than the code in Column 2. The Column 2 code differs from the Column 1 code in that it represents a lower work RVU value than the Column 1 code. In reality the definitions of Column 1 and Column 2 in the **Column 1/Column 2 Correct Coding Edits** table are simple but confusing. In short, Column 1 means comprehensive and major procedure with higher RVU, and Column 2 is a component code with a lesser RVU.

The second table is the **Mutually Exclusive Edits** table. This table includes edits pertaining to two codes that cannot be performed together because of reasonableness, code definitions, or anatomic considerations. Again, this table consists of Column 1 and Column 2 codes, but the Column 1 codes and the Column 2 codes carry different definitions relating to this table. In the **Mutually Exclusive Edits** table, Column 1 indicates the procedure or service with the lower RVUw and the Column 2 code indicates the procedure or service with the higher RVUw value. The **Mutually Exclusive Edits table uses definitions of Column 1 and Column 2 that are exactly opposite definitions of those used for Column 1 and Column 2 in the other CCI table.**

The **Mutually Exclusive Edits** addresses code pairs where the same beneficiary receives more than one service by the same provider on one date of service. It also provides the modifiers that should be used in these instances if the code is to be paid. Without the appropriate modifier, only the Column 1 code will be paid. Only if clinical circumstances exist such that an appropriate and justifiable modifier is added to the Column 2 code will both the Column 1 and Column 2 codes be paid. **When the higher work RVU code of Column 2 is reported with the Column 1 code, the Column 2 code is the procedure or service that will not be paid.** As noted, the **Mutually Exclusive Edits Table** outlines procedures or services that cannot reasonably "be performed at the same session by the same provider on the same beneficiary" and contains edits that dictate when both codes will be paid — both codes are paid only if indicated by clinical circumstances and billed with the appropriate modifier. CCI edits allow three kinds of modifiers: (1) Anatomical Modifiers, (2) Global Surgery Modifiers, and (3) Other Modifiers. Allowed modifiers can be found at the CMS Web site (www.cms.gov/NationalCorrectCodInited/).

To recap the difference in the definitions of the two columns in the two tables, Column 1 represents the higher work RVU in the first table — Column 1/Column 2 Correct Coding Edits — but Column 1 represents the lower work RVU in the second table — the Mutually Exclusive Edits. One the other hand, Column 2 represents the lower work RVU in the first table — Column 1/Column 2 Correct Coding Edits — but Column 2 represents the higher work RVU in the second table — The Mutually Exclusive Edits.

In the CCI, each code pair is assigned one of three modifier indicators — 0, 1, or 9: "0" indicates that a code pair cannot have any modifiers; "1" indicates that appropriate modifiers may be used; and "9" refers to effective dates, which are of little consequence to medical office insurance staff.

To complicate the CCI further, CMS identifies units of service (UOS) that are Medically Unlikely Edit (MUE) for HCPCS/CPT "code for services rendered by a single provider/ supplier to a single beneficiary on the same date of service." These MUEs are identified based on data collected from the vast majority of correctly reported claims. CMS states that the MUE "program provides a method to report medically reasonable and necessary UOS in excess of an MUE." However, CMS has not published MUEs because these "levels are confidential information that should not be published by third parties who have attempted to acquire them." You can download the NCCI policy manual at www.cms.gov/ NationalCorrectCodInitED.

CMS is clear that modifiers used inappropriately where clinical circumstances do not justify them constitutes fraud. Thus, compliance with CCI is necessary. CMS rejects any notion that the CCI program is secretive. CMS upholds that CCI is not isolated from input by organizations such as the AMA and other medical societies. In fact, comments from such organizations are seriously considered before changes in CCI are implemented. CCI edits are updated quarterly and, as stated at the beginning of the CCI discussion, the *CCI Edits Manual* is updated annually in October. However, the manual is not necessarily valid for a whole year because of the quarterly updates. In some quarters updates are substantial; in others there are relatively few changes.

It is incumbent on the physician's practice to be aware of the updates to the CCI edits. Although some software contains the CCI edits, CMS only recognizes the CMS Web site and NTIS as official sources of information. CMS suggests that if physicians' offices need to verify correctness in using modifiers, they should encourage the provider's representative to contact the local carrier's provider relations department to explain any issue that is unclear and to request an answer to the question in writing. When a physician's office disagrees with specific CCI edits, comments should be submitted in writing to:

National Correct Coding Initiative
Correct Coding Solutions LLC
PO Box 907
Carmel, IN 46082-0907

Medical office insurance staff members may also hear of Outpatient Code Editor (OCE) edits. OCE is a different editing system from the CCI edits and is used to process hospital outpatient services. While CCI edits are included in the OCE, medical practices should be aware that the CCI edits are only one version behind the current edits. OCE edits are arranged in numerical order and are accompanied by a description of each edit and a claim disposition for each edit. On the other hand, CCI edits consist of pairs of codes arranged in two tables. Should it be necessary request clarification on OCE edits, call the Division of Outpatient Care (DOC) of CMS at 410-786-0378.

It is important for medical office insurance staff to use the tools that CMS, the AMA, and other organizations have made available online to assist medical office staff needing to sort through complex issues such as NCCI. CMS has correct coding tools using the coding conventions that are defined by the AMA. The tool How to Use the National Correct Coding Initiative (NCCI) Tools can be found at www.cms.gov/NationalCorrectCodInitEd. The user must accept the CPT disclaimer before downloading the file. Files may be used in real time or may be downloaded for future use. However, it should be noted that the NCCI tables are updated quarterly. The medical office insurance staff will want to use the most recently updated tables.

The value of the CMS tools cannot be overstated. For example, a tool informs staff about whether a modifier is allowed for a code pair to bypass the NCCI edit. The Modifier Indicator Table, will indicate if a modifier is appropriate. Modifier indicator 0 means "not allowed." In other words, no modifiers are allowed to be used with a particular code pair. The 0 indicates that it has been determined that there are no circumstances where both procedure codes should be used on the same day, with the same beneficiary, by the same provider. Modifier indicator 1 means "allowed." Modifiers are allowed for this code pair. Modifier indicator 9 means "not applicable." NCCI edits do not apply for this code pair. Medical office insurance staff will mostly concern themselves with Modifier indicator 0 to learn what code pairs are not allowed.

DOCUMENTATION AND CODING

CMS mandates very specific requirements for documentation and coding of medical services provided, and those requirements are complex. Requirements for E/M codes were first laid out in 1995 and were followed by an additional set of 1997 requirements. The latest guidelines establish the general principles of documentation for medical records. Those principles rest on the belief that good documentation is critical to providing quality patient care. The patient record must give a chronological account of the patient's care in terms of pertinent facts relating to past and present illnesses along with findings and observations about the patient's health based on the examination, any tests ordered, treatment, and outcomes. The complete record aids in evaluating and managing the patient's health issues in the present and over time. The medical office insurance staff members, while not responsible for the content of documentation, can be adept at understanding when documentation for an encounter does not support the charge level that was billed. When medical office insurance staff members understand documentation guidelines, they can better help the practice avoid compliance issues with billing. Payers require accurate information from documentation relating to date of service, site of service, medical necessity, and appropriateness of the service to the diagnosis. Documentation must support the CPT and ICD-9 codes billed to the payers. The medical record must be legible even if hand written. Obviously, a typed, dictated, and transcribed or computer-generated record is preferable.

Principles of maintaining accurate patient records hold that the record should include the reason for the visit, an assessment of health risks including history, physical exam pertinent to the presenting problem, rationale for any tests ordered or procedures done, clinical impression and diagnosis, and the patient's progress with treatment and changes in treatment. The Documentation Guidelines for E/M services are laid out to reflect typical adults. Documentation guidelines may be downloaded at www.cms.hhs.gov/MLNProducts/Downloads/MASTER1.pdf.

The three key components of the patient's medical record that document a provider's encounter with a patient are history, examination, and medical decision-making. Each component is discussed in more detail the following paragraphs. The E/M aspect of their job is very important for insurance staff members to understand — not only in performing their day-to-day work, but also because they may be called at some point to serve on an organizational compliance committee. For both these reasons, the quick reference in Exhibit 11.2 E/M Elements Summary Tool is helpful to have on hand.

EXHIBIT 11.2 ■ E/M Elements Summary Tool

	[1]History			[2]Exam
	(HPI)	(ROS)	(PFSH)	
Problem focused	Brief 1–3	N/A	N/A	1–5 bullets
Expanded problem focused	Brief 1–3	Problem pertinent	N/A	6 or > bullets
Detailed	Extended 4 or >	Extended 2–9	Pertinent	2 or > bullets in 6 areas
Comprehensive	Extended 4 or >	Extended 10 or >	Complete	Record 2 elements in 9 areas

Note: HPI is location, severity, duration and associated signs/symptoms, etc.

[3]Medical Decision-making (Go with level when 2 of three are met)			
	# of Diagnosis or Options	Data to be reviewed	Risk: Complications, morbidity, mortality
Straightforward	Minimal	Minimal or none	Minimal
Low complexity	Limited	Limited	Low
Moderate complexity	Multiple	Moderate	Moderate
High complexity	Extensive	Extensive	High

E/M history

There are four components of documenting a patient's history as listed in Exhibit 11.2 and detailed here. They are:

1. **Chief complaint (CC).** The CC describes why the patient is seeing the provider at that encounter on that day. The CC can be stated in the patient's own words and should describe the problem and its signs or symptoms.

2. **History of present illness (HPI).** The HPI gives a chronological description, starting with the first sign or symptom (or last encounter) to the present. The elements that may be included in the HPI description are location, quality, severity, duration, timing, context, and modifying factors related to the main symptom, as well as associated signs and symptoms. Documentation relating to HPI may be brief or extended. If the HPI is brief, then three of the elements from the list provided by Medicare should be included. If the HPI is extended, then at least four elements from the list should be included.

3. **Review of systems (ROS).** The ROS relates directly to the body areas and organ systems and takes an inventory of the organ system(s) related to the problem. Providers use the ROS that best relates to the specialty medical services they provide. See Exhibit 11.3 for an example of an ROS form.

4. **Past, family, and/or social history (PFSH).** The PFSH reviews three areas: the patient's past illnesses, injuries, treatments, and operations; the patient's family history to look for hereditary or significant medical events that may impact the patient's risk; and the social history, which asks age-appropriate questions that may be related to the patient's problem. The history section of the guidelines is based on four billing levels impacting the extent of the HPI, ROS, and PFSH: (a) problem focused, (b) expanded problem focused, (c) detailed, and (d) comprehensive. See Exhibit 11.4 for an example of a PFSH form.

E/M examination

There are two types of examinations: a general multi-system examination and a single organ system examination. The four levels of billing apply to each of these types as listed in Exhibit 11.2 and detailed here.

- **Problem focused examination,** the lowest level of documentation, must show that one to five of the possible bulleted elements listed were examined in one or more organ systems or body areas.
- **Expanded problem focused,** the second level of exam, must show that at least six bulleted elements were examined in one or more organ systems or body areas.
- **Detailed,** the third level of exam, progresses to at least 6 organ systems or body areas documenting at least two bulleted elements in each or 12 bulleted elements in two or more organ systems or body areas.
- **Comprehensive,** the highest level of exam, progresses to at least 9 organ systems or body areas documenting at least two bulleted elements in each.

This discussion provides a very general overview of exam levels. A more detailed version of the guidelines, necessary for medical record auditing, can be found on the CMS Web site at www.cms.gov/MLNProducts/Downloads/MASTER1.pdf.

EXHIBIT 11.3 ■ Sample ROS Form

Always Best Medical Practice

REVIEW OF SYSTEMS

Name:______________________________ Date:____________________

Please check the box if you **NOW** have any of these symptoms.

CONSTITUTIONAL SYMPTOMS

- ❑ High blood pressure
- ❑ Recent weight loss
- ❑ Fever and/or shaking chills
- ❑ Recent weight gain

EYES

- ❑ Blurring and double vision
- ❑ Halos around lights
- ❑ Vision loss

EAR, NOSE, AND THROAT

- ❑ Ringing or buzzing in your ears
- ❑ Noticed a lump or fullness in your neck
- ❑ Difficulty hearing
- ❑ Get hoarse frequently

CARDIOVASCULAR

- ❑ Heart trouble
- ❑ Had a stroke
- ❑ Serious chest pain
- ❑ An irregular heartbeat
- ❑ Stop when climbing a flight of stairs

How far can you walk without leg pain? ❑ 1 Block ❑ 1 Mile Other____________

RESPIRATORY

- ❑ Chronic cough
- ❑ TB
- ❑ Cough up blood
- ❑ Asthma
- ❑ Get winded easily

GASTROINTESTINAL

- ❑ Stomach ulcers
- ❑ Pass blood in your stool
- ❑ Constipation/hemorrhoid problems
- ❑ Vomit blood
- ❑ Frequent diarrhea
- ❑ Heartburn/indigestion
- ❑ Bloating/abdominal pain
- ❑ Difficulty swallowing
- ❑ Black bowel movements
- ❑ Stomach pain
- ❑ Burp hot liquid

GENITOURINARY

- ❑ Have pain or burning when urinating
- ❑ Passed blood in your urine
- ❑ Get up frequently at night to urinate
- ❑ Kidney stones

MUSCULOSKELETAL

- ❑ Get swelling in ankles and/or legs
- ❑ Frequent joint pains
- ❑ Cramps in your legs when walking
- ❑ Muscle weakness
- ❑ Muscle spasms

SKIN

- ❑ Any skin problems
- ❑ Any recent skin rashes

NEUROLOGICAL

- ❑ Do you have numbness or weakness of an arm or a leg?
- ❑ Have you recently had dizziness or fainting spells?
- ❑ Have you recently lost sight in an eye for a short time?
- ❑ Do you have seizures or convulsions?

PSYCHIATRIC

- ❑ Have you ever been treated for, or are you susceptible to, depression?
- ❑ Have you ever been treated for, or are you susceptible to, anxiety disorder?

ENDOCRINE

- ❑ Do you have frequent urination?
- ❑ Do you have excessive thirst?
- ❑ Do you have a wound that will not heal?
- ❑ Have you been diagnosed with diabetes?
- ❑ Do you have a rapid pulse or palpitations?
- ❑ Do you have extreme nervousness or sweating?
- ❑ Have you had recent unexplained weight loss?

HEMATOLOGIC/LYMPHATIC

- ❑ Do you bruise easily?
- ❑ Do you bleed easily?
- ❑ Do you have swollen lymph nodes?
- ❑ Have you had recent chills or fever?
- ❑ Do you experience severe night sweats, loss of appetite, and/or persistent fatigue?

NEXT SIX QUESTIONS FOR WOMEN ONLY

At what age was your first menstrual cycle? ____________________

How many pregnancies have you had? ____________________

How old were you when your first child was born? ____________________

Did you breast feed? ____________________

How many living children do you have? ____________________

Have you gone through menopause? ____________________

Patient's Signature ____________________ Date ____________________

EXHIBIT 11.4 ■ Sample PFSH Form

Always Best Medical Practice

PATIENT HISTORY

Please complete both sides of the form.

________________________________ Date: ____________________
(First Name) (Middle Initial) (Last Name)

Date of Birth: ________________Age: _______ Sex: M F

Referring Physician: ________________ Family Physician ________________

CHIEF COMPLAINT (Reason you are here today, including symptoms): ________________

Have you had any tests done for this problem? If yes, please list. ________________

How long have you had this problem? ________________

Do you see any specialists? ❑ Cardiologist ❑ Gastrointestinal ❑ None Other ________

MEDICAL HISTORY

Illnesses

Have you ever had or do you have:

❑ High Blood Pressure	❑ Aneurysm	❑ Hepatitis
❑ Heart Disease	❑ Blood Clots	❑ HIV or AIDS
❑ Diabetes	❑ Asthma	❑ Emphysema/COPD
❑ Kidney Disease	❑ Cancer	❑ High Cholesterol
❑ Stroke	❑ TB	❑ None of the above

Please list other: ________________________________

Surgeries *(Please check ALL surgeries you have had in the past)*

❑ Appendectomy	❑ Hysterectomy	❑ Please list other surgeries:
❑ Mastectomy	❑ Ovaries Removed	________________
❑ Gallbladder	❑ Prostate	________________
❑ Stomach	❑ Hernia Repair	________________
❑ Colon	❑ Organ Transplant	________________
❑ Rectal	❑ Heart/Surgery Procedure	________________
❑ Lung	❑ None of the above	________________
❑ Thyroid		

Have you had any serious injuries? *(Please check the appropriate box/boxes below)*

❑ Broken Bones:

Location of fracture: ______________________________

❑ Lung ❑ Abdomen

❑ Head ❑ None ❑ Please list other ____________

DO YOU HAVE A HOSPITAL PREFERNCE? ❑ St. Francis ❑ Southeast ❑ Either

Family History

(Mother, father, sisters, brothers, grandparents, aunts, uncles)

Type	**What Kind**	**Who**
❑ Cancer	____________	____________
❑ Diabetes	____________	____________
❑ Heart Disease	____________	____________
❑ Vascular Disease (aneurysm, stroke)	____________	____________

❑ Other: ______________________________

❑ NO FAMILY HISTORY OF THE ABOVE

Tobacco Use

Do you smoke or have you ever smoked? Y N ❑ Cigarettes ❑ Cigars ❑ Smokeless/ Chewing

How much per day? ____________

How long have you smoked? ____________

Counseled to quit/cut down? Y N Passive smoke exposure? Y N

Have you ever used illegal drugs? Y N

Do you drink alcohol? Y N If yes, how often? ❑ Daily ❑ Weekly ❑ Monthly

A review of how the levels of examination build to satisfy documentation requirements to meet the 1997 guidelines can be illustrated from the General Multi-System Examination. The General Multi-System Examination presents 14 system/body areas for examination. Level 1, problem-focused exam, requires physicians to perform and document that they have performed any one through five elements or bullets. Physicians will decide what level of exam to do and which bullets and elements to record. However, medical office insurance staff members may be asked to participate in chart audits to ensure that physicians are documenting appropriately to support the level of exam charged. If so, the examples in this lesson will serve as a model that might be used to assess documentation. The examples in Exhibit 11.4 are not intended to suggest the item that a physician should document but to help medical office insurance staff understand the accumulative nature of the documentation requirements. It is fair to say that many physicians include more in the physical exam than they document in the patient's medical record. Review Exhibit 11.5 to evaluate what can be recorded. Note that bullets are designated by bullet symbol and elements are parts within a bullet. To reiterate, it is a good idea to download the *1997 Documentation Guidelines for Evaluation and Management Services* to see the full documentation options in each system/body area.

EXHIBIT 11.5 ■ Documentation Levels and Options

LEVEL 1: Problem Focused
(Can record the following, 1–5 elements or bullets)

System/Body Area	Exam Element
1. Constitutional	➢ Three of the seven vital signs: – Sitting or standing blood pressure (1) – Pulse rate and regularity (2) – Height (3) – Weight (4) ➢ General appearance – Comment on deformities, attention to grooming, etc. (5)
2. Eyes	
3. Ear, Nose, Throat, and Mouth	
4. Neck	
5. Respiratory	
6. Cardiovascular	
7. Chest (Breast)	
8. Gastrointestinal (Abdomen)	
9. Genitourinary: MALE FEMALE	
10. Lymphatic	
11. Muscles/Skeletal	
12. Skin	
13. Neurologic	
14. Psychiatric	

LEVEL 2: Expanded Problem Focused
(Can record the following, at least 6 elements or bullets)

System/Body Area	Exam Element
1. Constitutional	➢ Three of the seven vital signs: – Sitting or standing blood pressure (1) – Pulse rate and regularity (2) – Height (3) – Weight (4) ➢ General appearance – Comment on deformities, attention to grooming, etc. (5)
2. Eyes	
3. Ear, Nose, Throat, and Mouth	➢ External inspection of ears and nose – Overall appearance such as scars, lesions, etc. (6)
4. Neck	
5. Respiratory	
6. Cardiovascular	
7. Chest (Breast)	
8. Gastrointestinal (Abdomen)	
9. Genitourinary: MALE FEMALE	
10. Lymphatic	
11. Muscles/Skeletal	
12. Skin	
13. Neurologic	
14. Psychiatric	

(Exhibit continues on next page)

LEVEL 3: Detailed

(Can record the following, at least 2 elements or bullets from each of 6 areas/systems or at least 12 elements or bullets in 2 or more areas/systems)

System/Body Area	Exam Element
1. Constitutional (area 1 of 6)	➢ Three of the seven vital signs: – Sitting or standing blood pressure – Pulse rate and regularity – Height – Weight ➢ General appearance – Comment on deformities, attention to grooming, etc.
2. Eyes	
3. Ear, Nose, Throat, and Mouth (area 2 of 6)	➢ External inspection of ears and nose – Overall appearance such as scars, lesions, etc. ➢ Assessment of hearing – Whispered voice
4. Neck (area 3 of 6)	➢ Neck exam – Masses, overall appearance, etc. ➢ Thyroid exam – Enlargement, tenderness, etc.
5. Respiratory (area 4 of 6)	➢ Assessment of respiratory effort ➢ Auscultation of lungs
6. Cardiovascular (area 5 of 6)	➢ Auscultation of heart, note abnormal sounds or murmurs
7. Chest (Breast)	
8. Gastrointestinal (Abdomen) (area 6 of 6)	➢ Abdomen exam, note masses or tenderness ➢ Hernia exam, note presence or absence
9. Genitourinary: MALE FEMALE	
10. Lymphatic	
11. Muscles/Skeletal	
12. Skin	
13. Neurologic	
14. Psychiatric	

LEVEL 4: Comprehensive
(Can record the following, at least 2 elements or bullets from each of the 9 areas or systems)

System/Body Area	Exam Element
1. Constitutional (area 1 of 9)	➢ Three of the seven vital signs: – Sitting or standing blood pressure – Pulse rate and regularity – Height – Weight ➢ General appearance – Comment on deformities, attention to grooming, etc.
2. Eyes	
3. Ear, Nose, Throat, and Mouth (area 2 of 9)	➢ External inspection of ears and nose – Overall appearance such as scars, lesions, etc. ➢ Assessment of hearing – Whispered voice
4. Neck (area 3 of 9)	➢ Neck exam – Masses, overall appearance, etc. ➢ Thyroid exam – Enlargement, tenderness, etc.
5. Respiratory (area 4 of 9)	➢ Assessment of respiratory effort ➢ Auscultation of lungs
6. Cardiovascular (area 5 of 9)	➢ Auscultation of heart, note abnormal sounds or murmurs
7. Chest (Breast)	
8. Gastrointestinal (Abdomen) (area 6 of 9)	➢ Abdomen exam, note masses or tenderness ➢ Hernia exam, note presence or absence
9. Genitourinary: MALE FEMALE	
10. Lymphatic	
11. Muscles/skeletal (area 7 of 9)	➢ Gait and station exam ➢ Inspect/palpate digits and nails; note clubbing, ischemia, infections, etc.
12. Skin (area 8 of 9)	➢ Inspect skin/subcutaneous tissue; note rashes, lesions, etc. ➢ Palpate skin/subcutaneous tissue; note induration, tightening, etc.
13. Neurologic	
14. Psychiatric (area 9 of 9)	➢ Description of judgment and insight of patient ➢ Assessment of mental status orientation to time, place, person, OR mood and affect

Medical decision-making

Medical decision-making refers to the amount of complexity involved in establishing a diagnosis along with selecting management options for the patient. As listed in Exhibit 11.2 and detailed here, there are four types of medical decision-making:

- straightforward,
- low complexity,
- moderate complexity, and
- high complexity.

The elements of medical decision-making include the number of management options based on the number of diagnoses to be considered during the encounter; the data to be reviewed based on the amount of data and its complexity such as test ordered or planned; and the related risk of significant complications, morbidity, and/or mortality that are associated with the presenting problem.

Although medical office insurance staff members will not be accountable for medical decision-making, they need to be familiar with these types of medical decision-making and the elements to be considered in each. For example, informed insurance staff members will know that if decision-making for the presenting problem is straightforward and the level of risk is minimal, it is unlikely that a comprehensive examination is warranted or will pass a carrier's audit.

The importance of the documentation process in medical practices cannot be overstated. The volume of claims filed and the billions of dollars represented by those claims make the insurance claims process susceptible to mistakes, fraud, and abuse. It should be understood that most errors made in healthcare billing are not attempts at fraud but are made because of a lack of knowledge on the part of providers, administration, or medical office insurance staff. Mistakes can be costly to honest providers, and it is incumbent on medical office insurance departments to make every effort to ensure that pursuing accuracy is an abiding rule in the medical practice. On the other hand, fraud and abuse occupy a different space in the medical organization and, for the benefit of all parties, must not be engaged in or tolerated. Understanding the differences in and definitions of fraud and abuse is important.

All medical office insurance staff should have access to a current CPT codebook as published by the AMA. The Evaluation and Management section provides complete descriptions for new patient documentation, established patient documentation, and all other E/M coding for various settings. The examples in Exhibit 11.6 illustrate the information found in the CPT codebook. In these examples, the changes from one level to the next appear in bold type.

When considering the requirements that are different between new patient and established patient visits, you will note that for new patient documentation all three components — history, exam, and decision-making — are required. For established patients, only two of the three components — history, exam, and decision-making — are required. Additionally, the time expectation for new patients is longer than the time expectation for established patients.

EXHIBIT 11.6 ■ Sample Descriptions for Coding

NEW PATIENT

CPT code	Requires
99201	➢ Problem-focused history ➢ Problem-focused exam ➢ Straightforward decision-making (typical: time 10 minutes and presenting problem self-limited or minor severity)
99202	➢ Expanded problem-focused history ➢ Expanded problem-focused exam ➢ Straightforward decision-making (typical: time 20 minutes and presenting problem low-to-moderate severity)
99203	➢ Detailed history ➢ Detailed exam ➢ Low-complexity decision-making (typical: time 30 minutes and presenting problem moderate severity)
99204	➢ Comprehensive history ➢ Comprehensive exam ➢ Moderate-complexity decision-making (typical: time 45 minutes and presenting problem moderate-to-high severity)
99205	➢ Comprehensive history ➢ Comprehensive exam ➢ High-complexity decision-making (typical: time 60 minutes and presenting problem moderate-to-high severity)

ESTABLISHED PATIENT

CPT code	Requires
99211	Does not require the presence of a physician. Nurse visit, typical: time 5 minutes and presenting problem minimal
99212	2 of 3 listed below: ➢ Problem-focused history ➢ Problem-focused exam ➢ Straightforward decision-making (typical: time 10 minutes and presenting problem self-limited or minor severity)
99213	2 of 3 listed below: ➢ Expanded problem-focused history ➢ Expanded problem-focused exam ➢ Low-complexity decision-making (typical: time 15 minutes and presenting problem low-to-moderate severity)

(Exhibit continues on next page)

CPT code	Requires
99214	2 of 3 listed below: ➢ Detailed history ➢ Detailed exam ➢ Moderate-complexity decision-making (typical: time 25 minutes and presenting problem moderate to high severity)
99215	2 of 3 listed below: ➢ Comprehensive history ➢ Comprehensive exam ➢ High-complexity decision-making (typical: time 40 minutes and presenting problem moderate to high severity)

MODIFIERS

A complete list of modifiers for CPT codes is found in the CPT codebook, which is published and updated yearly by the AMA. It is important for every medical office's billing department to have a current CPT codebook. The list of modifiers is found on the inside of the front cover of the book, and broader definitions are found in Appendix A. Modifiers indicate that some special circumstance existed relating to the CPT code that describes the procedure or service provided. Medicare instructs that if one is in doubt about using a certain modifier, he or she should contact the provider relations department at the local Medicare contractor.

The following discussion addresses some situations that may cause confusion with modifiers. The term *global surgical package* refers to the usual pre- and postoperative care pertaining to a particular CPT code for a surgical procedure — that means preoperative visits after the decision is made to operate, intra-operative services, management of complications following surgery, postoperative visits, post-surgical pain management from the surgeon, most supplies, and miscellaneous services relating to the surgery. Services that may be paid for separately from global surgical packages are initial evaluation, services of another physician other than transfer of surgical care, visits unrelated to the surgical procedure, diagnostic tests, distinct unrelated surgical procedures, return trip to the operating room, and a more extensive procedure.

Global surgical packages carry certain billing requirements. Major procedures have a 90-day postoperative period — the global period for major surgeries includes the day before the surgery, the day of the surgery, and 90-days following the surgery. Counting the postoperative period for minor surgeries differs. Minor procedures have a 10-day postoperative period — the day of the surgery is counted with 10 follow-up days. For minor procedures, the initial visit (consultation or evaluation) is always included and not billed separately.

If a procedure has 0, 10, or 90 postoperative days in a global period, a -22 modifier can be billed to signify that the procedure was substantially more difficult than expected (unusual circumstances), but a -22 modifier cannot be used with an E/M service code. Documentation should detail how the procedure differed from the usual. On the other hand, when services are significantly less than usual, a -52 modifier is used. In the case of a procedure with zero postoperative days, a -25 modifier may be used to bill both a procedure and an E/M service code. The -25 modifier should be added to the E/M code, and the documentation of the E/M code must substantiate how the service provided went above and beyond the expected preoperative and postoperative service. To recap, a -22 modifier **is not** used with an E/M code and is used to substantiate difficulty of a procedure. A -25 modifier **is** used with an E/M code that occurs on the same day as a procedure. Use of the -25 modifier must be substantiated by documentation.

Modifier -25 should not be confused with a -57 modifier. Modifier -57 is used to identify that an encounter between a patient and physician took place in which the initial decision for a major surgery was made. When a patient is seen by a surgeon and during that visit the decision to perform surgery is made and the surgery occurs either that day or the next day, the E/M service code must be billed with a -57 modifier in order to be paid for the E/M service. The -57 modifier is not used with minor surgeries. The decision for minor surgeries is typically made on the spot, and a visit is not billed in addition to the procedure. Modifier -59 is used to signify a non-E/M service that is independent of another service such as two different procedures or a separate incision, lesion, or injury site.

Modifiers -54 and -55 deal with transfer of operative surgical care. Modifier -54 is applied to the surgical CPT code by the surgeon when the transfer of postoperative care occurs after the surgery, that is to say that another physician will provide the postoperative care. The other physician then uses modifier -55 for inpatient hospital care and post-discharge. The use of modifiers -54 and -55 require a written transfer agreement.

Modifier -58 is used for billing procedures that have been planned to be performed in stages. When the next step surgery occurs, a new postoperative period is set. Modifier -58 is not used when a return to the operating room is required because of complications.

Modifiers -79 and -24 are used during the postoperative period to identify visits and procedures that are unrelated to the surgery. Modifier -79 is used with a procedure, and modifier -24 is used with an E/M code. When modifier -79 is used for a procedure, the postoperative period is reset to the most recent procedure. The physician who has used modifier -55 denoting management in the postoperative period will also use modifier -24 when billing for unrelated visits. Modifier -51 is used to report multiple surgeries. In the case of multiple surgeries, the major surgical procedure should not carry a modifier, but modifier -51 should be used to report additional surgical procedures by the same surgeon on the same day.

A good rule of thumb when thinking about how to differentiate the modifiers just discussed is:

22 Procedure of substantially more work — not used with E/M code

25 On day of procedure — use with E/M code to note above and beyond

57 Use with E/M — decision for major surgery

59 Separate or different procedure — do not use with E/M code

54 Used by surgeon for surgical care only

55 Used by physician who assumes transfer for postoperative care

58 Planned staging of procedures — not used for complications

79 Used with an unrelated procedure in a postoperative period

24 Used with E/M code unrelated to postoperative period

52 Used to note services provided are less than usual

78 Return trip to operating room for complications

51 Used for additional procedures on the same day after reporting the most major procedure without a modifier

91 Used with lab test to indicate necessitated repeat test/not used because errors are made

CMS has detailed information on defining modifiers. For example, Medicare provides an article helping to understand modifier -59, separate or different procedure — do not use with E/M code. The Web site article (www.cms.gov/NationalCorrectCodInitEd/Downloads/modifier59.pdf) gives the entire CPT codebook definition and identifies how modifier -59 is often used incorrectly when applying NCCI edit. The discussion points out that modifier -59 is used primarily to identify two or more procedures at different anatomic sites and should only be used when no other modifier is more descriptive. One of the misuses pointed out is using modifier -59 to report two surgical procedures performed using the same anatomic site. It is appropriate to use modifier -59 when two different anatomic sites are affected. The article points out that modifier -59 does not require a different diagnosis code for the procedures and, on the other hand, using two difference diagnoses is not sufficient to use modifier -59. The key for using modifier -59 is different anatomic sites. The article defines different anatomic sites as "different organs or different lesions in the same organ."

Likewise, the MACs representing CMS are very responsible in assisting medical office insurance staff with appropriate use of modifiers. For example, WPS Medicare provides modifier fact sheets on its Web site (www.wpsmedicare.com).

A look at the modifier -52 fact sheet is instructive. First a definition is given, followed by appropriate usage situations and inappropriate usage situations. The fact sheet also provides additional instructive information. Modifier -52 represents reduced service; it indicates that the service or procedure was partially reduced or eliminated. The fact sheet points out that it is appropriate to use modifier -52 when the service was significantly less then would be normal and the less-than-normal service provided was at the physician's discretion. The documentation should describe how the service was less than normal, and the charge should be reduced. The fact sheet points out in the inappropriate usage section that modifier -52 is *not* a time-based code and is *not* to be used in the following circumstances: when procedures are terminated, if the patient does not have ability the to pay the full charge of the procedure, or with E/M codes.

The fact sheet also points out that item 19 on the CMS 1500 form, or its electronic equivalent, should indicate "documentation available upon request."

PLACE-OF-SERVICE CODES

Place-of-service codes are used on providers' claims to identify where the service to the patient was provided. These codes are also in the CPT codebook. Place-of-service codes should be available in an organization's administrative software system. Codes are given both names and descriptions to ensure appropriate identification. The codes must be available to ensure correct reporting and payment.

Some places of service are approved for the delivery of some services but not for others. Typically, payers base their place-of-service policies on the welfare of the insured. Payers want to ensure that a service is delivered in a facility that is equipped adequately to provide the support functions to meet safety standards for the patient. Place-of-service codes are reimbursed based on whether the service was provided in a facility or a non-facility as defined in the practice expense portion of RVU (RVU PE). A *facility (PE-f)* is defined as a hospital, a skilled nursing facility, or an ambulatory surgery center. A *non-facility (PE-nf)* is defined as a physician's office, patient's home, and/or all other facilities, institutions, and care settings except those specifically defined as a PE-f as listed above.

Medical office insurance staff members must know the language of healthcare to be effective in their work. This lesson has identified and defined terms that impact working insurance. Additionally, it has continued to build on the knowledge from an understanding of CPT, ICD-9, RBRVS, and correct coding (CCI) by adding information about modifiers and place-of-service codes.

KEY TERMS AND DEFINITIONS

Budget Neutrality (BN) — Accounts for program growth by reducing programmatic costs so total program cost does not grow.

CCI Edits Column 1 — In Column 1/Column 2 Correct Coding Edits is a comprehensive code, major procedure or service, and higher work RVU. In Mutually Exclusive Edits is procedure or service with lower work RVU.

CCI Edits Column 2 — In Column 1/Column 2 Correct Coding Edits is a component code that is an integral part of Column 1 code and lower work RVU. In Mutually Exclusive Edits is procedure or service with higher work RVU.

Conversion Factor (CF) — A fixed dollar amount that is multiplied by RVUs to establish the fee for a service provided.

Current Procedural Terminology (CPT) codes — The official standard system of codes maintained annually by the American Medical Association of the medical industry. Descriptive terms are coupled with numeric codes and paired with diagnosis codes to bill for services provided.

E/M Examination — The four levels of billing that dictate services provided and documented are: problem focused, expanded problem focused, detailed, and comprehensive.

E/M History — The four components are chief complaint (CC); history of present illness (HPI); review of systems (ROS); and past, family, and/or social history (PFSH).

Evaluation and Management (E/M) — Codes divided into three key components of the patient's medical record that document a provider's encounter with a patient — history, examination, and medical decision-making.

Geographical Practice Cost Indices (GPCI) — The indices vary by region and compare each region to a national average. Each of the established GPCIs is multiplied by its corresponding RVU element value to help determine physicians' fees.

Medical Decision-Making — The four levels are straightforward, low complexity, moderate complexity, and high complexity.

Modifiers — Numeric codes that increase or decrease the relative value unit (RVU) of a Current Procedural Terminology (CPT) code. A complete list of modifiers with definitions is found in the CPT codebook.

National Correct Coding Initiative (NCCI) — Developed to help control cost to the Medicare system; gives instruction about which codes can be reported together and which must be reported separately.

Place of Service — Codes that are used on providers' claims to identify where the service to the patient was provided.

Relative Value Units (RVUs) — Unit divided into three components — work, practice expense, and malpractice expense — that are totaled to measure the value of services and procedures.

Resource-Based Relative Value System (RBRVS) — A national uniform system that went into effect in 1992, used for reimbursing all physician services.

REVIEW OF OBJECTIVES

- **Overview of Current Procedural Terminology (CPT) impact on charges and payments**
  - CPT codes are designed to pay for physician services — both procedures and evaluation and management (E/M) services.
  - Payment on CPT codes is determined by medical necessity of the service provided combined with billing under the appropriate individual CPT code requirements.
  - The purpose of CPT codes is to provide uniformity across the medical spectrum of care — medical, surgical, and diagnostic services.
  - The directive is to use the CPT code that most closely describes the service or procedure that was provided to the patient.
- **Relative Value Units (RVUs)**
  - Resource-Based Relative Value System (RBRVS) is a national uniform system that went into effect in 1992, used for reimbursing all physician services.
  - The factors of RBRVS are (1) relative value units (RVUs), (2) Geographical Practice Cost Indices (GPCIs), and (3) conversion factor (CF).
  - RVUs are divided into three components — work, practice expense, and malpractice expense — when totaled they measure the value of services and procedures.
  - GPCI is a set of indices that vary by region. GPCI compares each region to a national average, and each of the established GPCI's is multiplied by its corresponding RVU element value to help determine physicians' fees.
  - CF — A fixed dollar amount that is multiplied by RVUs to establish the fee for a service provided.

- The fully implemented resource-based formula for calculating fees is [(RVUw × GPCIw) + (RVUpe × GPCIpe) + RVUm × GPCIm)] × CF

Correct Coding Initiative (CCI)

- The National Correct Coding Initiative (NCCI) was developed to help control cost to the Medicare system.
- The intent of the NCCI was to clarify how and when codes should be reported.
- NCCI breaks down edits into two sets of tables — Column 1/Column 2 Correct Coding Edits and Mutually Exclusive Edits.
  - Column 1, in Column 1/Column 2 Correct Coding Edits, is a comprehensive code denoting a major procedure or service and has higher work RVU.
  - Column 1, in Mutually Exclusive Edits, is a code for a procedure or service with lower work RVU.
  - Column 2, in Column 1/Column 2 Correct Coding Edits, is a component code that is an integral part of the Column 1 code and has a lower work RVU.
  - Column 2, in Mutually Exclusive Edits, is a code for a procedure or service with higher work RVU.

Documentation and coding evaluation and management (E/M) codes

- E/M codes have three key components of the patient's medical record that document a provider's encounter with a patient — history, examination, and medical decision-making.
- There are four components of documenting a patient's history.
  - The chief complaint (CC) describes why the patient is seeing the provider at that encounter on that day. The CC can be stated in the patient's own words and should describe the problem and its signs or symptoms.
  - The history of present illness (HPI) gives a chronological description, starting with the first sign or symptom (or last encounter) to the present. The elements that may be included in the HPI description are location, quality, severity, duration, timing, context, and modifying factors related to the main symptom, as well as associated signs and symptoms.
  - Review of systems (ROS) relates directly to the body areas and organ systems and takes an inventory of the organ system(s) related to the problem.
  - The past, family, and/or social history (PFSH) breaks down into three areas. First, the patient's past illnesses, injuries, treatments, and operations are reviewed. Second, the patient's family history is reviewed to look for hereditary or significant medical events that may impact the patient's risk. Third, the social history asks age-appropriate questions that may be related to the patient's problem.
- There are four billing levels that dictate service provided and documented in the exam.
  - Problem focused
  - Expanded problem focused

  - Detailed
  - Comprehensive
- There are four levels of medical decision-making.
  - Straightforward
  - Low complexity
  - Moderate complexity
  - High complexity

➢ **Modifiers**

- Modifiers serve to notify that some special circumstance existed relating to the CPT code that describes the procedure or service provided.
- Global surgical packages carry certain billing requirements.
  - Major procedures have 90-day postoperative period
  - Minor procedures have 10-day postoperative period
  - Some procedures have no (0-day) postoperative period
- A complete list of modifiers for CPT codes is found in the CPT codebook published yearly by the American Medical Association.
- It is important for every medical office's billing department to have a current CPT codebook. The content of the book is updated yearly.

➢ **Place of service**

- Place-of-service codes are used on providers' claims to identify where the service to the patient was provided.
- Place-of-service codes can be found in the CPT codebook.
- Place-of-service codes are reimbursed based on whether the service was provided in a facility or a non-facility as defined in the practice expense portion of RVU (RVU PE).
  - A *facility (PE-f)* is defined as a hospital, a skilled nursing facility, or an ambulatory surgery center.
  - A *non-facility (PE-nf)* is defined as a physician's office; patient's home; and/or all other facilities, institutions, and care settings except those specifically defined as a PE-f.

REVIEW EXERCISES: LESSON 11

MULTIPLE CHOICE

Please circle the best answer.

1. **CPT codes are used to code physicians':**
   a. Evaluation and management services
   b. Procedures
   c. Both a and b

2. **CPT codes provide uniformity:**
   c. Across medical and diagnostic services
   b. Across medical, surgical, and diagnostic services
   c. Across medical and surgical services

3. **The appropriate CPT code to use is:**
   a. Only the one that exactly describes the service
   b. Only the one that includes all the services provided
   c. The one that most closely describes the service or procedure that was provided to the patient

4. **A national uniform system used for reimbursing all physician services is:**
   a. HIPAA
   b. RBRVS
   c. RVU

5. **Which is a component of RVU?**
   a. Work
   b. Charges
   c. Both a and b

6. **Which is a component of RVU?**
   a. Practice expense
   b. Malpractice expense
   c. Both a and b

7. **Geographical Practice Cost Indices (GPCI) are used primarily to:**
   a. Count where people live
   b. Help determine physicians' fees
   c. Help determine U.S. census funding

8. **A fixed dollar amount that is multiplied by RVUs to establish the fee for a service provided is called:**
   - **a.** Budget neutrality
   - **b.** Conversion factor
   - **c.** Geographical Practice Cost Indices

9. **The number of components in documenting a patient's history is:**
   - **a.** Three
   - **b.** Four
   - **c.** Five

10. **The system that gives instruction about which codes can be reported together and which codes cannot is called:**
    - **a.** NCCI
    - **b.** RBRVS
    - **c.** NEPPS

11. **Global surgical billing carries certain billing requirements about postoperative days. They are:**
    - **a.** 10, 90, and 120
    - **b.** 0, 10, and 90
    - **c.** 0, 30, and 90

12. **The chief complaint describes:**
    - **a.** The reason the patient is seeing the healthcare provider on the day of service
    - **b.** The diagnosis code that is used in coding the service
    - **c.** The level of service that is provided to the patient on the day of service

13. **Place-of-service codes identify:**
    - **a.** Where the service was provided to the patient
    - **b.** Which services were provided on the first visit to the physician's office
    - **c.** Both a and b

14. **Which of the following is classified as a facility (PE-f)?**
    - **a.** Hospital
    - **b.** Ambulatory surgery center
    - **c.** Both a and b

15. **Which of the following is classified as a non-facility (PE-nf)?**
    - **a.** Patient's home
    - **b.** Skilled nursing facility
    - **c.** Both a and b

(Answers on page 260)

CASE STUDIES

Please select the best answer.

Case study 1: Mary, who works in the insurance department at Always Best Medical Clinic, has found a stack of unbilled tickets. When she inquired about the stack, her coworker who does the coding told Mary that the new procedure they are doing in the clinic is not listed in the CPT codebook, so they will not be able to bill for the service. How should Mary handle this situation?

- **a.** Mary does not do the coding and should leave resolving the issue to the coder.
- **b.** Mary should help her coworker find the CPT code that most closely describes the new procedure so that the procedure can be billed.
- **c.** Mary should call the AMA and find out when the new code will appear in the CPT codebook.

Case study 2: Dr. Jones is not documenting adequately. When he sees new patients he documents the level of the exam he performed and the decision-making level, but he doesn't document any history except the chief complaint. Mary has been put on a committee to conduct an in-house audit. She has discovered this issue and discussed the problem with her supervisor. The supervisor talked with Dr. Jones, who said that he is recording two out of three of the requirements in keeping with documentation guidelines. The supervisor has told Mary that Dr. Jones has been practicing for 30 years and that undoubtedly he knows what to record. The supervisor has also told Mary that because they file claims electronically, nobody will ever ask to see the documentation on E/M codes. How should Mary handle this situation?

- **a.** Mary should pull together the documentation guidelines in an understandable format so that she can help her supervisor understand that Dr. Jones using established-patient guidelines and ask if she can have some time to talk with Dr. Jones.
- **b.** Mary should pull together the documentation guidelines in an understandable format so that she can help her supervisor understand the requirements, and if her supervisor doesn't understand she should tell her she is going to turn Dr. Jones in for fraud.
- **c.** Mary should turn in the audit information and leave the problem to someone else.

(Answers on page 260)

COMPLETION QUESTIONS

Please fill in the blank.

1. What are the factors of RBRVS?

2. What are the six sections of the CPT codebook?

3. What organization maintains the CPT codebook?

4. Name four licensed professionals whom, when collaborating with physicians, Medicare recognizes and pays for their E/M services.

5. List the three components of RVUs.

6. Define *Column 1* as used in Column 1/Column 2 Correct Coding Edits and as used in Mutually Exclusive Edits.

7. Define *Column 2* as used in Column 1/Column 2 Correct Coding Edits and as used in Mutually Exclusive Edits.

8. What is the fully implemented resource-based formula for calculating fees?

9. What are the three components of E/M codes?

10. What are the four components of a patient's history that should be recorded in the medical record?

11. Define *chief complaint*.

12. Define *history of present illness*.

13. Define *review of systems*.

14. Define *past, family, and social history*.

15. List the four levels of E/M billing.

16. List the four levels of medical decision-making.

17. What are modifiers used to signify?

18. How are place-of-service codes used?

19. How do place-of-service codes impact reimbursement?

20. How are *facility* and *non-facility* defined?

(Answers on pages 260–261)

MATCHING

Please match the letter of the definition to the term.
Write the letter of the definition next to the term.

Relative value units (RVUs) _____	**a.** A fixed dollar amount that is multiplied by RVUs to establish the fee for a service provided.
Budget neutrality (BN) _____	**b.** In Column 1/Column 2 Correct Coding Edits is a comprehensive code, major procedure or service, and higher work RVU. In Mutually Exclusive Edits is procedure or service with lower work RVU.
National Correct Coding Initiative (NCCI) _____	**c.** The four levels of billing that dictate services provided and documented are problem focused, expanded problem focused, detailed, and comprehensive.
Conversion factor (CF) _____	**d.** The four levels are straightforward, low complexity, moderate complexity, and high complexity.
Geographical Practice Cost Indices (GPCI) _____	**e.** Codes that are used on providers' claims to identify where the service to the patient was provided.
Resource-Based Relative Value System (RBRVS) _____	**f.** The official standard system of codes maintained annually by the American Medical Association of the medical industry. Descriptive terms are coupled with numeric codes and paired with diagnosis codes to bill for services provided.
E/M examination _____	**g.** Numeric codes that increase or decrease the relative value unit (RVU) of a Current Procedural Terminology (CPT) code. A complete list with definitions is found in the CPT codebook.
Column 1 _____	**h.** Accounts for program growth by reducing programmatic costs so total program cost does not grow.
Column 2 _____	**i.** Unit divided into three components — work, practice expense, and malpractice expense — that are totaled to measure the value of services and procedures.
Medical decision-making _____	**j.** The indices vary by region and compare each region to a national average. Each is multiplied by its corresponding RVU element value to help determine physicians' fees.
Evaluation and management (E/M) _____	**k.** In Column 1/Column 2 Correct Coding Edits is a component code that is an integral part of Column 1 code and lower work RVU. In Mutually Exclusive Edits is procedure or service with higher work RVU.

Modifiers _____	**l.** The four components are chief complaint (CC); history of present illness (HPI); review of systems (ROS); and past, family, and/or social history (PFSH).
Place-of-service _____	**m.** Codes divided into three key components of the patient's medical record that document a provider's encounter with a patient — history, examination, and medical decision-making.
E/M history _____	**n.** Developed to help control cost to the Medicare system. Gives instruction about which codes can be reported together and which must be reported separately.
CPT codes _____	**o.** A national uniform system that went into effect in 1992, used for reimbursing all physician services.

(Answers on page 261)

ANSWERS: LESSON 11

MULTIPLE CHOICE

1-c; 2-b; 3-c; 4-b; 5-a; 6-c; 7-b; 8-b; 9-b; 10-a; 11-b; 12-a; 13-a; 14-c; 15-a

CASE STUDIES

Case study 1-b; Case study 2-a

COMPLETION QUESTIONS

1. (1) Relative value units (RVUs), (2) Geographical Practice Cost Indices (GPCIs), and (3) conversion factor (CF)
2. The book is divided into six sections — E/M, Anesthesia, Surgery, Radiology, Pathology and Laboratory, and Medicine.
3. The AMA
4. Medicare will pay for E/M services provided by a physician assistant (PA), nurse practitioner (NP), clinical nurse specialist (CNS), or certified-nurse midwife (CNM).
5. Work, practice expense, and malpractice expense
6. In Column 1/Column 2 Correct Coding Edits is a comprehensive code, major procedure or service, and higher work RVU. In Mutually Exclusive Edits is procedure or service with lower work RVU.
7. In Column 1/Column 2 Correct Coding Edits is a component code that is an integral part of Column 1 code and lower work RVU. In Mutually Exclusive Edits is procedure or service with higher work RVU.
8. $[(\text{RVUw} \times \text{GPCIw}) + (\text{RVUpe} \times \text{GPCIpe}) + \text{RVUm} \times \text{GPCIm})] \times \text{CF}$
9. The three key components are history, examination, and medical decision-making.
10. The chief complaint (CC); history of present illness (HPI); review of systems (ROS); and past, family, and/or social history (PFSH)
11. The chief complaint (CC) describes why the patient is seeing the provider at that encounter on that day.
12. The history of present illness (HPI) gives a chronological description, starting with the first sign or symptom (or last encounter) to the present describing location, quality, severity, duration, timing, context, and modifying factors related to the main symptom, as well as associated signs and symptoms.
13. Review of systems (ROS) relates directly to the body areas and organ systems and takes an inventory of the organ system(s) related to the problem.

14. The past, family, and/or social history (PFSH) breaks down into three areas. First, the patient's past illnesses, injuries, treatments, and operations are reviewed. Second, the patient's family history is reviewed to look for hereditary or significant medical events that may impact the patient's risk. Third, the social history asks age-appropriate questions that may be related to the patient's problem.

15. Problem focused, expanded problem focused, detailed, and comprehensive

16. Straightforward, low complexity, moderate complexity, and high complexity

17. Modifiers serve to notify that some special circumstance existed relating to the CPT code that describes the procedure or service provided.

18. Place-of-service codes are used on providers' claims to identify where the service to the patient was provided.

19. Place-of-service codes are reimbursed based on whether the service was provided in a facility (PE-f) or a non-facility (PE-nf) as defined in the practice expense portion of RVU (RVU PE).

20. A facility (PE-f) is defined as a hospital, a skilled nursing facility, or an ambulatory surgery center. A non-facility (PE-nf) is defined as a physician's office; a patient's home; and/or all other facilities, institutions, and care settings except those specifically defined as PE-f as listed above.

MATCHING

__ Relative value units (RVUs): **i**

__ Budget neutrality (BN): **h**

__ National Correct Coding Initiative (NCCI): **n**

__ Conversion factor (CF): **a**

__ Geographical Practice Cost Indices (GPCI): **j**

__ Resource-Based Relative Value System (RBRVS): **o**

__ E/M examination: **c**

__ Column 1: **b**

__ Column 2: **k**

__ Medical decision-making: **d**

__ Evaluation and management (E/M): **m**

__ Modifiers: **g**

__ Place-of-service: **e**

__ E/M history: **l**

__ CPT codes: **f**

LESSON 12

ICD Coding

OBJECTIVES

- Explain the purpose of ICD.
- Review a brief history of ICD-9-CM.
- Characterize the move from ICD-9 to ICD-10.

OVERVIEW

Coding using diagnosis codes is best preformed by certified staff. Certification requires extensive study and is outside the scope of this training. However, medical office insurance staff should have a working understanding of ICD-9-CM coding. Certified coders are encouraged to work with healthcare providers to ensure the best outcome for getting coding right. The World Health Organization (WHO) maintains the International Classification of Diseases (ICD) in order to track and classify morbidity and mortality across the globe for statistical purposes. ICD-9 refers to the Ninth Revision. The most recent version is ICD-10. That version has not been well received for use in the United States but will be implemented on October 1, 2013.

Before that date, ICD-9-CM is used in the United States and is compatible with the parent system ICD-9. The CM stands for Clinical Modification, and ICD-9-CM has been designated by the Centers for Medicare & Medicaid Services (CMS) as the coding system to be used by physicians when billing for services. ICD-9-CM, coupled with Current Prodedural Terminology (CPT), describes precisely the clinical picture of the patient. ICD-9-CM expands using a fifth-digit to allow for a greater level of detail or specificity that is retained in the medical record for better tracking purposes. ICD-9 uses a three-digit rubric that is adequate for statistical purposes at an international level to classify manifestations of disease but is not precise enough to describe medical necessity of a procedure. Like the CPT codebook, the ICD-9-CM codebook is a valuable resource for individuals working in the insurance department to find diagnosis, condition, or disease codes. The codebook lays out the following 10-step plan for correct coding:

1. Describe the reason for the visit. Do not code based on uncertainty (that is, suspected or probable conditions).
2. Use Volume 2, the Alphabetic Index, first before referring to the Tabular List.
3. Find the main entry term in the Alphabetic Index, which is arranged by condition.
4. Review and interpret italicized notes listed with the main term.

5. Review modifiers.
6. Pay attention to cross-references, abbreviations, and brackets.
7. After choosing a tentative code, locate it in the Tabular List.
8. Determine the highest level of specificity — assign a five-digit code if possible.
9. Use the key at the bottom of the page for definitions of colors and symbols.
10. Assign the code.

Like CPT, ICD-9-CM codes are revised annually, and medical practices should accommodate staff by purchasing new books to optimize efficiency.

BRIEF HISTORY

In 1977, the International Classification of Diseases, Ninth Revision, was published. That same year a division of the U.S. Centers for Disease Control and Prevention (CDC), the National Center for Health Statistics (NCHS), began preparing a modification of ICD-9 to be used in the United States. In 1997 the WHO approved ICD-9 as a universal system statistical classification of diagnoses.

In 1979, ICD-9-CM was implemented in the United States and has been used since. The two departments in the federal government that have authority over ICD-9-CM are CMS and NCHS. A committee, ICD-9-CM Coordination and Maintenance Committee (C&M), composed of members from the two departments, is formed to do the work implied by its name. The committee meets twice each year in sessions open to the public to hear modification proposals that are incorporated in the next update.

In 1992, the WHO published the 10th revision of ICD in order to expand the scope of the system. In response to the 10th revision of ICD, the United States developed ICD-10-CM and ICD-10-PCS. The Final Rule for the adoption and implementation of ICD-10-CM and ICD-10-PCS as code sets to replace ICD-9-CM, Volumes 1, 2, and 3, was published January 16, 2009, by the Department of Health and Human Services (HHS). The Final Rule mandates that any healthcare claim filed for payment of services on or after October 1, 2013, use the code sets as outlined in the 10th revision. Services provided before October 1, 2013, will continue to use ICD-9-CM. This situation will require organizations to run parallel code sets for a period of time.

ICD-9-CM

While ICD-9-CM is a modification of the WHO's ICD-9 system, it is completely compatible with its parent system. ICD-9-CM is expanded, but it collapses back to the parent ICD-9 system's three-digit rubrics. The contents and the sequence of the rubrics are just as in ICD-9. When necessary, however, ICD-9-CM subdivides the rubrics for clinic detail and clinical accuracy. Another difference is that dual classifications do not exist in ICD-9-CM; they have been deleted. ICD-9-CM adds a fifth digit to provide greater specificity to substantiate the clinical record. The fifth digit is required but easy to overlook. Because ICD-9-CM has been modified to fit the United States, even the spelling of medical terms has been converted to conform to U.S. spelling.

The ICD-9-CM codebook is set up so that individuals intending to use it must spend some time familiarizing themselves with the book's format. It is a mistake to try to use the ICD-9-CM codebook without using its self-guided tutorial. The book begins with a discussion of the symbols and conventions used throughout, providing excellent

examples. Part I of the book provides an introduction, followed by Part II, the Alphabetic Index — Volume 2. Part III is Disease: Tabular List — Volume 1. To reiterate, ICD-9-CM coding is very complicated; those individuals intending to participate with healthcare providers in coding should become certified coders through an extensive training program.

MOVING TO ICD-10-CM AND ICD-10-PCS

As we start the discussion of moving to the U.S. versions of ICD-10, it is important to point out that the move will have no impact on CPT or Health Common Procedure Coding Sytem (HCPCS) codes, which will continue to be used to report physician and ambulatory services. Even though medical office insurance staff will likely not be coding claims, the working of claims requires an understanding of diagnosis codes. An introductory knowledge of ICD-10 helps to take the mystery out of the new system.

Most industrialized countries had already implemented ICD-10 well before the 2009 Final Rule was published requiring the United States to move to ICD-10-CM and ICD-10-PCS. The move is required to adequately support the tracking of disease in the 21st century. ICD-9-CM does not have the capacity to provide accommodation for the advances of detailing disease nor to record new technology of the day at the level that is useful for comparison. In *Basic ICD-9-CM Coding, 2011 Edition* (Chicago: AHIMA Press, p. 391) Lou Ann Schraffenberger outlines how the move will make better data available.

CMS has reported the implementation date of October 1, 2013, as a *final* date with no delays and no grace period. ICD-10-CM will be used by providers to report diagnoses, and ICD-10-PCS will be used to report inpatient hospital procedures only. ICD-10-PCS will *not* be used on physician claims at all — even for services provided in the hospital. On or after October 1, 2013, any provider services, regardless of the setting, must be reported using ICD-10-CM, replacing ICD-9-CM Volumes 1 and 2.

On the same date ICD-10-PCS, replacing ICD-9-CM Volume 3, will be used to report procedures on hospital claims. Any inpatient discharge occurring on or after October 1, 2013, will use ICD-10-CM and ICD-10-PCS codes. Any providers using ICD-9-CM to report services that occurred on or after October 1, 2013, will be rejected. Similarly, any claims reporting ICD-10-CM before October 1, 2013, will be rejected.

It cannot be overstated that the Health Insurance Portability and Accountability Act (HIPAA) standard changes on October 1, 2013, and all providers and payers must be ready to make that change. It will be necessary to have computer systems that accommodate the new HIPAA standard. Preparation for those changes, as well as training for coping with the new system, must start months in advance of the October 1, 2013, date. Medical office insurance staff members need good resources to cope with the new system.

The ICD-9-CM C&M has been charged with developing General Equivalence Mappings (GEMs) to help provider organizations make the conversion from ICD-9-CM to ICD-10-CM and ICD-10-PCS. Forward and backward mapping has been developed, and the most recent updates can be found at www.cms.gov/icd10 as well as all the latest resources for providers. GEMs may be useful to organizations making the change initially. However, organizations should not rely on GEMs in lieu of training staff. While GEMs are very worthwhile, some organizations may find it more convenient and expeditious to use the ICD codebooks.

We have reviewed the case for moving to ICD-10-CM and will now review how the structure differs from ICD-9-CM. First, the level of specificity reflected in ICD-10-CM requires many more codes and codes with more characters. The side-by-side comparison in Exhibit 12.1 demonstrates the structural difference.

EXHIBIT 12.1 ■ ICD-9-CM vs. ICD-10-CM

ICD-9-CM (Volumes 1 & 2)	ICD-10-CM
Number of characters: Three to five	**Number of characters:** Three to seven
First character: Numeric or alpha (E or V) *Note:* Alpha characters are case sensitive	**First character:** Alpha (A–Z except U) *Note:* Alpha characters are **not** case sensitive
Second character: Numeric	**Second character:** Numeric
Three to five characters: Numeric *Note:* At least three characters required	**Three to seven characters:** Alpha or numeric
Decimal: Used after character 3	**Decimal:** Used after character 3 *Note:* Uses "x" as dummy placeholder

To summarize:

- **ICD-9-CM** consists of three category characters, followed by a decimal, with two more characters referring to etiology, anatomic site, or manifestation.
- **ICD-10-CM** consists of three category characters, followed by three more characters referring to etiology, anatomic site, or severity, then a seventh character for an extension that may represent a visit or any abnormal condition that follows injury or external causes.

The side-by-side comparison in Exhibit 12.2 demonstrates the structural difference between ICD-9-CM and ICD-10-PCS

EXHIBIT 12.2 ■ ICD-9-CM vs. ICD-10-PCS

ICD-9-CM (Volume 3)	ICD-10-PCS
Number of characters: Three to four	**Number of characters:** Seven
Characters: All numeric *Note:* At least three characters required	**Characters:** Each can be either alpha or numeric. Numeric characters are 0–9. Alpha characters are A–H, J–N, P–Z (alpha characters I and O are not used) *Note:* Seven characters required *Note:* Alpha characters are not case sensitive
Decimal: Used after character 2	**Decimal:** None

As you can see from the comparison, ICD-10 uses many more alpha codes and the codes are longer to accommodate greater detail and specificity. A partial code freeze before the implementation date will offer vendors, payers, and educators an opportunity to be prepared for the implementation date. A regular update made to both ICD-9-CM and ICD-10 on October 1, 2011, will be the last regular update. Then on October 1, 2012, only a limited group of codes will be updated to both systems to accommodate new technology and new diseases, allowing only a limited number of updates to occur on the implementation date, October 1, 2013. Regular updates for ICD-10 will start on October 1, 2014.

CMS will deal with "unspecified" ICD-10 codes the same way it has handled unspecified ICD-9-CM codes. Payment and coverage policies for unspecified codes in place before ICD-10 will continue to be at the discretion of the payers, who will make independent judgments about how to handle unspecified codes. Other payers, as well as CMS, will announce how conversion to ICD-10 will impact specific payment and coverage policies.

KEY TERMS AND DEFINITIONS

General Equivalence Mappings (GEMs) — A forward and backward mapping between ICD-9-CM and ICD-10-CM and ICD-10-PCS developed to help provider organizations make the conversion more smoothly.

ICD-9 — International Classification of Diseases (ICD), Ninth Revision.

ICD-9-CM Coordination and Maintenance (C&M) — Committee charged with developing General Equivalence Mappings (GEMs) to help provider organizations make the conversion from ICD-9-CM to ICD-10-CM and ICD-10-PCS.

ICD-9-CM Volume 1 — The Disease: Tabular List.

ICD-9-CM Volume 2 — The Alphabetic Index.

National Center for Health Statistics (NCHS) — A department within the Centers for Disease Control and Prevention that has control over ICD-9-CM maintenance.

October 1, 2013 — Implementation date for ICD-10-CM and ICD-10-PCS.

World Health Organization (WHO) — Maintains the International Classification of Diseases in order to track and classify morbidity and mortality across the globe for statistical purposes.

REVIEW OF OBJECTIVES

- **Explain the purpose of ICD.**
  - The World Health Organization (WHO) maintains the International Classification of Diseases (ICD) in order to track and classify morbidity and mortality across the globe for statistical purposes.
  - The CM stands for Clinical Modification, and ICD-9-CM has been designated by the Centers for Medicare & Medicaid Services (CMS) as the coding system to be used by physicians when billing for services.
  - ICD-9-CM, coupled with CPT, describes precisely the clinical picture of the patient.

- **Review a brief history of ICD-9-CM.**
  - In 1977, The International Classification of Diseases, Ninth Revision (ICD-9), was published.
  - In 1977, a division of the U.S. Centers for Disease Control and Prevention (CDC), the National Center for Health Statistics (NCHS), began preparing a modification of ICD-9 to be used in the United States.
  - In 1979, ICD-9-CM was implemented in the United States and has been used since.
  - In 1992, the WHO published the 10th Revision of ICD in order to expand the scope of the system.
  - On January 16, 2009, HHS published the *Final Rule* for the adoption and implementation of ICD-10-CM and ICD-10-PCS as code sets to replace ICD-9-CM Volumes 1, 2, and 3.
  - The *Final Rule* mandates that any healthcare claim filed for payment of services on or after October 1, 2013, use the code sets as outlined in the 10th Revision.

- **Characterize the move from ICD-9 to ICD-10.**
  - ICD-9-CM (Volumes 1 & 2):
    - Three to five characters
    - First character is numeric or alpha (E or V — case sensitive)
    - Second character is numeric
    - Third to fifth characters are numeric
    - At least three characters required
    - Use decimal after third character
  - ICD-10-CM:
    - Three to seven characters
    - First character is alpha (A–Z except U — not case sensitive)
    - Second character is numeric
    - Third to seventh characters are alpha or numeric
    - Uses decimal after third character
    - Uses "x" as dummy placeholder
  - ICD-9-CM (Volume 3):
    - Three to four characters
    - Characters all numeric
    - Uses decimal after second character
  - ICD-10-PCS:
    - Seven characters
    - Characters alpha or numeric. Numeric characters are 0–9. Alpha characters are A–H, J–N, P–Z. (I and O are not used.) Alpha characters are not case sensitive.
    - No decimals are used.

REVIEW EXERCISES: LESSON 12

MULTIPLE CHOICE

Please circle the best answer.

1. **ICD-9:**
   - **a.** Uses a two-digit rubric
   - **b.** Uses a three-digit rubric
   - **c.** Uses a four-digit rubric

2. **ICD-9-CM expands for greater level of detail to:**
   - **a.** Five digits
   - **b.** Six digits
   - **c.** Seven digits

3. **When coding using ICD-9-CM, it is accurate to say that:**
   - **a.** The Tabular List should be used before the Alphabetic Index
   - **b.** The Alphabetic Index should be used before the Tabular List
   - **c.** Neither a nor b

4. **The organization responsible for making the ICD-9 modification to ICD-9-CM is:**
   - **a.** World Health Organization
   - **b.** Centers for Medicare & Medicaid Services
   - **c.** National Center for Health Statistics within CDC

5. **When discussing ICD-9 and ICD-9-CM it is accurate to say that:**
   - **a.** The two systems are not compatible
   - **b.** ICD-9-CM is completely compatible with ICD-9
   - **c.** ICD-9 is identical to ICD-9-CM

6. **The implementation date for ICD-10-CM and ICD-10-PCS in the United States is:**
   - **a.** October 1, 2012
   - **b.** October 1, 2013
   - **c.** October 1, 2014

7. **ICD-10-CM will be used to report services by:**
   - **a.** Providers in every healthcare setting
   - **b.** Providers of outpatient services
   - **c.** Providers of inpatient services

8. **ICD-10-PCS will be used to report:**
   a. Hospital observations services
   b. Hospital claims for inpatient procedures
   c. Hospital outpatient services

9. **For services provided after the ICD-10-CM implementation date:**
   a. Only ICD-10-CM claims will be accepted
   b. ICD-9-CM claims will be accepted
   c. Either ICD-9-CM or ICD-10-CM claims will be accepted

10. **Patients discharged from an inpatient setting after the implementation will use:**
   a. ICD-9-CM or ICD-10-CM
   b. ICD-10-CM and ICD-10-PCS
   c. ICD-10-CM and ICD-10

11. **ICD-10-CM replaces:**
   a. ICD-9-CM Volume 1
   b. ICD-9-CM Volumes 1 & 2
   c. ICD-9-CM Volume 3

12. **ICD-10-PCS replaces:**
   a. ICD-9-CM Volume 1
   b. ICD-9-CM Volumes 1 & 2
   c. ICD-9-CM Volume 3

13. **ICD-9-CM and ICD-10-PCS differ in that:**
   a. Maximum number of characters used
   b. Number of alpha characters used
   c. Both a and b

14. **ICD-9-CM and ICD-10-CM differ in that:**
   a. ICD-10-CM uses “x” as a dummy placeholder
   b. ICD-10-CM uses “o” as a dummy placeholder
   c. Neither a nor b

15. **It is true that alpha characters are:**
   a. Not case sensitive in ICD-10-CM
   b. Not case sensitive in ICD-10-PCS
   c. Both a and b

(Answers on page 274)

CASE STUDIES

Please select the best answer.

Case study 1: Susan works in a small medical practice with limited resources. The organization has one person, John, who manages the information technology. John told Susan that the organization was not getting a new computer server to accommodate ICD-10-CM, because it didn't have the resources to purchase the server. Therefore, the practice will continue to use ICD-9-CM. How should Susan handle this situation?

- **a.** Susan should know that she is not responsible for information technology.
- **b.** Susan should make sure that the decision-makers in the organization know that all claims filed after October 1, 2013, must use ICD-10-CM or they will be rejected.
- **c.** Susan should find a new job in an organization that has more resources.

Case study 2: Mary works in an organization that has two coders. The date is October 31, 2013, and Mary has noticed that several claims have been rejected. After researching the problem, Mary discovered that the rejected claims represented patients who were admitted as inpatients in the hospital before October 1, 2013, but were discharged early in October. She also discovered that claims were submitted using ICD-9-CM codes. How should Mary handle this situation?

- **a.** Mary should share what she has discovered with the coders and explain that inpatients discharged after October 1, 2013, must have claims filed using ICD-10-CM.
- **b.** Mary should worry about working claims and not get involved in coding because that is not her job.
- **c.** Mary should find a new job in an organization that trains its staff.

(Answers on page 274)

COMPLETION QUESTIONS

Please fill in the blank.

1. What are the organizations involved in maintaining and modifying ICD codes?

____

____

2. What are ICD-9-CM Volumes 1 and 2 called?

____

3. The implementation date for ICD-10-CM and ICD-10-PCS is:

____

4. What purpose do GEMs serve?

____

5. How many characters does ICD-9-CM have?

____

   How many characters does ICD-10-CM have?

____

6. What are the alpha characters used with ICD-9-CM?

____

7. What are the alpha characters used with ICD-10-CM?

____

8. What alpha characters are not used in ICD-10-PCS?

____

9. Describe how unspecified codes will be handled with ICD-10-CM.

____

10. How will vendors, payers, and educators keep up with the ICD-10-CM and ICD-10-PCS changes?

____

____

(Answers on page 274)

MATCHING

Please match the letter of the definition to the term.
Write the letter of the definition next to the term.

ICD-9-CM Volume 2 _____	**a.** International Classification of Diseases (ICD), Ninth Revision.
World Health Organization (WHO) _____	**b.** A department within the Centers for Disease Control and Prevention that has control over ICD-9-CM maintenance.
ICD-9-CM Volume 1 _____	**c.** Implementation date for ICD-10-CM and ICD-10-PCS.
National Center for Health Statistics (NCHS) _____	**d.** The Disease: Tabular List.
ICD-9-CM Coordination and Maintenance (C&M) _____	**e.** The Alphabetic Index.
General Equivalence Mappings (GEMs) _____	**f.** Committee charged with developing General Equivalence Mappings (GEMs) to help provider organizations make the conversion from ICD-9-CM to ICD-10-CM and ICD-10-PCS.
ICD-9 _____	**g.** A forward and backward mapping between ICD-9-CM and ICD-10-CM and ICD-10-PCS developed to help provider organizations make the conversion more smoothly.
October 1, 2013 _____	**h.** Maintains the International Classification of Diseases in order to track and classify morbidity and mortality across the globe for statistical purposes.

(Answers on page 275)

ANSWERS: LESSON 12

MULTIPLE CHOICE

1-b; 2-a; 3-b; 4-c; 5-b; 6-b; 7-a; 8-b; 9-a; 10-b; 11-b; 12-c; 13-c; 14-a; 15-c

CASE STUDIES

Case study 1-b; Case study 2-a

COMPLETION QUESTIONS

1. World Health Organization (WHO), U.S. Centers for Disease Control and Prevention's (CDC's) National Center for Health Statistics (NCHS), and Centers for Medicare & Medicaid Services (CMS)
2. Tabular List and Alphabetic Index
3. October 1, 2013
4. Provide forward and backward mapping from ICD-9-CM to ICD-10-CM and ICD-10-PCS
5. ICD-9-CM has five characters.
   ICD-10-CM has seven characters.
6. E or V
7. A–Z except U
8. I and O
9. The same way they are handled with ICD-9-CM. Payers use their discretion to make independent decisions.
10. A partial code freeze is enacted to provide an opportunity to prepare for the implementation on October 1, 2013.

MATCHING

__ ICD-9-CM Volume 2: **e**

__ World Health Organization (WHO): **h**

__ ICD-9-CM Volume 1: **d**

__ National Center for Health Statistics (NCHS): **b**

__ ICD-9-CM Coordination and Maintenance (C&M): **f**

__ General Equivalence Mappings (GEMs): **g**

__ ICD-9: **a**

__ October 1, 2013: **c**

LESSON 13

Regulations

OBJECTIVES

- Review HIPAA.
- Review the HITECH Act.
- Recognize fraud and abuse.
- Explain compliance guidelines.

The healthcare industry is heavily regulated due to several reasons. Contributing factors include unchecked usage and unchallenged charges in the early days of Medicare. Over time Americans have gotten in the habit of high utilization in an attempt to seek the best possible healthcare. As technology has kept up with the demand for better care, costs have skyrocketed.

To address the financial crisis in healthcare, the government has initiated many regulations in an effort to contain cost. This lesson reviews some of the regulations that impact medical office insurance staff.

HIPAA

The Health Insurance Portability and Accountability Act (HIPAA) of 1996 is public law to amend the Internal Revenue Code of 1996. The purpose of HIPAA in the healthcare system is to promote standardization and efficiency. The Office for Civil Rights (OCR) has authority to administer and enforce HIPAA provisions. HIPAA consists of five titles:

- Title I: Healthcare Access, Portability and Renewability
- Title II: Preventing Healthcare Fraud and Abuse; Administrative Simplification; Medical Liability Reform
- Title III: HIPAA Tax-Related Health Provisions
- Title IV: Application and Enforcement of Group Health Plan Requirements
- Title V: Revenue Offsets

HIPAA covers anyone who conducts business with electronic transactions for claims submission that:

1. Contains encounter information,
2. Sends or receives payment or remittance advice,

3. Makes claims status inquiry or give responses to inquiry,
4. Makes eligibility inquiry or give responses to inquiry, and
5. Conducts referral authorization inquiry or gives responses to inquiry.

On January 16, 2009, the U.S. Department of Health and Human Services (HHS) published two separate final rules to update HIPAA standards. One rule adopted a new electric standard, X12 Version 5010, to replace the old electric standard, Version 4010/4010A1. The other rule adopted the International Classification of Diseases, 10th Revision, Clinical Modification (ICD-10-CM) along with International Classification of Diseases, 10th Revision, Procedural Coding System (ICD-10-PCS). The compliance date for X12 Version 5010 is January 1, 2012. The ICD-10-CM and ICD-10-PCS compliance date is October 1, 2013. Staggering implementation will allow adequate time for the healthcare industry to complete testing of Version 5010 that is necessary to support ICD-10.

Title I

HIPAA Title I and HIPAA Title II are of most importance for the medical office insurance staff members, so we will discuss them in detail. Title I, Healthcare Access, Portability and Renewability, offers people who change jobs either voluntarily or involuntarily the opportunity to stay insured with health coverage. Prior to HIPAA Title I, when individuals with pre-existing conditions changed jobs, they could not be insured by the new group health plan for treatment of the pre-existing condition. This inability to be covered by health insurance caused people to stay in jobs when they preferred to change jobs or careers.

HIPAA prohibits group health plans from imposing pre-existing condition eligibility limitations for coverage. In addition it says that when calculating premiums, these plans cannot consider an individual's health status or medical history. HIPAA regulates pre-existing condition exclusion by outlining a provision for creditable coverage. If an individual has had creditable coverage for 12 consecutive months, with no greater lapse than 63 days, he or she must be permitted to have medical problems, as outlined in the benefits plan, covered by the group health plan. Not all health insurance meets the definition of creditable coverage. Those that do are group health plans and plans offered by local, state, or federal government. When an individual leaves employment and is not covered immediately by a new plan, he or she may choose to be covered by Consolidated Omnibus Budget Reconciliation Act (COBRA) insurance. Individuals may also be eligible under HIPAA when purchasing individual health plan coverage. For individuals not covered under a group plan, HIPAA also provides coverage provisions. For individuals, 18 months of continuous creditable coverage, with no greater lapse than 63 days, is required to avoid pre-existing condition limitations.

Title II

HIPAA Title II, Preventing Healthcare Fraud and Abuse; Administrative Simplification; Medical Liability Reform, is often referred to as Administrative Simplification. There are four parts to Administrative Simplification: (1) Electronic Transaction Code Set Standards and Requirements, (2) National Identifier Requirements, (3) Privacy Requirements, and (4) Security. (See Exhibit 13.1 for an overview of HIPAA and its parts.)

EXHIBIT 13.1 ■ Overview of HIPAA

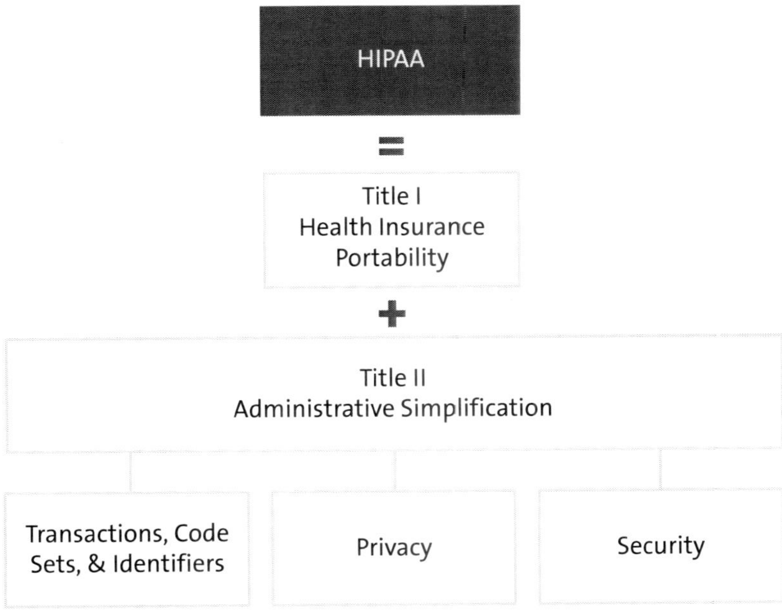

Healthcare providers and the billing services and clearinghouses representing them have rules impacting the electronic transmission of data. Those requirements are a provision of HIPAA and responsible for CMS adopting national standards (X12N 837) for electronic data interchange (EDI) transactions as well as for the paper claims that correspond with those electronic claims. These rules apply to claims that are submitted to or from Medicare. The information governing claims transfer and outlining the requirements relating to the coordination of benefits (COB) can be found in the *Medicare Claims Processing Manual,* Chapter 24.

The HIPAA regulation has provided *Transaction and Code Sets Standards,* uniform standards for transactions, which are defined as any activity that transfers health information from one entity to another for a specific purpose, as well as for code sets and identifiers. The transactions standard impacts claims information, claims payment, claims remittance advice, claims status, and claims inquiry. Although the language is different, medical office insurance staff members are already familiar with code sets (for example, CPT, ICD-9, and HCPCS codes). These code sets identify evaluation and management (E/M) services, procedures, and diagnoses. A series of 10 papers that discuss the transaction and code sets standards in depth can be found on the CMS Web site at www.cms.gov/TransactionCodeSetsStands/.

It is important for medical insurance office staff members to have an understanding of the EDI system. They must be aware that each new provider is required to participate in EDI enrollment in order to exchange transaction information. The agreement, called the CMS Standard EDI Enrollment Form, confirms the provider's responsibility to safeguard all data relating to personal health information. Additionally, the agreement specifies who is authorized to exchange data on behalf of the provider and instructs that the provider notify the Medicare contractor if that information should change. This national standard also supports electronic funds transfer (EFT), so that funds can be deposited directly into the provider's account in a financial institution. The EFT authorization form, as a part of Medicare enrollment, should be completed and sent with a voided blank check indicating the facility and account in which funds from Medicare will be transferred. EFT facilitates a faster fund transfer to providers whether claims are filed electronically or on paper. It takes Medicare funds approximately two weeks to be transferred into the account directed by the provider. These elements of healthcare insurance billing and payment are largely initiated and directed by CMS for Medicare beneficiaries.

To reiterate, commercial carriers follow the lead of Medicare. Due to regulatory requirements, it is important for *every* medical office insurance staff member to be well acquainted with Medicare regulations.

Identifiers, code sets, and transactions

Administrative Simplification has been brought about by necessity to create uniformity for electronic health information. The Office of E-health Standards and Services (OESS), which is a part of CMS, enforces compliance with the HIPAA Administrative Simplification standards for transactions, code sets, and national identifiers. HIPAA standard transactions will compress over 400 different ways to submit claims as required by various local codes to use the same healthcare identifiers, code sets, and transaction method. HIPAA requires healthcare providers, as well as health plans and employers, to have a national identifier to use on standard transactions.

Identifiers

An example of standardized identifiers is the Employer Identification Number (EIN), which is issued by the Internal Revenue Service as the identifier for employers. Providers are identified by a unique National Provider Identifier (NPI). The NPI, a 10-digit number, does not contain identifying information. For example, the NPI will not reflect a medical specialty or state in which the provider practices. The NPI must be used on standard transactions, replacing the original Medicare number assigned to providers (called the legacy provider number).

Code sets

Code sets are used to identify the service or procedure code and the diagnosis codes on claim forms. *Code sets* are encoded data elements used to describe health services, procedures, tests, diagnoses, and so on. Exhibit 13.2 shows a list of approved medical code sets.

Under HIPAA, local codes are not permitted. Standard code sets will replace local codes that have been used by various payer organizations in unique circumstances. In addition to medical code sets, non-medical code sets also exist. Non-medical code sets are used for administrative functions. Some examples of non-medical code sets are provider taxonomy codes, claim adjustment reasons codes, remittance advice remarks, and claim status category codes. These are discussed in Lesson 10 "Reading an Explanation of Benefits."

EXHIBIT 13.2 ■ Approved Medical Code Sets

1. HCPCS	Healthcare Common Procedure Coding System	**Responsibility:** CMS **Used for:** Items, supplies, and nonphysician services not covered in CPT
2. CPT	Current Procedure Terminology	**Responsibility:** AMA **Used for:** Medical procedures and physician services
3. ICD-9-CM Volumes 1 & 2	International Classification of Diseases, 9th Revision, Clinical Modification	**Responsibility:** National Center for Health Statistics, CDC **Used for:** Diagnosis codes
4. ICD-9-CM Volume 3	International Classification of Diseases, 9th Revision, Clinical Modification	**Responsibility:** CMS **Used for:** Inpatient hospital procedures/services
5. ICD-10-CM	International Classification of Diseases, 10th Revision, Clinical Modification	**Responsibility:** CDC **Used for:** Replacing ICD-9-CM Volumes 1 & 2. Oct. 1, 2013
6. ICD-10-PCS	International Classification of Diseases, 10th Revision, Clinical Modification	**Responsibility:** CDC **Used for:** Replacing ICD-9-CM Volume 3. Oct. 1, 2013
7. NDC	National Drug Codes	**Responsibility:** HHS
8. CDT	Code on Dental Procedures and Nomenclature	**Responsibility:** ADA

Note: Sets 1–6 will consistently be used in medical practices. ICD-10 will be used to replace ICD-9 starting October 1, 2013.

Transactions

HIPAA requires standard electronic transaction formats that allow for convenience in exchanging information relating to healthcare information. Each transaction has an associated identifying number and purposeful flow of information in a distinct direction such as information going from provider to health plan or information from health plan to provider (see Exhibit 13.3).

Two other standard transactions that do not apply to providers are:

- 820 — Payroll Deducted and Other Group Premium Payment and
- 834 — Benefit Enrollment and Maintenance.

HIPAA requirements, effective October 16, 2003, for all Medicare claims to be submitted electronically have result in a massive movement to electronic claims submission. CMS reports that 99 percent of Part A claims and 96 percent of Part B claims are received

EXHIBIT 13.3 ■ Identifying Numbers and Code Sets

Identifying Number and Format	Type of Information	Information Direction
Identifying Number: 837 Format: ASC X12N 837	Claims or encounter submission	From provider to health plan
Identifying Number: 835 Format: ASC X12N 835	Claims payment remittance advice	From health plan to provider
Identifying Number: 276 Format: ASC X12N 276	Claims status inquiry	From provider to health plan
Identifying Number: 277 Format: ASC X12N 277	Claims status response	From health plan to provider
Identifying Number: 270 Format: ASC X12N 270	Eligibility benefit inquiry	From provider to health plan
Identifying Number: 271 Format: ASC X12N 271	Eligibility benefit response	From health plan to provider
Identifying Number: 278 Format: ASC X12N 278	Prior authorization and referral	From provider to health plan and health plan to provider

electronically. While medical office insurance staff members are not likely to be involved in claims formatting for moving data electronically, it is valuable for them to be familiar with transaction standards when working with covered entities and business associates and to understand the importance of adhering to the format requirements of each standard.

Privacy

In general the most important aspect of HIPAA for medical office insurance staff members may be the Privacy Rule. The intent of the Privacy Rule is to protect an individual's personal and identifiable health information. HIPAA defines the use and disclosure of protected health information (PHI) and allows the individual as a patient to be secure in the knowledge that his or her personal health information will not be shared except as minimally necessary. The entire HIPAA rule can be found at www.hhs.gov/ocr/hipaa. The OCR within HHS has responsibility for enforcing the HIPAA Privacy Rule.

Covered entities

All covered entities must adhere to the standards required for electronic exchange of health information. A *covered entity* is any healthcare provider, person, or organization, regardless of size, that provides medical or health services, including health plans, and healthcare clearinghouses that transmit health information electronically. These entities are bound by HIPAA. In other words, as stated in the Privacy Rule, any person or organization "that furnishes, bills, or is paid for healthcare" is subject to HIPAA regulations. HIPAA protects all PHI held or transmitted by a covered entity in any form whether electronic, paper, or oral. The Privacy Rule is intended to define the circumstances of disclosure and to limit the disclosure of an individual's health information, but it is not intended to halt the flow of heath information that is needed to provide high-quality healthcare.

Disclosure

The limits of disclosure are specific. A covered entity may disclose an individual's PHI when relating to treatment, payment, and other healthcare operations such as quality and improvement activities, medical reviews or audits, insurance functions, and public interest and benefit activities. Individuals have a right to their own PHI, and a covered entity must disclose information when requested by patients or their representatives. The Privacy Rule requires healthcare providers to:

1. Make patients aware of their privacy rights,
2. Implement privacy procedures in their organization,
3. Name a privacy official to ensure adoption of privacy procedures, and
4. Secure records with individually identifiable health information.

Although organizations must make patients aware of their privacy rights and make an effort to acquire acknowledgment that the patient received notice of rights, it is not necessary to notify patients again if the facility changes its privacy policy. Organizations have the latitude to adopt privacy procedures that fit its needs.

Organizations must train employees relating to the privacy policy — training may be as simple as reviewing and documenting knowledge of it. The Privacy Rule permits an organization to charge a reasonable fee to cover the cost of copying and postage, if medical records are requested. The organization cannot charge staff labor costs for searching and retrieving information.

The Privacy Rule allows covered entities to cooperate with law enforcement officials without the patient's written authorization. In general the rule recognizes the importance of the legal process and is not at odds with answering court orders; reporting child or adult abuse, neglect, or domestic violence; and acting reasonably to prevent a health or public safety event. In the occurrence of any of these events, the covered entity may rely on the law enforcement officials to define the minimum amount of information to suit the lawful purpose. It is the covered entities' responsibility to verify the identity and authority of law enforcement officials prior to disclosing information.

Role of HIPAA in Privacy Rule

Across the industry providers have misunderstood the role of HIPAA. It is important for medical office insurance staff members to know the importance of respecting a patient's right to know that his or her health information is protected. It is also important for insurance staff members to know what is included in the HIPAA Privacy Rule (and what is not) to avoid misunderstanding. For example, the Privacy Rule does permit the disclosure of a complete medical record for treatment purposes, including old records created by a previous provider. All disclosure must be permitted in the Privacy Rule.

Exhibit 13.4 briefly summarizes the HIPAA Privacy Rule for medical office insurance staff. The outline in Exhibit 13.5 (compiled from the HHS Office for Civil Rights Privacy Brief, HIPAA Compliance Assistance) will help staff know where to quickly access specific information in the Privacy Rule. Items in bold type are likely to be of most importance to insurance staff members.

EXHIBIT 13.4 ■ Brief Summary of HIPAA Privacy Rule

I	What is a **Covered Entity**?
II	Who are **Business Associates**?
III	What Information is Protected?
IV	General Principle for **Uses and Disclosures**
V	**Permitted** Uses and Disclosures **without Individuals' Authorization**
VI	**Authorized Uses and Disclosures — require permission by patient**
VII	**Limiting Uses and Disclosures to the Minimum Necessary**
VIII	**Notice and Other Individual Rights**
IX	Administrative Requirements
X	Organizational Options — issues that may affect privacy protections
XI	**Other Provisions: Personal Representatives and Minors**
XII	State Law
XIII	Enforcement and Penalties for Noncompliance
XIV	Compliance Schedule

EXHIBIT 13.5 ■ Brief Outline of HIPAA Privacy Rule

I. The **Privacy Rule** Applies to Covered Entities. What is a Covered Entity?
   - A. Health Plans
   - B. Healthcare Providers
     - a. Regardless of size
     - b. Whether it electronically transmits transactions or uses someone on its behalf
     - c. Healthcare Clearinghouses

II. Who are **Business Associates**?
   - A. Business Associates Defined
     - a. Person or organization
     - b. Performs a function or service on behalf of a covered entity
     - c. Functions or activities include claims processing, data analysis, utilization review, and billing
     - d. Services limited to legal, actuarial, accounting, consulting, data aggregation, management, administrative accreditation, or financial services.
   - B. **Business Associate Contract** Defined
     - a. Performs function or service on behalf of a covered entity under contract
     - b. Contracts must specify safeguards of individually identifiable health information

III. What Information is Protected?
   - A. **"Individually Identifiable Health Information"** called **"Protected Health Information (PHI)**
     - a. Demographic data
     - b. Any information relating to past, present, or future health condition
     - c. Healthcare provided to individual
     - d. Any information relating to past, present, or future payment for services provided
   - B. **De-Identified Health Information** have No Restrictions

(Exhibit continues on next page)

a. De-identifies by statistician
b. Specific identifiers removed

IV. General Principle for **Uses and Disclosures**
 A. **Basic Principle** for Disclosure
  a. Release only as Privacy Rule specifies
  b. Release only to individuals or their designated representative when authorized in writing
 B. **Required Disclosures**
  a. Must provide to individuals access to health records or provide the number of times their protected health information has been disclosed
  b. Must disclose to HHS when conducting a compliance investigation or enforcement action

V. **Permitted** Uses and Disclosures **Without Individuals' Authorization**
 A. To the Individual Who is the Subject of the Information
 B. **Treatment, Payment, and Healthcare Operations**
  a. **Treatment** — providing, coordinating, and managing healthcare services
  b. **Payment** — obtaining premiums, cover and provide benefits, payment for services
  c. **Healthcare operations**
   1. Quality activities
   2. Competency activities
   3. Medical reviews, audits, or legal services including fraud and abuse/compliance
   4. Insurance functions — underwriting, risk rating, and reinsurance
   5. Business planning, development, management, and administration
   6. Business management and general administration
 A. Opportunity to Agree or Object Using Professional Judgment with Best Interest of Patient
  a. Facilities directories — patient contact information
  b. For notification and other purposes — informal permission to disclose to patient's family
 B. **Incident to** Situations — within covered entities, adopt safeguards when incident to occurs information is minimum necessary
 C. **Public Interest** and Benefit Activities
  a. Required by law — court orders, statutes, and regulations
  b. Public health activities
   1. Preventing or controlling disease, injury, etc.
   2. FDA activities
   3. Communicable disease
   4. Employers — work related to allow compliance with OHSA
  c. Victims of abuse, neglect, or domestic violence
  d. Health oversight activities — release to agencies
  e. Judicial and administrative proceedings — release to the courts
  f. Law-enforcement purposes
   1. Court orders
   2. Identify or locate individuals
   3. Information related to a crime
   4. On death of individual
   5. Protected health information is evidence in a crime
   6. Medical emergencies related to crime
  g. Decedents — identify deceased person, cause of death
  h. Cadaveric organ, eye, or tissue donation — facilitate donation and transplantation
  i. Research
   1. Release to Institutional Review Board (IRB) or Privacy Board
   2. Prepare a research protocol
   3. Covered entity may disclose solely for research
  j. Serious threat to health or safety — to prevent or lessen threat

(Exhibit continues on next page)

k. Essential government functions — military, intelligence, or national security
l. Worker's compensation

VI. **Authorized Uses and Disclosures — Require permission by patient**
A. Authorization — written in specific terms, not for treatment
B. Psychotherapy Notes
C. Marketing — communication about a product or service

VII. **Limiting Uses and Disclosures to the Minimum Necessary**
A. **Minimum Necessary** — central concept of Privacy Rule
a. Only amount of information required to accomplish intended purpose
b. Minimum Necessary not imposed when:
1. Requested by provider for treatment
2. Released to individual or designee
3. Outlined in authorization
4. HHS use
5. Required by Law
6. Compliance with compliance with HIPAA
B. Access and Uses — covered entity's internal use
C. Disclosures and Requests for Disclosures — entities develop protocols, criteria
D. Reasonable Reliance — another covered entity or professional

VIII. **Notice and Other Individual Rights**
A. Privacy Practices Notice
a. **Notice distribution**
1. Not later than first service encounter
2. Notice posted at care delivery site in prominent place
3. In emergency treatment, as soon as is practicable
b. **Acknowledgement of notice receipt**
1. **Obtain written acknowledgement**
2. If not obtained, document reason
B. **Access — Patients Have Right to Review and Receive Copy of PHI**
C. **Amendment**
a. **If record is inaccurate or incomplete, patient may submit statement of disagreement**
b. **Covered entity may or may not accept amendment**
c. **If not accepted, covered entity must give patient written denial**
d. **If not accepted, patient can respond requesting amendment**
e. **If another covered entity sends amendment information, covered entity must amend record**
D. **Disclosure Accounting**
a. **Give individuals accounting on disclosures of records**
b. **No requirement for disclosures:**
1. Treatment
2. If to individual or designee
3. Of limited data set
4. For national security
5. Law enforcement
6. Incident to situations
E. **Restriction Request**
a. Individuals have right to restrict PHI related to treatment, payment, or health operations
b. Covered entity is under no obligation to comply with restriction request
F. **Confidential Communications Requirements** — covered entity and health plans
a. Both must allow individuals alternative means or location to receive communications — designated address or phone number, closed envelope not postcard
b. Health plans must accommodate request without question

IX. Administrative Requirements
   A. Privacy Policies and Procedures
   B. Privacy Personnel
   C. Workforce Training and Management
   D. Mitigation
   E. Data Safeguards
   F. Complaints
   G. Retaliation and Waiver
   H. Documentation and Record Retention
   I. Fully-Insured Group Health Plan Exception

X. Organizational Options — Issues that may affect privacy protections
   A. Hybrid Entity
   B. Affiliated Covered Entity
   C. Organized Healthcare Arrangement
   D. Covered Entities with Multiple Covered Functions
   E. Group Health Plan disclosures to Plan Sponsors

XI. **Other Provisions: Personal Representatives and Minors**
   A. Personal Representatives
      a. Same as an individual (including parents)
      b. Covered entity may deny for reasonable belief of abuse or neglect, or endangerment
   B. Special case: Minors — Parents have rights
      a. Unless state law prohibits — Privacy Rule defers to state law on issue
      b. When state law silent, covered entity has discretion to provide or deny parental access based on professional judgment

XII. State Law
   A. Preemption — in general Privacy Rule applies
   B. Exception Determination — HHS make determination

XIII. Enforcement and Penalties for Noncompliance
   A. Compliance
   B. Civil Monetary Penalties
   C. Criminal Penalties

XIV. Compliance Schedule
   A. Covered Entities — April 14, 2003
   B. Small health plans — April 14, 2004

Not all of the Privacy Rule summary is pertinent to medical office insurance staff, but the portions that may create question are described in the Exhibit 13.5 to use as a quick reference. The entire rule can be found at www.hhs.gov/ocr/hipaa.

Security

Any entity that maintains or transmits electronic PHI must comply with HIPAA security provisions. The Security Rule applies to covered entities regardless of size, and these standards are enforced by the OCR. In general medical office insurance staff should know certain facts regarding the Security Rule:

- A unique name or number, used for identity tracking, should be assigned to every workforce member. The Security Rule will not allow employees to use the same log-in.
- There is no single strategy for compliance for covered entities; rather, it is up to the entity to ensure the protection of electronic protected health information (e-PHI) as outlined for confidentiality, integrity, and availability of information.

- Security is an ongoing process. Covered entities should perform periodic evaluations — both technical and non-technical — to verify security.
- HHS does not recognize or endorse any private vendor's certification.
- The Security Rule does not prohibit the use of e-mail for e-PHI, but each entity is responsible for addressing transmission security to ensure that the open network is adequately protected.
- Encryption must be implemented if a risk assessment by the covered entity has determined encryption reasonable and appropriate to safeguard protected health information. If the risk assessment finds encryption not necessary, the rationale should be documented.
- Automatic log-off must be implemented if it is reasonable and appropriate. If not implemented, documentation should provide the rationale and outline how the standard will be met. This includes employees who are working outside the covered entity's physical space.
- Employees who work physically away from the covered entity's space and have access to protected health information must implement safeguards to protect the entity's data. This includes workers who telecommute. Home-based offices must be secure.

There are three primary types of security requirements about which medical office insurance staff members must be aware: (1) administrative safeguards, (2) physical safeguards, and (3) technical safeguards.

Administrative safeguards

To satisfy administrative safeguards, each organization should establish comprehensive policies and procedures that outline who has access to PHI. Organizations are required to conduct a risk analysis outlining sanctions if security is breached. Security responsibility should be assigned for both the information system and the workforce. Data backup and recovery should be addressed. Contingency plans should be in place in case of disaster.

Physical safeguards

Physical safeguards encompass more than just safeguarding the physical space, for example, making sure that areas containing PHI are private and inaccessible to unauthorized individuals. Workstation use and security policies are required throughout the organization if PHI is accessible. Data disposal must be addressed. Organizations should conduct a risk analysis relating to:

- Natural disasters (for example, flood, earthquake, tornado, hurricane);
- Human actions, intentional or unintentional (for example, a network attack or unauthorized access to confidential information); and
- Environmental issues (for example, power failures or chemical spills).

Technical safeguards

Technical security includes unique user identification, automatic log-off, encryption, and integrity controls. Firewalls help ensure that no unauthorized person gains access. Each organization must ensure that data integrity is maintained and that all electronic PHI is held confidentially.

A security incident can occur when unauthorized access, successful or unsuccessful, is attempted in an effort to interfere in any way with a covered entity's information system. All covered entities should have a security incident procedures policy. An organization may have a process to alert staff to an unauthorized attempt. If alerted, the organization must assess whether information was breached and potential harmful effects. The incident should be documented. Response on to an unauthorized intrusion is directly related to the incident's severity.

HITECH ACT

The Health Information Technology for Economic and Clinical Health (HITECH) Act was signed into law February 17, 2009, as a part of the American Recovery and Reinvestment Act of 2009. The purpose of the HITECH Enforcement Rule is to promote the adoption and meaningful use of health information technology. HITECH promotes the meaningful use of electronic health records (EHRs) by describing the criteria that organizations must meet and report to CMS if they are to take advantage of the incentive program outlined by CMS. The incentive program allows eligible professionals who use certified EHR systems in a meaningful way to receive incentive payments from CMS through Medicare or Medicaid.

Regardless of practice size, each qualifying professional who meets the criteria may receive payment up to $44,000 from Medicare or $63,750 from Medicaid beginning with 2011 participation. Medicare will distribute payment over a five-year period to participating providers who show evidence of meeting meaningful use in a 90-day consecutive period during the first incentive year, and Medicaid will distribute payments over a six-year period to participating providers without evidence requirements.

Medicaid will distribute incentive money based on the implementation of an EHR where 30 percent of the physician's practice is Medicaid, or for pediatricians, 20 percent. The Medicare and Medicaid incentive programs define qualifying professionals differently.

Medicare qualifying professionals are within the following categories:

- Doctors of medicine or osteopathy
- Doctors of dental surgery or dental medicine
- Doctors of optometry
- Chiropractors

Medicaid qualifying professionals are within the following categories:

- Physicians
- Dentists
- Certified nurse-midwives
- Nurse practitioners
- Physician assistants practicing in federally qualified health centers (FQHCs) or rural health clinics (RHCs)

Professionals within either of these categories whose reported place-of-service codes demonstrate that 90 percent of their services are hospital based, are not eligible to participate in the incentive program.

Providers who qualify for participation are eligible for incentive payments when they have met a set of criteria consisting of all 15 core objectives listed in Exhibit 13.6, five objectives selected from a menu set of 10 objectives (Exhibit 13.7), and a total of six Clinical Quality Measures (CQMs). Of these six, three must be from the core set CQM or from the Alternative Core Set, and the remaining three measures must come from an additional set of CQMs out of a set of 38. All measures must be met to be eligible to meet meaningful use criteria.

The Office of the National Coordinator (ONC) for health information technology will determine certified EHR systems based on their ability to meet meaningful use. Only professionals using those systems will be eligible for incentive payments. ONC will work through authorized testing and certification body groups to certify systems.

Regional extension centers (RECs) have been established along with extension programs and research centers to provide education, outreach, and technical assistance to providers. These 60 RECs are set up to help providers in a defined geographic area select and successfully implement a certified EHR to meet meaningful use.

EXHIBIT 13.6 ■ Eligible Professional Core Measures

1. Use a computerized provider order entry (CPOE).
2. Perform drug–drug and drug–allergy interaction checks.
3. Maintain up-to-date problem list of diagnoses.
4. Use electronic prescriptions (eRX).
5. Maintain an active medication list.
6. Maintain an active medication allergy list.
7. Maintain demographic records:
    - Preferred language
    - Gender
    - Race
    - Ethnicity
    - Date of birth
8. Record and chart vital sign changes
    - Height
    - Weight
    - Blood pressure
    - Body mass index (BMI)
    - Plot growth charts children 2–20 years
9. Record smoking status for patient 13 years and older.
10. Report Clinical Quality Measures to CMS (Medicaid reports to states).
11. Implement one clinical decision support rule relevant to specialty.
12. Provide patients with an electronic copy of their health information if requested — diagnostic test results, problem list, medication list, medication allergies.
13. Provide clinical summaries for patients for each office visit.
14. Have capability to exchange key clinical information with authorized entities electronically.
15. Protect electronic health information.

Source: www.cms.gov/EHRIncentivePrograms. (Accessed 8/2/11.)

EXHIBIT 13.7 ■ Eligible Professional Menu Set of Measures

1. Perform drug formulary checks.
2. Input clinical lab test results into EHR as structured data.
3. Generate patient list by condition.
4. Send patient reminders — patients older than 65 years or younger than 5 years.
5. Provide patients with timely (four-day) access to health information.
6. Use certified EHR to identify and provide as appropriate patient-specific education resources.
7. Perform medication reconciliation.
8. Create summary care records per care visit.
9. Submit electronic data to immunization registries.
10. Send syndromic surveillance data to public health agencies.

Source: www.cms.gov/EHRIncentivePrograms. (Accessed 8/2/11.)

Although responsibility for the EHR incentive program would likely not be that of the medical office insurance staff members, their familiarity and knowledge relating to meaningful use may serve as a valuable resource in the medical practice. For full information on and registration in the program visit www.cms.gov/EHRIncentivePrograms.

HITECH strengthens the civil and criminal enforcement of the HIPAA rules through creating four categories of violations tied to the responsibility of establishing fault. The categories of violations are:

- Did Not Know
- Reasonable Cause
- Willful Neglect: Corrected
- Willful Neglect: Not Corrected

As shown in Exhibit 13.8, those four categories match up with four tiers of penalty amount.

EXHIBIT 13.8 ■ Violation Categories and Penalty Amounts

Violation Category	Each Violation $ Range	Maximum $ Violations per Calendar Year — identical provisions
Did Not Know	$100–$50,000	$1,500,000
Reasonable Cause	$1,000–$50,000	$1,500,000
Willful Neglect: Corrected	$10,000–$50,000	$1,500,000
Willful Neglect: Not Corrected	$50,000	$1,500,000

The *Federal Register* (Vol.74, No. 209, October 30, 2009, Rules and Regulations) provides definitions that are helpful when considering the categories of violations that correspond with civil monetary penalties. Per the *Federal Register, reasonable diligence* means "the business care and prudence expected from a person seeking to satisfy a legal requirement under similar circumstances." In other words, if a covered entity was exercising reasonable efforts to avoid a breach of protected information, but a breach occurred, then the entity would be subject to the fines under the category Did Not Know. *Reasonable cause* means "circumstances that would make it unreasonable for the covered entity, despite the exercise of ordinary business care and prudence, to comply with the administrative simplification provision violated." The strongest violation categories deal with willful neglect. *Willful neglect* means "conscious intentional failure or reckless indifference to the obligation to comply with the administrative simplification provision violated. HITECH's enforcement regulation provides the time period for correcting a violation as 30 days.

FRAUD

During the past decade conversations on the topic of fraud in healthcare have caused many providers concern. Medicare has pursued and prosecuted providers who have not adhered to the Medicare program guidelines. Medicare has also used its resources to help states monitor providers for dishonest practices in order to retain billions of dollars that could be vulnerable to fraudulent practices. *Fraud* is defined in Title XVIII, of the U.S. Code of Federal Regulations as:

> knowingly and willing executing, or attempting to execute, a scheme or artifice to defraud any healthcare benefit program or to obtain (by means of false or fraudulent pretenses, representations, or promises) any of the money or property owned by, or under the custody or control of, any healthcare benefit program.

HIPAA established the Medicare Integrity Program (MIP) to achieve accuracy in healthcare reimbursement. Its goal is to ensure that healthcare billing is for the right amount, the right service, the right provider, and the right beneficiary. CMS has established four strategies to reduce payment errors:

1. Effective program enrollment and education;
2. Medical Review and data analysis for early detection;
3. Close cooperation with its partners such as quality improvement organizations, Office of Inspector General (OIG), Federal Bureau of Investigation, Department of Justice, and its contractors and providers; and
4. Enforcement of policy.

Examples of fraud include:

- False statements or misrepresentation
- Altering records — claim forms or medical records — to receive higher payments
- Billing for services that were not provided
- Misrepresenting services provided
- Misrepresenting diagnoses to justify providing more services or furnishing equipment

- Soliciting or receiving a kickback or bribe
- Completing Certificates of Medical Necessity when the provider does not have a professional relationship with the patient
- Knowingly filing duplicate claims with the intent to be paid twice
- Using another person's Medicare card to obtain medical care.

ABUSE

Abuse differs from fraud in intent. An unintentional mistake, depending on the situation, is unlikely to constitute fraud, but it can constitute abuse. Abuse does not need to meet the knowledge, willfullness, and intentionality threshold of fraud. *Abuse* is typically defined as a mistake that results in unnecessary costs to any healthcare benefit program. When payment is made in situations where there is no legal entitlement to payment, abuse exists. Examples of abuse include:

- Charging in excess for services
- Unbundling charges
- Providing services that do not meet professional standards
- Billing Medicare for services that are the responsibility of another carrier
- Not accepting assignment as agreed
- Providing unnecessary medical services

In short, receiving unauthorized payment is abuse. Lack of knowledge by members of an organization is no excuse. Therefore, medical office insurance staff members *must* be educated about the rules and regulations pertaining to medical insurance and trained to deal with the nuances in healthcare insurance billing. *The detrimental impact on a medical practice of the allegation of fraud or abuse cannot be overstated.*

COMPLIANCE

Further impacting physicians is the OIG's Compliance Program for Individual and Small Group Physician Practices. In October 2000 in an attempt to encourage self-policing in the healthcare industry, the OIG issued guidelines for medical practices to develop and implement voluntary compliance programs (*Federal Register,* October 5, 2000, p. 59434). The compliance guidelines evolved from the Federal Sentencing Guidelines. Although the OIG compliance guidelines do not have the same legal significance as the Federal Sentencing Guidelines, they are very significant. Most healthcare matters do not go before federal judges; rather, enforcement agencies such as the OIG initiate healthcare investigations.

> "Having a corporate compliance program which OIG considers effective can influence the enforcement environment in many ways, including:
>
> - Who gets investigated and how;
> - Whether investigation is civil or criminal;
> - What matters are prosecuted, and by whom;

- Whether and on what terms the government will settle;
- Whether the government will impose its own compliance program through a corporate integrity agreement, and how stringent that will be; and
- Who gets excluded from Medicare and Medicaid"

Brandt, K, and Santer, R.J. (Speakers) 2000. *Final Rule — OIG Small Group Compliance.* Englewood, CO: Medical Group Management Association (Audio Conference, November 7, 2000).

The OIG guidance focuses on reimbursement and regulatory issues of federal healthcare. As noted in the title of the guidance, the guidelines apply to small groups. However, because the OIG does not define the term *small group,* it is generally understood that these guidelines apply to any physician medical practice that does not have a full-time compliance department (Brandt and Saner, 2000, p. 8). The OIG is particularly interested in reducing fraudulent claims in the areas of coding and billing, medical necessity, documentation, kickbacks, and self-referral. The guidance outlines the following seven-step approach:

1. Conduct internal monitoring and auditing.
2. Create written standards and procedures.
3. Appoint a designated compliance officer.
4. Provide education and training.
5. Conduct investigations and disclosure.
6. Have open lines of communication.
7. Enforce disciplinary standards. (*Federal Register,* October 5, 2000, p. 59434)

The cornerstone of the compliance guidance is the evaluation and management (E/M) guidelines. Physician practices may use either 1995 or 1997 E/M guidelines to begin the first step of the seven-step compliance approach. Internal monitoring and auditing are predicated on compliance with the E/M guidelines. Each of the other six steps, as outlined above, follows, based on the degree of conformity with the E/M guidelines. The presence of a formalized compliance plan in a healthcare organization signals that a physician organization intends to conduct all its affairs by the rules and regulations governing federal health policy.

KEY TERMS AND DEFINITIONS

Administrative Simplification — A provision of HIPAA that defines standards for (1) electronic transaction requirements including the adoption of code sets; (2) national identifier requirements; (3) privacy requirement; and (4) security requirement.

Authorization — Required by the Privacy Rule. Authorization must specify several elements to include:

- Description of the protected health information relating to use or disclosure
- The person receiving the disclosure information
- Expiration date
- Purpose of information — use or disclosure of information

Consent — Defined as an individual giving written permission to use and disclose his or her own protected health information for treatment, payment, or healthcare operations. Consent in the Privacy Rule is not mandatory but voluntary, unlike authorization, which is required.

Creditable Coverage — The term used to convey the criteria for an individual who has had insurance coverage for 12 consecutive months with no lapse greater than 63 days with a group health plan or a plan offered by local, state, or federal government and can change insurance without penalty for pre-existing conditions.

Health Insurance Portability and Accountability (HIPAA) of 1996 — Passed by Congress to (1) establish healthcare standards in several areas, (2) provide health insurance portability to individuals changing jobs — individuals who can prove continuous health insurance coverage cannot be denied benefits for pre-existing conditions when moving to another health plan for coverage — and (3) reduce fraud and abuse.

HIPAA Title I — Healthcare Access, Portability and Renewability offers people who change jobs either voluntarily or involuntarily the opportunity to stay insured with health coverage.

HIPAA Title II — Preventing Healthcare Fraud and Abuse; Administrative Simplification; Medical Liability Reform — referred to as Administrative Simplification.

Limited Data Set — Protected health information when specific identifiers have been removed and data used for research, public health, or healthcare operations.

Local Codes — Codes set up by various payer organizations to use in unique circumstances.

Minimum Necessary — A major concept in the Privacy Rule intended to ensure that covered entities limit the amount of protected health information to the minimum that is necessary to accomplish the goal at hand. Minimum necessary does not apply with an authorized disclosure that outlines the specific information to be disclosed.

Office for Civil Rights (OCR) — Has authority to administer and enforce HIPAA provisions.

Privacy Rule — Requires healthcare providers to make patients aware of their privacy rights, implement privacy procedures in their organization, name a privacy official to ensure adoption of privacy procedures, and secure records with PHI.

Protected Health Information (PHI) — Protected health information that is personal and identifiable.

REVIEW OF OBJECTIVES

- **Review HIPAA.**
  - The purpose of HIPAA in the healthcare system is to promote standardization and efficiency.
  - HIPAA covers anyone who conducts business with electronic transactions for claims submission in the following circumstances:
    - shares encounter information,
    - sends or receives payment or remittance advice,
    - makes claims status inquiry or gives responses to inquiry,
    - makes eligibility inquiry or give responses to inquiry, and
    - conducts referral authorization inquiry or gives responses.
  - HIPAA consists of five titles.
  - HIPAA Title I and HIPAA Title II are of most importance to medical office insurance staff.
  - HIPAA Title I — Healthcare Access, Portability and Renewability
  - HIPAA Title II — Administrative Simplification:
    - Electronic transaction code sets standards and requirements,
    - National identifier requirements,
    - Privacy requirements, and
    - Security.
  - The HIPAA regulation has provided a uniform standard for transactions, defined as any activity that transfers health information from one entity to another for a specific purpose, as well as for code sets.
  - Identifiers
    - EIN for businesses
    - NPI for physicians
  - Code set
    - HCPCS
    - CPT
    - ICD-9-CM Volumes 1 & 2
    - ICD-9-CM Volume 3
    - ICD-10-CM
    - ICD-10-PCS
    - NDC
    - CDT
  - Transactions
    - 837, 835, 276, 277, 270, 271, 278, 820, and 834
  - Privacy
    - The intent of the Privacy Rule is to protect an individual's personal and identifiable health information.

    - The Privacy Rule requires healthcare providers to (1) make patients aware of their privacy rights, (2) implement privacy procedures in their organization, (3) name a privacy official to ensure adoption of privacy procedures, and (4) secure records with individually identifiable health information.
  - Security
    - There are three primary types of security requirements of which medical office insurance staff members must be aware: (1) administrative safeguards, (2) physical safeguards, and (3) technical safeguards.

- **Review the HITECH Act**
  - The purpose of the HITECH Enforcement Rule is to promote the adoption and meaningful use of health information technology.
  - HITECH promotes the meaningful use of electronic health records by spelling out criteria that organizations must meet and report to CMS if they are to take advantage of the incentive program outlined by CMS.
  - The incentive program allows eligible professionals who use certified EHR systems in a meaningful way to receive incentive payments from CMS through Medicare or Medicaid.
  - Medicare qualifying professionals are:
    - Doctors of medicine or osteopathy
    - Doctors of dental surgery or dental medicine
    - Doctors of optometry
    - Chiropractors
  - Medicaid qualifying professionals are:
    - Physicians
    - Dentists
    - Certified nurse-midwives
    - NPs
    - PAs

- **Recognize fraud and abuse.**
  - *Fraud* is defined as "knowingly and willing executing, or attempting to execute, a scheme or artifice to defraud any healthcare benefit program or to obtain (by means of false or fraudulent pretenses, representations, or promises) any of the money or property owned by, or under the custody or control of, any healthcare benefit program."
  - *Abuse* is defined as an unintentional mistake that results in unnecessary costs to any healthcare benefit program.

- **Explain compliance guidelines.**
  - The presence of a formalized compliance plan in a healthcare organization signals that a physician organization intends to conduct all its affairs by the rules and regulations governing federal health policy.

REVIEW EXERCISES: LESSON 13

MULTIPLE CHOICE

Please circle the best answer.

1. **Healthcare is a heavily regulated industry, largely in an attempt to control:**
   - **a.** Cost
   - **b.** Eligibility
   - **c.** Autonomy

2. **The purpose of HIPAA is to:**
   - **a.** Pay providers less
   - **b.** Lessen provider autonomy
   - **c.** Promote standardization and efficiency in the healthcare system

3. **An organization that sends or receives payment or remittance advice is:**
   - **a.** Covered by HIPAA
   - **b.** Covered by Medicare
   - **c.** Covered by Medicaid

4. **When an individual has been covered by a group health plan for 12 consecutive months, with no lapse greater than 63 days, it is said that he or she has had:**
   - **a.** Insurance coverage
   - **b.** Creditable coverage
   - **c.** Minimal coverage

5. **HCPCS is:**
   - **a.** An approved medical code set
   - **b.** A transaction code set
   - **c.** Administrative simplification

6. **For which approved medical code set does the AMA have responsibility?**
   - **a.** HCPCS
   - **b.** CPT
   - **c.** ICD

7. **Under HIPAA:**
   - **a.** Local codes are not permitted
   - **b.** Local codes are permitted
   - **c.** Local codes are limited

8. **Standard electronic transactions:**
   a. Allow for convenience in exchanging healthcare information
   b. Allow lower reimbursement due to efficiency
   c. Allow physicians to see more patients

9. **Each standardized transaction has:**
   a. An associated identifying number
   b. A purpose with a distinct direction of information
   c. Both a and b

10. **The intent of the Privacy Rule is:**
    a. To protect physicians from saying too much
    b. To protect individuals' personal and identifiable health information
    c. Both a and b

11. **The Privacy Rule requires providers to:**
    a. Make patients aware of their privacy rights
    b. Name a privacy official to ensure adoption of privacy procedures
    c. Both a and b

12. **Which of the following is a covered entity?**
    a. Large group healthcare providers
    b. Small group healthcare providers
    c. Both a and b

13. **PHI refers to:**
    a. Public health information
    b. Protected health information
    c. Physician health identifiers

14. **Permitted uses and disclosures without an individual's authorization can take place for purposes of:**
    a. Treatment, payment, and healthcare operations
    b. Treatment and payment
    c. Healthcare operations

15. **Authorization specifies certain elements including:**
    a. The person receiving the disclosure information
    b. Expiration date
    c. Both a and b

(Answers on page 305)

CASE STUDIES

Please select the best answer.

Case study 1: Dr. Jones has just interviewed and hired Mary to work in his insurance department. Mary was impressed with Dr. Jones. She was very upset for him when he explained how much his practice writes off, how little he collects, and how much his expenses have gone up. He said that he was specifically hiring her because he was sure that she could help him get better receipts. Dr. Jones told Mary that he is considering dropping participation with Medicare and Medicaid because of low payments. Mary approaches her new job determined to help Dr. Jones collect more of the money owed to him. Karen, in the process of training Mary, has spent a great deal of time explaining the Medicare regulations, including the serious issue of fraud and abuse. As they worked together, Mary watched Karen write off a large amount of money that was not paid by Medicare. Even though Karen explained what she was doing and why, Mary has decided that she will bill the patient the amount between the charge and what Medicare paid so that Dr. Jones will be able to collect the money due to him. Is Mary handling this situation correctly?

- **a.** No. What Mary is doing in the practice would be considered abuse.
- **b.** No. Mary should call the patient and let him know that if he does not pay the difference between what Medicare paid and the standard charge, Dr. Jones will drop Medicare participation and the patient will have to find a new physician.
- **c.** Yes. Mary can charge up to the limiting charge that Medicare sets but not the standard fee.

Case study 2: Beth is working at home doing coding for Always Best Medical Practice. When it comes to complying with HIPAA regulations, she is unconcerned because she is the only person who is at home during the day when she is working. Jane in the insurance department went to Beth's house for lunch one day and noticed that Beth's computer was on and didn't have automatic log-out installed. How should Jane handle this situation?

- **a.** Explain that HIPAA covers even workers who physically work outside the covered entity and take steps to help her become compliant.
- **b.** Tell Beth's supervisor she is not in compliance and that it isn't fair that she gets to work from home anyway.
- **c.** Don't go to Beth's house for lunch again.

Case study 3: Joe, who works in the IT department, has started a company called Certified HIPAA Compliance. He explained to the physicians that they should have the practice go through the certification process and has given a bid to Dr. Smith for certifying that Always Best Medical Practice is HIPAA compliant. Dr. Smith told Patricia, who is the practice's insurance supervisor, that the group had made the decision to spend $15,000 to get the organization certified as compliant. How should Patricia handle this situation?

- **a.** Patricia should do the research and present the information to Dr. Smith to verify that HHS does not recognize or endorse certifications from private vendors.
- **b.** Patricia should tell Dr. Smith that Joe is a fraud and that she is going to call the OIG to report him.
- **c.** Patricia should do the research and present Dr. Smith with the information that is included in a good certification process.

Case study 4: Patricia has discovered that Julie, who works in the insurance department, told her neighbor that the neighbor's sister-in-law is pregnant. Julie told her neighbor because she knows that the couple is getting a divorce. Julie is one of Patricia's best insurance staff members, and Patricia likes Julie as a friend. Patricia knows that Julie has gone through HIPAA training. How should Patricia handle the situation?

- **a.** She shouldn't worry about it, because it is only one person.
- **b.** She should go through the proper reporting process as set out in the organization's policy for reporting breaches in PHI.
- **c.** She should tell Julie that if she does this again, she will report her.

Case study 5: Always Best Medical Practice has experienced an unauthorized access to its computer system. Several patients have telephoned saying that they have reason to believe that their protected health information and demographic information has gotten into the hands of individuals outside the organization. Always Best Medical Practice has been careful to exercise reasonable effort to avoid any breach of protected information. Always Best will be subject to fines under the category:

- **a.** Did Not Know
- **b.** Reasonable Cause
- **c.** Willful Neglect

(Answers on page 305)

COMPLETION QUESTIONS

Please fill in the blank.

1. What is the intent of HIPAA Title I?

____

2. What does *creditable coverage* mean?

____

3. What are the four parts of HIPAA Title II — Administrative Simplification?

____

4. What is the purpose of the Privacy Rule?

____

5. What does the Privacy Rule require providers to do?

____

____

____

6. Define *PHI.*

____

7. What are the permitted uses of PHI without an individual's authorization?

____

____

8. What are the three primary types of security requirements?

____

9. What is the intention of HITECH?

____

10. What are the seven steps outlined for a formalized compliance plan in a healthcare organization?

____

____

____

(Answers on page 305)

MATCHING

Please match the letter of the definition to the term.
Write the letter of the definition next to the term.

HIPAA Title I _____	**a.** Has authority to administer and enforce HIPAA provisions.
Health Insurance Portability and Accountability Act (HIPAA) of 1996 _____	**b.** Requires healthcare providers to make patients aware of their privacy rights, implement privacy procedures in their organization, name a privacy official to ensure adoption of privacy procedures, and secure records with PHI.
HIPAA Title II _____	**c.** Defined as an individual giving written permission to use and disclose his or her own protected health information for treatment, payment, or for healthcare operations. Is not mandatory in the Privacy Rule but voluntary, unlike authorization, which is required.
Local codes _____	**d.** The term used to convey the criteria for an individual who has had insurance coverage for 12 consecutive months with no lapse greater than 63 days with a group health plan or a plan offered by local, state, or federal government and can change insurance without penalty for pre-existing conditions.
Authorization _____	**e.** Protected health information that is personal and identifiable.
Limited data set _____	**f.** A major concept in the Privacy Rule intended to ensure that covered entities limit the amount of protected health information to the minimum that is necessary to accomplish the goal at hand. Does not apply with an authorized disclosure that outlines the specific information to be disclosed.
Minimum necessary _____	**g.** Protected health information when specific identifiers have been removed and data used for research, public health, or healthcare operations.
Consent _____	**h.** Required by the Privacy Rule. Authorization must specify several elements to include: ➢ Description of the protected health information relating to use or disclosure ➢ The person receiving the disclosure information ➢ Expiration date ➢ Purpose of information — use or disclosure of information

PHI _____	**i.** Codes set up by various payer organizations to use in unique circumstances.
Privacy Rule _____	**j.** A provision of HIPAA that defines standards for (1) electronic transaction requirements including the adoption of code sets; (2) national identifier requirements; (3) privacy requirement; and (4) security requirement.
Creditable coverage _____	**k.** Passed by Congress to (1) establish healthcare standards in several areas, (2) provide health insurance portability to individuals changing jobs — individuals who can prove continuous health insurance coverage cannot be denied benefits for pre-existing conditions when moving to another health plan for coverage — and (3) reduce fraud and abuse.
Office for Civil Rights (OCR) _____	**l.** Preventing Healthcare Fraud and Abuse; Administrative Simplification; Medical Liability Reform — referred to as Administrative Simplification.
Administrative Simplification _____	**m.** Healthcare Access, Portability and Renewability offers people who change jobs either voluntarily or involuntarily the opportunity to stay insured with health coverage.

(Answers on page 306)

ANSWERS: LESSON 13

MULTIPLE CHOICE

1-a; 2-c; 3-a; 4-b; 5-a; 6-b; 7-a; 8-a; 9-c; 10-b; 11-c; 12-c; 13-b; 14-a; 15-c

CASE STUDIES

Case study 1-a; Case study 2-a; Case study 3-a; Case study 4-b; Cast study 5-a

COMPLETION QUESTIONS

1. To offer people who change jobs either voluntarily or involuntarily the opportunity to stay insured with health coverage
2. That an individual who has had insurance coverage for 12 consecutive months with no lapse greater than 63 days with a group health plan or a plan offered by local, state, or federal government and can change insurance without penalty for pre-existing conditions
3. Electronic transaction code sets standards and requirements, national identifier requirements, privacy requirements, and security
4. To protect an individual's personal and identifiable health information
5. It requires making patients aware of their privacy rights, implementing privacy procedures in their organizations, naming a privacy official to ensure adoption of privacy procedures, and securing records with individually identifiable health information.
6. Protected health information
7. PHI may be released to the individual who is the subject of the information or for treatment, payment, or healthcare operations.
8. They are administrative safeguards, physical safeguards, and technical safeguards.
9. The intent is to promote the adoption and meaningful use of health information technology.
10. Internal monitoring and auditing, written standards and procedures, a designated compliance officer, education and training, investigation and disclosure, open communication lines, and enforced disciplinary standards

MATCHING

__ HIPAA Title I: **m**

__ Health Insurance Portability and Accountability Act (HIPAA) of 1996: **k**

__ HIPAA Title II: **l**

__ Local codes: **i**

__ Authorization: **h**

__ Limited data set: **g**

__ Minimum necessary: **f**

__ Consent: **c**

__ PHI: **e**

__ Privacy Rule: **b**

__ Creditable coverage: **d**

__ Office for Civil Rights (OCR): **a**

__ Administrative Simplification: **j**

ABOUT THE AUTHOR

Sarah J. Holt, PhD, FACMPE, is the administrator of several healthcare organizations in Cape Girardeau, Missouri. Sarah provides practice management for Cape Girardeau Surgical Clinic, Inc., & Breast Care Center and for Cape Medical Billing Corp., a medical practice billing company. Additionally, she is the administrator of Cape Girardeau Doctors' Park, which offers a full range of medical services on an 80-acre complex of 35 medical buildings.

Sarah received a PhD in Policy Analysis with a healthcare emphasis from St. Louis University, a master's in counseling from Southeast Missouri State University, and an undergraduate degree in education. She has done extensive research on how medical office insurance staff members make decisions relating to insurance reimbursement and how complexity influences organizations. She teaches health policy and healthcare reimbursement at the graduate level at Southeast Missouri State University and speaks on healthcare management topics to audiences of physicians, management, and staff.

Sarah's leadership has led Cape Girardeau Surgical Clinic, Inc., to be recognized as a Medical Group Management Association (MGMA) Better Performer numerous times. For many years Sarah has been an active participant of the American College of Medical Practice Executives (ACMPE) and in MGMA at local, state, and national levels. She is a Fellow in the American College of Medical Practice Executives and a past chair of the ACMPE Board of Directors.

Sarah is also the author of MGMA's *Get the Money in the Door: Physician Billing Basics* (2010).